'*Uneasy Translations* is a work of extraordinary imaginative power, literary sophistication and moral insight. It is a mediation of the pressing questions of our time. What does it mean to represent suffering? How does language both enable us to access other lives and selves, and yet also limit our understanding? What pedagogical practices are appropriate to a society where the bonds of sympathy are broken, or where the easy comforts of taking a position prevent the attainment of genuine moral knowledge. Through nuanced readings of literary texts, pedagogical practices and reflections on the art of translation, Kothari brilliantly opens up new theoretical and moral conversations.'

—Pratap Bhanu Mehta

Laurence S. Rockefeller Professor, Princeton University

'The relationship between language and experience is complex in India because of caste and class dynamics. To negotiate through this space is an act of courage and Rita Kothari does this from the vantage point of an insider. This exceptionally insightful book posits Kothari as an important thinker of language and literature.'

—Vivek Shanbhag

Author, *Ghachar Ghochar*

'Using stories and songs that chafe and struggle to express caste- and gender-specific ways of being in the world, the essays in this book enact its basic premises—that knowledge is born out of experience, that languages and their hierarchies profoundly shape us but also provide some space for reinvention, and that uneasy translation is something we do and live every day. A wonderfully rich example of theorising, the book will delight, stimulate, and reward every reader interested in how words and languages work on us, their power and their magic.'

—Francesca Orsini

Professor Emerita, SOAS, University of London

'This provocative book is going to make many stand on their toes. The artifice of language and expression is taken to task. English will have to pass the difficult tests put by the author.

The page-turner tract will find an audience in many. Written with vivid details and punchy scholarly takes, *Uneasy Translations* is an extraordinary achievement. Rita Kothari is an outstanding metonym witnessing the metamorphosis of her calling—as a child of Sindhi migrants to a professional language hustler—rejoicing the critique of English and translations. *Uneasy Translations* is vital for the culture of languages and the discipline in general. It assures diverse India, rich with its long registers of languages, sub-languages, accents and dialects, to not rely on the hegemonic parlance of the English language to seek validations. It is a holler for writers and readers alike.'

—Suraj Yengde
Author, *Caste Matters*

Uneasy Translations

Uneasy Translations

Self, Experience and Indian Literature

Rita Kothari

B L O O M S B U R Y
NEW DELHI • LONDON • OXFORD • NEW YORK • SYDNEY

BLOOMSBURY INDIA
Bloomsbury Publishing India Pvt. Ltd
Second Floor, LSC Building No. 4, DDA Complex, Pocket C – 6 & 7,
Vasant Kunj, New Delhi, 110070

BLOOMSBURY, BLOOMSBURY ACADEMIC INDIA and the Diana logo are trademarks of Bloomsbury Publishing Plc

First published in India 2022
This Paperback edition published in 2025

Bloomsbury Academic
An imprint of Bloomsbury Publishing Plc

ISBN: PB: 978-93-69529-15-5

Typeset in Manipal Technologies Limited
Printed in India by Manipal Technologies Limited, Manipal

To

Kamala Makhija

There's more of you in me than I knew

Contents

Acknowledgements

How does one account for ongoing conversations with friends and family that inform not only the questions of the book but rescue us from self-doubt? To this end, Abhijit Kothari, Abir Bazaz, Aparna Vaidik, Tridip Suhrud, Shamini Kothari, Sarvar Sherry Chand, Mathangi Krishnamurthy, Shuchi Kothari and Sumana Roy need to be mentioned. I am also thankful to Ravindranchandran Sriramachandran and V. Geetha for their input. Urvashi Butalia has been a constant source of support and taught me what she is best at—listening. Prashant Ingole, my former student, was also a valuable interlocutor. Thanks are also due to Joshua Price, Valerian Rodrigues, Rajeev Bhargava, Robert J.C. Young, Debjani Ganguly, Kamalakar Bhat, Ira Pande, Udaya Kumar, Alok Rai, Apurva Shah, Shabnam Virmani and Shruthi Viswanath. I am grateful to the many quiet workers who make our work possible—for instance, Vimlaben who provided me with endless nourishment while I wrote and the library team at Ashoka University that made every single book and article accessible. Bibhutinath Jha deserves a special mention in this regard. I am grateful to the institutions where I have taught for giving me students who taught me important lessons about life, and it is from them that I learnt the finitude of institutionalised knowledge.

A very special thanks to Angana Sinha-Ray. Technically, she was my research assistant, but that is such an inadequate expression for the engagement she has had with me and the project. She heard the thoughts in my head, and that was such a relief. Sanchit Toor has reinforced my faith in the teaching profession. A very big thank you, Sanchit. I am grateful to Pratap Bhanu Mehta, Suraj Yengde, Francesca Orsini and Vivek Shanbhag for their endorsements. Thank you Sundar Sarukkai for all the words before and after.

Finally, the book has taken risks of infusing the intellectual with the personal; the body with the psychic; and collapsed many things that are usually kept separate. Prices, if any, are mine to pay.

Prologue

> *Is it not possible that the entire society is seen as a vast university, every community in it an open treasurer of knowledge, as if they were collectively a vast reference library, and the institution of learning a co-curator, a co-supervisor of that knowledge?*
>
> —Devy 2017: 50

It must have begun as some kind of transaction. Otherwise, how would a 15-year-old have been expected to teach? I lived with my parents at that time in a house that left me quite ashamed. The house was perched on a mound in a colony that was next to a defecation pit. We called it *tekre vaaro ghar*. The house on a mound. Our next-door neighbour, whom my mother called Savitri Bhabhi, would on and off lend money to my mother for *ghar-kharch*, household expenses. My father was out of business. And my angry brother was trying in vain to make ends meet for us. As the youngest person in the house, there was not much else I could do, but, at the very least, I could help Savitri Aunty's children to study in return for the money and kindness she extended to my mother. So, I would go to the house next door and teach Savitri Aunty's two children English and social studies. Frankly, I seethed with resentment and felt quite poor. But, each time I came out of their home, I also felt a strange sense of power. Teaching *is* power. It was also an escape from a grim home where we tiptoed around unhappy and angry men. Transaction, joy, power, refuge and, to a certain extent, inexplicable helplessness and vulnerability—these characterise, even today, some of the primal feelings I have in a classroom.

There are profound experiences attached to our lives in the classroom, regardless of our being a 'student' or 'teacher'. I use both terms tentatively for students also teach and teachers also learn. This does not mean a denial of the power equation that characterises this relation; this equation has more complexity and a greater dialectical dimension that does not get captured in unidirectional phrases like a teacher's power. As such, every transaction—however functional it may appear—is underpinned by a social experience. The transactionality of giving and receiving knowledge in a classroom is also an experience-produced and experience-producing phenomenon. The tendency to extricate 'knowledge' from the experiences that students and teachers come with—the ones that produce the texts taught in class—draws my attention in particular. This is not only the result of my own deep investment in this profession but also an investment in questions of knowledge and conditions producing it, institutionalising what can be legitimately considered 'knowledge'.

Enriching and humbling, unsettling and despairing, the 'experience' of being in a classroom in India is multifold and, frankly, unsummarisable. This, by itself, is not an object of study for me or a site of research and publication. It is rather a mediation with the self and a self that mediates a relation with the classroom. Many discussions in this book stem from reflections inspired by and constrained by the classroom. And I use the word 'classroom' as a shorthand to include physicality of location and also acts of engagement over knowledge with students. These engagements have held me deeply, sometimes scarred me, sometimes led to adulation in frightening ways, but almost always brought lessons on what constitutes knowledge and its democratic moment. The self-exclusion of the subaltern student (which I later discuss through Aniket Jaaware's essay) or the privilege of the 'paying' student at the elite university where I teach form two extreme ends. Between the two ends are also many forms of mediations informed by situations that cannot be easily captured through sympathy or censure.

Almost 30 years ago, when I was in my early 20s and struggling as a Sindhi in an upper-caste vegetarian joint-family Gujarati household, I took up my first job in the old city of Ahmedabad. Smt Sadguna C U Arts College for Girls had Dalit and Muslim girls to whom I had to teach literature. It was clear to me on the first day that I had to teach William Wordsworth and John Keats in Gujarati—a language with which I was developing a new relationship. Hitherto, I had not received any formal education in Gujarati. But this memory is not about me; it is about those girls who were learning English poetry in a native language. Was this a postcolonial condition of agency or one of tragic dissonance? The same college had a teacher of Persian to whom no students went, and I witnessed one of the last teachers of Persian vanish, taking with him knowledge we had ceased to have use for. During those years, I merely processed my job as a transition towards better things in the future. However, when I now look back, I can think of several instances in divergent institutional contexts when the conditions of its production have imperceptibly interrupted my relationship with knowledge. Neither from my own nor others' experiences do I take knowledge and 'merit' for granted; they almost always involve lives that have a greater relationship with labour. The English language, which forms the basis of my livelihood, has a particularly complex place in that context.

This awareness that the source of my livelihood—the English language—had discursive effects and relations has been central to the way I see knowledge and what passes off as legitimate knowledge. Simultaneously, the inalienable connection between subjectivity and experience on the one hand and knowledge on the other is also an important fulcrum of the humanities. That is to say, the 'truth' of the humanities is inseparable from its subjectivity and experience, as also the conditions framing it. As teachers and students of English in India, we have come into this linguistic–literary zone by embracing the most dominant sign of symbolic power and, at times, at the cost of other languages that have shaped us—provided us with subliminal idioms and metaphors. They did not, for a number of reasons, have the power to beckon us into their world, but it is a relation that is manifest for many of us in the uneasy translations we make of meaning between English and our other selves. Entering Lecture Room 25 in St. Xavier's College as a literature student, I left my film songs outside the room. It was the only tangible inheritance I carried—one that informed me that hyperbole was to say, 'I can pluck down the moon for you' or that there was no oxymoron in the idea of *meetha dard* (sweet pain). But these lives of the bhashas were distant from English learning and teaching. Over the years, they infiltrated my classroom, now fighting, now collaborating with the English language. In fact, English seldom appears by itself in India, there is nearly always a *chhaya* or shadow of another language lurking behind it somewhere. Really speaking, no language appears by itself; each is haunted by acknowledged and unacknowledged shadows of other languages. It is useful to think of Anandavardhan's concept of *dhvani* (suggestion or hint) here, for meaning carries itself as a trace[1] of something unintended, inhering in elements that are not always identifiable. They may well be other languages we thought didn't matter.

Meanwhile, when I taught at St. Xavier's College (Ahmedabad) for almost 17 years, I saw how I wielded a powerful language that had not only brought me out of a conventional Sindhi home but also given some of my tribal students the jobs of a teacher or *talati* in villages they came from. Some of them accessed the power of language because their families were part of a Christian parish. Occasionally, they would continue to worship their own gods, and early on, I learnt a lesson that different gods give different things. This was not a phenomenon of the way liberals celebrate religious fluidity but also a pragmatism that characterised religious conversions. St. Xavier's College's own commitment to the goals of social justice made the rich and well-to-do students feel that their goals of learning 'pure' literature were getting marginalised, and competing forms of democracy played out in that unusual and valuable institution that taught me some of the most formative lessons. In his moving and very pointed essay, 'The Silence of the Subaltern Student' (1994), Aniket Jaaware says that it is common for teachers of English in urban centres of education to find that their classes are divided from the word go into two groups who define themselves as essentially different from each other—the urban and the rural students. Jaaware troubles the category further down in the essay as he thinks through 'oppositional structures: urban/rural, dominant/subaltern, coloniser/colonised, legitimised-intelligence/illegitimate-power to think, privileged/underprivileged, etc.' (Jaaware 1994: 107). At the Jesuit missionary college where I taught the longest, these divides

1 I have taken liberties in interpreting both *dhvani* and trace. Anandavardhana's concept of *dhvani* refers to secondary and tertiary levels of meaning, and he moves away from denotative to connotative meaning. However, an unintended shadow lingers over the concept which is resonant for me in Derrida's concept of the 'trace'. Neither Anandavardhana nor Derrida speaks of a language in particular, but both concepts suggest for me the leaking effects of words that may be produced through other spectres that lie hidden in language. In India's multilingual environment, this may be seen as a spilling over of specific and muted languages that are not visible in contexts of English academia (Ingalls 1990; Derrida 2016).

were also troubled by Dalit and Adivasi students (as opposed to 'rural' students). The students came with Gujarati, Vasavi, Chaudhari, Rathvi and a host of other languages in Gujarat that do not make it to being considered standard 'Gujarati'. There were also pre-novices wishing to join various Christian orders, who came with languages such as Kho and Santhali. The affective and psychological, cultural and political words produced through these languages became invisible, and what mattered to most teachers and the students themselves was how they needed to learn English. Caught between the goals of making students experience the 'love of literature' and strengthening the English of marginalised students who could find empowerment through jobs and mobility, the English department at Xavier's and elsewhere lived with multiple forms of dissonance. In some sense, dissonance is what my journey has been about, and the discipline was emblematic of that state but not its only site.

I wish to talk of one particular category that functioned under a non-identitarian label but revealed to some of us the most bitter truth about the English language in the subaltern constituencies. For students coming to the urban centre of Ahmedabad from tribal towns in South Gujarat such as Dediapada and Zankhvav, the road to literature was inconceivable. They were the 'B' stream students, that is, they had been made to drop English in their tenth and twelfth standards so as not to fail and thereby bring disrepute to the schools they came from. Our tasks as teachers of English were to cover the range of tenses and articles for the 'B' stream students. In another section called the 'A' stream students, we could do simple exercises and storytelling in English. The 'A' stream students (like the 'B' stream students) also belonged to the Gujarati medium; however, they had passed their tenth and twelfth standards with English. In fact, 'with' and 'without English' were common phrases found even in a Gujarati sentence and conveyed their own graded inequality. If the 'B' stream was predominantly tribal in its composition, the 'A' stream students were mostly Dalits. The 'literature' class had a mix of some upper-caste and well-to-do students as well as students from relatively marginal constituencies. The same language performed different empirical and symbolic functions—preparing some to pass an examination and become school teachers or *talati*s and others to go on to do graduate studies in the United States. Within the literature class, they were always students who, in the words of Jaaware, marginalised themselves and remained silent. Apart from what such day-to-day complexity does to an academic is also what it does to academic knowledge, which on some days appears a highly specious entity. Jaaware rightly points to the 'silence of the subaltern student' produced through academic knowledge. He encapsulates the condition with the following equation: Language of Knowledge = Knowledge of Language (1994: 113).

After the year 2007, I joined a premier private and management institution where a student once asked me, 'Professor, what is the ROI [Return-on-investment] of learning Kabir in your class? How is that going to help in my job in the industry?' I have often wondered whether the overt instrumentalism of the latter or the non-English speaking students' demand for Gujarati represent a conundrum about privilege and knowledge. *The demand for another language is from the lack of privilege, the demand for another knowledge is from excess of it.* And as teachers of the humanities what contextual apparatus do we possess to understand these? Cut to another context of a technology institution where I taught before joining Ashoka University. A senior colleague said to me, '*Arre aap aurton ki expectations hame samajh mein naheen aati*. We, engineers, are straightforward people.' Subjectivity stood not just erased but pronounced as an illegitimate, messy business, which in the 'straightforward' path of skill education had clearly no place. Both the humanities education and gender I represented collapsed into each other. Clearly, different disciplines construct their own versions of truths. As a student of the humanities, I am thankful for the room it makes for subjectivity and experience; also, as Martha Nussbaum has persuasively argued, for making societies more democratic (Nussbaum 2010). However, the conditions of inequality that drive some of the research in the humanities are also ones that shrink the possibility of disseminating that knowledge. The marginalisation of the non-metropolitan student who studies texts in a language and idiom that is distant from her affective and lived reality makes even the humanities education violent. In effect, I carry both belief and cynicism in the project of the humanities, and this makes my relationship with my own discipline of English particularly ambivalent. The belief stems from possibilities of social transformation I have witnessed in the lives of vulnerable students; the cynicism stems from the way knowledge produced and flaunted gets disembodied from our own experiences and the experiences of those we claim to 'teach'. Really speaking, the metropolitan theory has no room for the homes we come from. Those experiences must order theory. A student who evidently experienced this disjuncture between her lived reality and theory during her studies at Ashoka University, later remarked to me,

> My home holds the absence of a sibling, Kashish, younger than me, who we lost way too soon. If there is ever pain in my or my parents' lived experience, it's almost always linked a little to the trauma of losing a child or the trauma of watching your parent lose a child. When I decided to pursue a liberal arts education, I had to fight my way into it. I have been trying to find theory on that but so far I have only been able to gather concrete lived experience of Muslim women having to fight so hard for their needs.... First two years of college, apart from courses in politics, I read just about women from the west. They talked about beauty and law and male gaze and the politics of a woman but it swiftly moved past their home. They can never equip me to deal with my very Indian, very Muslim parents who are not letting me move out of the house without threatening to cut all ties. And me? I am also not like a theorist. I am here, in this house, with a family I can die for but for the life of me cannot live with. Because I cannot afford to cut ties with my family. Theory equipped me to debate feminism vs misogyny in a conference, on the internet, in a paper, with men and women. But it failed me in my own home. Theory did not equip me to tell my parents that they are hurting me. (Varisha Tariq, personal communication, 18 October 2020)

Varisha's sense of dissonance is not unique; and yet we must refrain from universalising it and asking ourselves which analytical categories are missing in how we teach that lead to such dissonance. It might seem that Varisha and, by extension, I are looking for a theory to provide recipes and answers from a theory that it does not provide. However, Varsiha may well be looking for resonances of her South Asian urban Muslim home in the concerns of 'gender' theory. Perhaps, the entire category of home missing in a theory class, consigned as it were to a discussion of particular novels in a literature class, if at all they are taught. As someone who has had to spend a considerable amount of time cooking for different generations in an undivided large family, I have begun to notice how the domestic is missing as an analytical category from our discussions of theoretical literature. Projecting the cosmopolitanism of the immigrant, the traveller and the troubadour, literary theory has ignored what came into the house and transmuted the self that lay flattened by banality. Analogous to this is a language of movement; of heroic action; of tragedy-as-death rather than non-action and ennui; of repetition and recursiveness of being-at-home. The 'home' occurs as a site of diasporic longing and not as-its-own epistemological and experiential site. One of the major themes of this book is experience and how that mediates the production, dissemination and naming of knowledge. In fact, the marginalisation of experience in the institutionalisation of knowledge makes us not name experience as knowledge. The sites of this reflection are certain texts, classroom situations and many episodes from outside class, but from within life stories, including mine. Hence the business of being a teacher of texts is particularly important, even though every chapter in this book is not about pedagogy. And while I ruminate on this, a horrific video has been leaked from IIT Kharagpur where an English teacher who writes on subalternity and postcolonialism abuses her Dalit students in class. In a situation where signposts of meaning are lost because life is fragile and short-lived, this development imbues our discussion on shaping forces with a sense of urgency and relevance. It's worth asking how a powerful upper-caste English teacher has so far concealed such forms of epistemic violence? This is not to say that caste abuse does not happen in other languages, but it gets projected as exceptional when it happens in a prestigious institution with English-speaking teachers. The exceptionalism is evident in the element of 'surprise' and 'indignation' many of us feel, instead of thinking of this as business-as-usual. Underlying this phenomenon is our investment in emancipatory goals in education of a particular kind. In fact, this is also our blindness to experience. Human beings don't change by using postcolonial jargon; they remain the prejudiced people they have been.

Not to recognise this is also to not see what shaping role experience performs.

The first chapter, 'Texts, Pre-texts and Experience', is not only a rumination on the ungraspable element of experience that eludes language but also puts pressure upon words that get used in particular ways. My mother's use of the plural for an autobiography is a simple point, perhaps particular to her, but it also demands deep thought into how modern genres are institutionalised by being evacuated of collective selves. My point is not to valorise experience. Aparna Vaidik's book *My Son's Inheritance* has an important conversation about experience. A morning-walk conversation with a hatred-spewing neighbour leads the narrator and her husband to a discussion of whether the hatred was a result of the Partition experience and therefore understandable or if the experience is itself an 'inescapable dungeon, trapping everything inside' and defies reason. Is it possible to think outside of experience? The narrator/author replies, 'Perhaps not' (Vaidik 2020: xiii). What is it to recognise that experience mediates the outside world, but also know when it becomes a dungeon? This is perhaps one of the most challenging human situations and central to reflection. The tussle between the upper-caste reader's experience and location and that of the short story 'Creamy Layer' in the chapter on 'Scripting Caste' is in some sense about recognising your experience but also listening to another's. This simultaneity is attempted through a back and forth of languages, locations and voices so that a classroom is not left with an easy translation and transition to a 'Dalit' story. English does not allow caste its euphemisms. So, while translating caste into English, the elliptical becomes overt. This also means that English has no memory of caste since it does not have in its deep crevices words, idioms and indexical signs that point to caste. It is quite casteless in that sense, even if it does create a hierarchy. It also collaborates with upper-caste, merit-touting groups and helps preserve privileges for them. It helps produce the myth of the casteless secular modern. So, its transactional power makes it far from innocent. It is in its translational avatar that English needs to make caste overt, almost embarrassing. All these statements are heavy mouthfuls and mean little without examples.

I asked a publisher recently if she would be interested in a project of translation from Sindhi into English. The project involved a collaboration between me and a Sindhi writer from Pakistan. It had seemed to me that she would jump with excitement, a language this rare written in the Perso-Arabic script, almost a dying language, rarer to have its translation into English and rarest to have a collaboration from both sides of the border—it seemed like, well, rare. She said, 'Well, we are not looking into expanding that much. We will stick to major languages, big languages that have readerships.' I thanked her, and she reminded me that my project on Gujarati was very much on target. 'Of course,' I said. I was not pitting one language; against another. Sindhi and Gujarati are my everyday languages, however, they come with enormously different significance in my system. Their hierarchy is consolidated by the academic and publishing world, which has almost always taken cognisance of the social and economic significance of Gujarati, and not the historical, linguistic, psychological burden of Sindhi. The truth is that the experience of Sindhi has been made to turn into a footnote. One of the ways this book approaches experience is by examining language-as-experience. In 'Language and Incomplete Travels', I examine how desires for renewed self-definition may show themselves in changes from syllables and phonemes to the entire shedding or embracing of a language. This may or may not be enough; nonetheless, there are powerful accounts of how members of socially marginalised groups negotiate with hegemonic forms through forms of linguistic play and democracy. That said, we also need to remember that while no meaningful experience is possible without language, all meanings are not contingent upon language. As Mark Johnson reminds us, meaning goes deeper than language. In his words, 'meaning, understanding, thinking, and valuing all have to be enacted as embodied processes' (Johnson 2014: 14). This comes out much clearer in the chapter on Hindi film songs. Words such as *dil* and *aankhein* gesture to a signification that has little relation with anatomy; at the same time, they are embodied expressions of desires that do not have a social legitimacy to be openly communicated. Language is both central and incidental, but that judgement is always made contextually here. As such, my deep investment in language comes from the twin and inseparable contexts of translation and ethnography. The act of listening, of being arrested by certain words that seemed important to the interlocutors, the words thrown back at me reminding me who I was—female, urban, upper-caste—all of this has helped in addition to physical texts in not separating language from people. This approach is intimate with what B. Matilal refers to as the tradition of *sabdapramana* in Indian philosophy—that is we 'derive knowledge from linguistic utterances' (Matilal 2001: xiii). Matilal asserts that we understand the world in terms of our language, and this would imply that our thinking about the world necessarily involves the use of language.

One of the running forms of insistence in this book is also that we look at the quotidian modes of living and not think of the literary lying only in the literate spaces. It is the proximate world of the everyday—the familiar and the familial—that might have lessons of contexts shaping language and self. In 'Elsewhere: Language, Gender, Translation,' my interest lies in the ways in which language bears the implicitness of gender, inviting us to 'read' through translation what lies hidden in plain sight. In doing so, I draw attention to vignettes from multilingual sites and hope to demonstrate that questions of gender and translation are before and beyond the paradigms of translation studies, and it is those we need to study to nuance the existing positions on how to do feminist translation, which may simply be about how to listen as a feminist. In acts of listening, words arrest my attention. I find both the presence and the absence of words important sites of knowledge production. For instance, in the chapter 'The Illegibility of Shame', I ask what it means to not have quite that word, quite in the semantic range of the Indian languages. Does absence in language mean an absence of experience or oblivion regarding that experience? Are the groups institutionalising language and those experiencing a quiet, visceral shame different from each other? What is to make language accountable for not holding the experience of the marginalised? The chapter spends considerable time on the particular forms of self-repulsion in Dalit and other subaltern bodies to understand if shame is legible.

As such, with the chapter 'Saying It, Not Saying It: The "Hindi" Film Song', we may appear to make a strange shift. We move away from classrooms discussing texts, from questions of knowledge in academic contexts or understanding shame and humiliation. However, the book has been imbued with the personal, popular and everyday. It has situated discussions of self and knowledge in a way that the 'given-ness' of our bodies and memories, homes and surroundings are made to knock on the doors of the more 'academic' questions. As teachers and students, many of us are/were constituted by songs and images that we left behind outside classrooms as we entered the holy echelons of both English and literature or even other disciplines. The songs that played in our heads—by listening to or overhearing others at home—remained a 'personal' and 'unofficial' aspect of our lives, and their experience was muted in studying other things. Except for the occasional parlour or picnic game of *antakshari*, we give little thought to how songs shape our journeys. For those who pursued film studies, films became objects of study; however, the subjective and beyond-the-ideological world of songs and images seldom informs our larger questions of the everyday social in India. As such, this book has moved in and out of experience in its sensory meaning; in its distillation of knowledge produced through life; in its formation resulting from social class, caste and other forms of location. Instead of enumerating these different sites of experience, it has allowed experience to inform the discussion, reinforcing thereby the inarticulateness that surrounds this subject. One of the aspects of experience we examined is how its references appear through a proxy language—that it gets gestured at rather than mentioned. This displacement from the origins, so to speak, of language—the fact of its not emanating from where expected but appearing elsewhere—has also been a recurring theme in this book. The site of elsewhereness is discussed and demonstrated much more vividly when we put in conversation translation and gender. At the heart of all these ineffable formulations lies the transfer of experience as a unit of meaning—the act of translating a life, trauma or pain into another discourse or words.

Shabdon ke Peechhe: Chasing Words

Lata Mani reminds us that

> we apprehend the world through the words we use and the ways in which we have come to understand them. Words can open our consciousness or narrow our perception, deepen sensation or deaden our capacity to feel. The struggle over language is intrinsic to politics. We invent new words to speak of things our vocabulary cannot quite express. Or we reclaim existing terms in ways that alter the meanings they have accrued. (2013: 85)

'You are angry,' my therapist said. 'No, I am disappointed.' 'What do you feel when you say angry?' Substituting one word for another may serve as intralingual translation, that is translation within the same system. However, its effects can be staggering in the form of 'naming' an experience that we are reluctant to name with a less pleasant word. From 'disappointment' to 'anger' is a problem of translation and also a denial of reality. And so from a psychoanalytic point view it is an evidence of anxieties at work. Adam Phillips reminds us:

> Psychoanalysts don't tend to think of themselves as translating people. The analyst interprets, reconstructs, re-describes, returns the signifier, as Lacanians say, but he rarely describes what he does as translating the patient's so-called material. Translation is what we do to texts, and we can't read people like books. Even though words are the thing in analysis, translation isn't often the word that comes to mind, at least for the analyst. And yet, each of these techniques, or rather practices, both overlap with the work of the translator, or are just simply of a piece with what translation entails. To interpret, reconstruct, to describe, to question—even to return the signifier, if only to the dictionary, or the author's other work—this is what the translator also does with his text. Such disparate practices share a likeness. (2000: 126)

My mother noticed early on this obsession with words: 'Why did you remember every single word I said? Learn to *let go*.' She would say 'let go' like 'late go.' She would 'quote' perhaps Guru Nanak, '*Akharan je vich je koi atkya; ishq di chaadi mul na chadiya*.' This hybrid part-Punjabi, part-something else couplet says this in effect: One who gets lost in words cannot climb the ladder of love. Whether the couplet was by Guru Nanak or not is difficult for me to establish; for us, it carried Nanak's authority. It helped to suggest that love is about transcending language. Should we hang on to words or let them go? To chase words is to be *shabdon ke peechhe*, in pursuit, but it is also an unnecessary tenacity. This book believes in the centrality and untranslatability of the word. In making the word central, the book urges us to pay attention to it; it acknowledges human finitude in relation to not just language as a system but, at times, just a word.

'At the beginning of translation is the word,' Derrida says. 'The unit of measurement is the unit of the word' (2001: 180). Derrida's philosophy rests upon the paradox of translating and untranslating the word; it is the site where, in Walter Benjamin's oft-quoted words, one language licks another like a flame or caress. Paradoxically, words travel the most and the least, much like translation, which is both possible and not. They linger, reminding us of the incompleteness of translation. Finding equivalents or homonyms for them is not the point—I may well have done that. But their traces haunt my thinking, interrupting the neat English prose. They push their way into my writing, reminding me of how my English must see them and beat a retreat to think anew about what it has thought. My differently literate mother's word, *atamkatha*, a story of the soul, not of the self—stands next to 'autobiography'; it refuses to be replaced and therefore erased. It is no surprise that Indian philosophy considers meanings and words as the key to knowledge creation. Jonardan Ganeri begins his study of meaning in Indian philosophical traditions by the word, a beginning that Derrida would mark as one of translation.

> Words have powers, as do the people who understand them. A word has the power to stand in for or take the place of a thing. Vibrations in the air, or ink marks on paper, manage somehow to act as substitutes for people and places, planets and atoms, thoughts and feelings. It is to this extraordinary function that the Sanskrit term for 'meaning' calls attention: Shakti—the power or capacity of a word to stand for an object. People who understand words have powers as well; most remarkably, the capacity to acquire knowledge about people, places,

> planets, and so on, just by hearing noises or seeing marks. This too is power, just as surely is the power to see or remember or reason. It is the power to receive knowledge from the testimony of others. (Ganeri 2011: Introduction)

In her detailed commentary on Kabir's 'upside-down language', Linda Hess makes a fleeting reference to the 'crooked words' of a Zen master. At the beginning the Zen master did not emphasise the importance of the word, rather he argued against it: 'Even more foolish is one who clings to words and phrases and thus tries to achieve understanding. . . . It has nothing to do with the Truth'. The Zen master was clear that his 'talks would serve to stir up waves where there is no wind, to gash a wound in a healthy skin' (Hess and Singh 2002: 129), but it is not his words that he wanted to be pursued. There indeed was power in them but perhaps not the Truth. The sant poet Kabir also resonates with a view that words are everywhere, ubiquitous, but their existence is not only on the tongue. 'True words' need to be tested and tasted.

> Everyone says words, words.
> That word is bodiless.
> It won't come
> on the tongue.
> See it, test it, take it.
> —Kabir
> (ibid.: 93)

From the perspective of translation as well, chasing words and phrases for equivalence might help us track down the small acts of translation; it might also make us 'blind' to the experience of the word that, essentially, makes the endeavour of translation uneasy. Calling translation 'uneasy' as I do, in both the title of this book and the last chapter, does not mean that translation does not happen. It surely does, but 'we are always on a journey back to find something that we might almost have had' (Gunesekera quoted in Young 2006: 1)—often just a word that escaped in plain sight. It can thus be argued that the truth, if any, of translation lies not in the words or phrases but elsewhere—an experiential elsewhere that this book attempts to map for we must acknowledge that this business of chasing words is a futile exercise at some level. Words keep hiding themselves not only from us but also from other words, from other linguistic and non-linguistic expressions, teasing us into the space of the 'untranslatable'—not what is not or cannot be translated but 'rather what one keeps on (not) translating' (Apter 2014: xvii). Amidst a plenitude of words or lack thereof, we, the customers of the word, just move on by, for 'the price is high./Without paying you can't get it' (Hess and Singh 2002: 128) as Kabir confronts us. Exhausted, we let the matters be, abandoning them in favour of an afterlife that remains forever incomplete, though not entirely irredeemable. Restless, then, we wander back and forth, often hiding ourselves from the word in response. Such meanderings across words necessarily require the 'translating body moving through space and time [not to be] isolated, but [to be] engaged in social worlds' (Hess 2018: 25–26). It is, essentially, this awareness that turns the wanderer into a wonderer, the translated into a translation, and the finished into unfinished.

In essence, this book is but a series of interminable conversations in and about translation, eluding a conclusion, for even experience (the loss and mourning of translation) cannot be concluded. The book meditates upon different intensities emerging out of texts and 'real-life' situations almost as if the two were not separable. Mani remarks that

> It would not be considered radical to propose that the world is an interdependent singular whole of which everything is an integral, albeit complexly related, part. Yet the ways of thinking and being we have come to privilege tend to disaggregate self and phenomena from the multiple dimensions with which they are inextricably bound. (Mani 2013: 7)

This is not to say that all texts and experiences are available to us, let alone integral to us. *However, the attempt is to understand how in their movement from one to the other, from mind to body, from one body to another, one of the many things that go missing in translation may well be 'experience'.* The gaps left by experience are not visible, neither in the linguistic act of translation nor in the everyday forms of carrying over from context to context; experience to abstraction; teacher to student and back. In saying thus, the idea is not to valorise experience and resist historical and political narratives of the universes we occupy, in which our own and others' experiences both coalesce and clash. It is also not to make some bodies be consigned to 'experience' and to leave the rest of us unaccountable as if we had no role to play in creating those universes of experience. However, the forging of the experience as a translational challenge is to complicate both the invisibly resident meaning and the illegibility of experience itself as knowledge. The book is an experiment and experience in its attempt to write about experience. Is it a 'book' with chapters, or a book of essays? The book, if it is one, is neither fiction nor non-fiction; neither fully academic nor fully personal, deriving its unity from the approach. It's a gendered genre, for both words have their origins in the same root.

1

Texts, Pre-texts and Experience

... અખા, કથની થી અનુભવ તે અલગ

Akho says, experience is different from description.

—Joshi (2011: 3)

Look, all of you
All the Vedas, Shastras, Agamas, Puranas
Are the grit and husk
From beaten paddy.
Why beat it? Why strike it?
Once you purge the mind
From flowing here and there
Pure light dawns
Channamallikarjuna

—Akkamahadevi, trans. Shivaprakash (2010: 92)

My mother was married by the time she was 14, if not earlier, and then she moved to Ahmedabad. She had studied up to the third or fourth standard, but she doesn't quite remember. It gave her enough literacy to write Sindhi letters in Devnagari script to her family in Ajmer. The Sindhi schools in Rajasthan had adopted the Devnagari (as opposed to the Perso-Arabic) script after Partition. I remember her large handwriting on postcards and inland letters that she used to send to her family. The visual memory of those letters now feels like a slice from a distant past, for at some stage, she must have stopped writing. Perhaps the phone calls substituted the letters, or she was occupied with navigating a web of conflicts in her life and felt she had no leisure of that kind. From about the mid-1980s, she also joined what is called the 'Geeta Bhagwan jo Satsang', a spiritual group, one of many that Sindhi families follow. These *satsangs* are, perhaps, a continuation of both the pir and Guru Nanak *satsang* traditions that were strong in Sindh. Her large handwriting had now moved from the inland letter to diaries, where she would write down *satsang ji vaani*—the speeches given by the guru or the spiritual discourses. 'Secular' writing, for want of a better word, disappeared. Ordinarily, she would have dismissed writing letters about her life and herself as a form of maya. However, in the period following COVID, I often found her lost and suggested that she write something from her life. A woman of 77 today, my mother, like any other non-elite woman, had had a long journey with myriad challenges—social, financial and personal. Even as I write the word 'personal', I wonder if she would have used that as a separate term from the rest. Be that as it may, she entertained the possibility for the first time, and instead of making notes about *gyan* (used not as a term of mockery that the English language in India has recruited), she decided to try.

'I was trying to write *hinan jee ain muhanji atamkatha*,' she said to me. The word *hinan* is a respectful honorific used as a third-person pronoun by Sindhi women to refer to their husbands. Literally, it means 'him' and substitutes for the husband's name since mentioning his name is considered inauspicious for women. Basically, my mother was saying she was writing two autobiographies, my father's and her own, or rather using the word 'autobiography' loosely to cover the story of not one, but two people. She had spent over 50 years with my father before he passed away. It is only understandable that a self outside that conjugality was unimaginable in the telling of her life story. But she realised in the course of recalling and writing that she would violate my father's memory for me, and she simply could not continue. One day, she called up to say that she couldn't continue and said, 'Let me tell you, nobody who says *maan atamkatha mein sach likhyo aa, sach to galaye*.' (Nobody claiming to have been truthful while writing an autobiography is truthful.) This by itself is not profound knowledge for us about the genre of the autobiography, except that she was using the word *atamkatha* (note that Sindhis find it hard to use consonants in succession so it's not *atmakatha*) as a life story, but not just her own. She laughed at the end of our conversation and said, 'I am best left with *gyan*, should just go back to write *satsang jee vaani*.' My persuasion that I would consider her narrative of my father's life as a perspective and not an absolute truth, for he may have had his own, was incomprehensible to her. 'No, no,' she said, 'Truth hurts.' The matter ended there.

There are echoes in this story that take us to Tanika Sarkar's brilliant study *Words to Win: The Making of Amar Jiban* (2013). However, no autobiography is written here, first or otherwise. And there is no special case to be made of an unusual life in my mother's case. She is neither fully lettered nor fully unlettered. She is not an upper-caste bhadramahila, nor is she an underprivileged and marginal woman in terms of other locations. I use my mother's example because it has an immediacy and refuses to be sealed away as a neat formulation. It niggles me, forcing me to own up to the question of how experience poses serious challenges to theoretical positions. The experience of hurtful truth made my mother not write. As such, we seldom think of non-writing as a world of possibilities that were on the verge of being realised. The fact that the noun 'writing' is accompanied by the desideratum 'non' opens up questions of contexts that produce, but also in some cases, inhibit writing. Do our theories of writing account for the number of times writing does not happen, I asked myself. My aim in this chapter is to move between this immediate experiential context and intellectual impulses around the relationship between theory and experience. Since I can't help retreating to texts and classrooms with the messiness of life inside both, the last section ends with a text I taught around the same time.

Experience and the 'Autobiography'

The realisation that my mother Kamla could not continue had come to her from her experience with non-writing. Her excessive experience made her not write; and yet in many cases, as James Baldwin suggests, 'One writes out of one thing only—one's own experience. Everything depends on how relentlessly one forces from this experience the last drop; sweet or bitter, it can possibly give' (Baldwin 2017: 7). There must be a covenant with experience that is allowed to be written; a life to be narrated and sometimes not. I could schematise the difference in race and gender between my mother and Baldwin; however, I want to stay for the moment with the idea of experience as both generative and inhibiting, depending of course on a range of contexts.

Meanwhile, it begs discussion whether my father would have found it equally hard and whether we are witnessing a gendered relationship with the genre of the autobiography. Perhaps, he would have had a lot to document from leaving Karachi by ship to arriving in refugee camps, and living through life with tribulations and courage and despair and failure. It is equally true that when I needed to hear about Partition, it is to him that I first went—not only did he have memories, but he had seemed to me then to be that history's chosen candidate. The women followed instructions as the men planned the logistics of leaving Sindh. The autobiography as well as my testimony of Partition was about my father—the do-er. The 'home' was absent from my former inquiries too. What interests me today is not the action around my parents; but the language surrounding their selves and mine, especially the marking out of *satsang jee vaani* as a safe space for my mother. She is told by her guru to neither endure nor practise injustice and to neither valorise nor give up a sense of self. She said to me one day that her guru said the sense of *maan* (as in I, in Sindhi) is both good and bad. When Krishna uses it in the Gita, it is a good 'I' but when we humans use it as a form of egotism, it is not a good 'I'. This was perhaps a rare occasion when she would have asked herself if she had any 'I' at all. It is understandable then that there was more validation for her in the spiritual space of the satsang than in the modern space of the autobiography for the latter had the possibility of a bad 'I'. There is also another way of looking at this experience of non-writing. The satsang has provided my mother with the freedom of leaving behind the memory of a marriage that seems to do little for her. Her euphoria at having found that freedom is almost like this Therigatha poem:

> The name I am called by means freed
> And I am quite free, well—free from three crooked things,
> Mortar, pestle, and husband with his own crooked thing.
> I am freed from birth and death,
> What leads me to rebirth has been rooted out.
> (Hallisey 2015: 11)

Moreover, the *satsang jee vaani* is also a set of 'universal truths' about the transience of life; the importance of devotion; betrayal of maya and so on. The women who go to the satsang treat them as a set of principles and modify their lives around pithy statements made by the guru. I remember my mother (who doesn't know English) had learnt the sentence, 'nothing new under the sun'. It helped her to think she wasn't encountering a unique situation for the guru had said we have been there before. Mythologies help situate individuals in a larger network of rationalisation—of justifying the ways of god to us. They reduce the loneliness of being special. Also, there's safety and anonymity in universals that particularisms do not allow. Particularisms carry the odour of experience. My mother was repulsed by that odour and sought to take refuge in her guru's sanitised discourse. Her 'self' could be curated in that interaction; it was not a rough and jagged path over which many travels had happened, but a volitionally spliced side that waited to receive peace and grace. Neat universalisms provide relief as opposed to chaotic particularisms that cling to the skin.

Something about the universalisms versus particularisms reminds me of the flight Indian students take into theory instead of theorising the particularisms they come with. The comparison is not fair to my mother, and it also does not work all the way. However, the resonances are striking. I ask students what they feel about a text, and they quote a higher authority. They turn away from feelings, perfecting the art of hiding behind an avalanche of words like Brahmins hiding behind Sanskrit shlokas. The theoretical gems they regurgitate may have been produced out of particularisms; but in the tradition of handing down theory, they become sacred verses—empty universalisms. I also want to think of this 'particularism' of my mother's experience against the backdrop of her formulation *hinan jee ain muhinji atamakatha* that complicates both the self and genre. It does not allow me those words in English, 'his and my autobiography'. The genre of autobiography, by and large, does not carry a plural, as if it were possible for us to tell only our story.[1] Its pronoun 'I' occupies in the logic of the genre a full room, not an undivided joint family. The uneasiness of translation lies in the fact that the English-produced genre that I am used to does not

1 This requires qualification. Personal accounts of spiritual life both in South Asia and in Europe may be found inseparable from the objects of devotion and allow a collapsing of the self with virtually 'everyman' (for instance, Augustine's *Confessions*).

recognise a scope for more than one story. Isn't 'self' only a sliver of larger stories, as a poem by A.K. Ramanujan reminds us:

> I resemble everyone
> but myself, and sometimes see
> in shop-windows
> despite the well-known laws
> of optics,
> the portrait of a stranger,
> date unknown,
> often signed in a corner
> by my father.
> (Ramanujan 1997: 23)

Ramanujan gestures towards the difficulty of consolidating our 'original' selves—without our people and our histories—that constantly shape, interrupt and travel with us. The exercise of extracting one's identity as independent of its relationality with others is not one that always bears fruit. But how do I, schooled into modernity's promise of producing an individual self, account for my mother's use of the plural in whatever it is that she wanted to write, rather not write? What is the genre for me to translate her story? This translation, this naming and a woman who speaks from experience remind me of the following lines of another translation, another woman:

> For a long time when colleagues would ask me what I was 'working on', I found myself alternating between calling what Esperanza was telling me a 'life history' and a 'life story.' It finally dawned on me that the most appropriate term was obviously Esperanza's own, the Spanish word historia, which she often used in the plural, describing her account as her historias, making no distinction between history and story. (Behar 2003: 16)

Closer home, the book *Playing with Fire* (2006) undertakes the difficult task of providing each story with its dignity but also retaining a collective 'we' as a methodological resistance to both grammar and patriarchy. The book comprises autobiographical writing by seven women working in the Sitapur district of Uttar Pradesh. The autobiographical account and discussion 'enacts and theorizes experiences' and puts together 'personal' accounts and discussion as 'ground for analysis and transformation of self' (Mohanty, Foreword, Sangtin Writers 2006). Of course, its larger context of development politics makes it different from the example I began with. But *Playing with Fire* is an instructive book in bringing together women who understood poverty, sexuality and caste through both childhood experiences and the subsequent of these in NGOs. Knowledge is built upon experience, which is then translated to make uneasy the NGOs they work with. I am also reminded of the slipping and sliding of 'I' into 'we' in Bama's autobiography, *Karukku* (2000). Bama's experiences as a Dalit Tamil, living first in the village and then in a convent, are marked by caste discrimination meted out to her through the community and sometimes to the community through her. The definitional basis of the autobiographical genre turns out to be inadequate in determining how experience can be held within its confines, which is rather ironic. As a genre, the autobiography is meant to be an account of the narrator's experiences, but it seems to have difficulty accepting the slipperiness of experience. The two examples of *Playing with Fire* and *Karukku* (far from being the same) convey collective ownership and solidarity whereas the *hinan jee ani muhinjee atamakatha* does not translate into a Sindhi *asaanjee* (ours). It remains his and mine—separate and conjoined; hence my rumination over its absent vocabulary. Nonetheless, we may want to think of relationships between genres and lives they claim to define, and for this theoretical question, we may want to look at lived experiences of women and other marginalised groups. They remind us of intertwining contexts of methodological and political questions. Meanwhile, my mother made me think of the problematic nature of not just autobiography but the perennial problem of female autobiography.[2] She had also helped me think of how the

2 In this regard, also see Partha Chatterjee's 'Women and the Nation' in *The Nation and Its Fragments* (1993). Chatterjee begins by acknowledging the difference between male and female autobiographies. The latter are more about the domestic spheres, the family, the clan and surroundings. However, Chatterjee adds men do the same, and remarks that 'the difference lies in the textual strategies employed' (1993: 138). In the case of women's autobiographies, the striking feature is the way in which 'the very theme of self remains suppressed under a narrative of changing times…' (ibid.). It is interesting that Chatterjee should see this only as a difference of textual strategy for it is precisely the subsumption of self that does not even let women tell their stories; let alone tell them differently!

first-person account is a construction, invented when other selves are held in abeyance. Or, perhaps there's another way of thinking of autobiographies, in this case, the ones not written. Udaya Kumar makes penetrating arguments on this form in his study, *Writing the First Person* (2016). His focus on Kerala and the autobiographies written there bring attention to an illuminating discussion on agency. What is the relation between the individual and autobiographical expression? The question may take us to reductive places and get embroiled in seeing the autobiography—the capacity and the ability to tell one's story—as a testimony of the individual self. Instead, Kumar draws attention away from the original source of action to structures of authorisation—in other words, under what authority does one gain the right to speak about one's life, write one's autobiography? If writing the self-narrative is a testimony of agency (a myth circulated through modernity), did my mother feel more agency in not writing it? And yet, my mother is not a writer who made a conscious decision to not write; she only fleetingly thought of writing as a mode of expressing herself and then moved away from the idea.

I believe that she was operating from both active and passive positions, and this mixedness is seldom included in our understanding of the agential allure. Experience teaches us to not think of 'agency' in terms of stark positions of having it or not having it. For if asked to write about her experiences of satsang, she would certainly write them in the first person and see that as her story. This also means that the 'self' is not distinctive from other larger truths; at best, it curates its alignment with certain truths. Neither fully present nor fully absent, the self is inseparable from experience and its encounters with language, as I will explore in the next section.

Theoretical Impulses

This recent episode with my mother seems like a good place for me to begin ruminations on language, experience and translation, albeit not in any particular order. Experience that is as much in the body as in life. Experience is often made to masquerade as an anecdote in the social sciences, at best a case study. It lies as the invisible presence at the periphery, not in need to be held up as a foundation to theory.

And when experience and theory look into each other, it is available only through a cracked mirror, as Guru and Sarukkai's title reminds us (Guru and Sarukkai 2012).

The two books by Gopal Guru and Sundar Sarukkai—*The Cracked Mirror: An Indian Debate on Experience and Theory* (2012) and *Experience, Caste, and the Everyday Social* (2019) have shaped some of the approaches in this book. The primacy of experience and its shaping force as social theory is most compellingly articulated in *The Cracked Mirror.*[3] Situated squarely as an 'Indian debate', the discussion on experience and theory makes for a much-needed intervention in our intellectual history. Without valorising experience as a form of inherent indigeneity or the basis of rights and authority, Guru and Sarukkai manage to show the ethics of theorising out of experience. The strength of the book lies rather in overturning the terms of our relation with knowledge and drawing attention to the asymmetrical contexts of receiving and generating knowledge, which puts the underprivileged outside the pale of significance. Guru and Sarukkai emphasise that experience is prior to thinking and knowing but is susceptible to radical improvement using theory and philosophy. Guru makes a very pertinent observation about Gandhi and Ambedkar in this regard. He says,

> Both Gandhi and Ambedkar shared one thing in common: for both of them, experience provides the vantage point for making epistemological moves and also for ideological or political mobilization of the masses. However, there is a fundamental difference between the two. Gandhi experiments with the experience of the self and others. Thus, the experience of Ambedkar and his community becomes an object of Gandhi's experiment. Ambedkar and his entire untouchable community to not have to experiment in order to produce experience —in fact, untouchables are born into it. (Guru 2012: 75)

3 A much-needed qualification must be made here: All oppositional social theory originates in experience and highlights it in order to make its theory (I am thinking, for instance, of feminist consciousness raising, Black studies, gender studies, etc.). It is in its institutionalised orthodox forms that theory appears and is received as such without the experience that produced it. It may be digressive here to dwell further on this matter. However, bringing back 'experience' to the discussion every now and then reminds us in fact of the relevance of theory, instead of living with its bereft and empty existence.

Both Guru and Sarukkai underscore the lived experience, one that leaves no room for an exit clause, as the source of reflective consciousness. Attending upon those questions lies a judgment of what might be 'authentic' telling. Guru and Sarukkai bypass the settled nature of this judgment but activate experience as a category for theory-making. They critique the subordination, where experience is posterior to theory in the sense that theory orders experience. The nucleus around which the Guru and Sarukkai debates cohere was an essay, 'Egalitarianism and the Social Sciences in India', which points to a 'pernicious divide between theoretical Brahmins and empirical Shudras' (Guru 2012: 10). Guru interrogates the 'hierarchical division that suggests that some are born with a theoretical spoon in their mouth and the vast majority with the empirical pot around their neck' (11). To those familiar with caste practices, it is quite evident that Guru employs caste both as a metaphor as well as a sociological reality to implicate the hegemonic nature of knowledge creation by the upper castes, who feed upon the experiences of the marginalised sections. Before we continue, I would like to express a reservation here and in some sense, this book is also a mode of filling that unfilled gap. Guru does not address literature, except perhaps in a dismissive way, marking its existence beyond and outside theory. He quotes a Marathi ditty in the opening chapter:

> Brahmanchi ghari lihina (at the Brahmin's, you write and learn)
> Kanbay ghari dana (at the tiller's you thrash)
> Mahara ghari gana (at the Dalit's you sing).
> (Guru 2012: 16)

Guru rightly points out that the space for philosophising and engaging with abstract ideas and learnings has been considered exclusively the Brahmin's territory. He further states that Dalits and women have not had the access to formal education that is necessary if one is to speak in an abstract universal language. However, as Guru and Sarukkai themselves argue, this abstract universal language is not the only form of knowledge. I argue that regardless of whether one is formally educated or not, folk tales, idioms and songs are also literature that constitutes knowledge. While it is true that certain bodies may be kept outside of the realms of knowledge creation, what is considered knowledge must itself be expanded out of its ambit of universal abstractions to that of literature for it comes closest to giving voice to the particularisms of experience. To consider the poetic as knowledge is to lend credential to experience. Is that the same thing as saying all forms of poetry are contingent upon experience? This book is concerned with expanding—for our consideration—forms of knowledge that miss our serious attention for they get written off as anecdotal experiences. However, it is not arguing for all writing to be 'authenticated' by experience. Creative writing is formed through multitudes of possibilities and may emerge from experience lived or imagined, and sometimes neither. The locus is critical pedagogies and not a prescription for creative writing.

In (the sequel to *The Cracked Mirror*) *Experience, Caste and the Everyday Social*, Guru and Sarukkai examine the arena of the social. Arguing that the everyday social is made of senses—things we see, touch, smell—Guru and Sarukkai attempt to apprehend this undescribable flow. The social is not simply constituted by the sensory; in fact, the sensory provides an insight into social theory around un/touchability and difference. In a literary context, this would mean that upper-caste readers and researchers (like me, for instance) 'use' Dalit literature to build theoretical arguments. But it's also important to see the following: What is the nature of experience embedded in a narrative; what forms of proximate and distant experiences does the text encounter through the senses, and how might we put our own sensory world in conversation with that of the text in forms of reading, sharing and forming a social space of the text.[4]

The Homonyms of Experience

An experience is a form of knowledge. Indian philosophical theories tell us that. However, contemporary discourses of experience are mute and hidden behind identity politics, which in cruder words is about who can speak for whom. This book treats experience as a constant—an epistemology rather than a back-story or anecdote. Experience in

4 For a detailed discussion on this, see Galp Lok's panel discussion. Available at: https://www.youtube.com/watch?v=DTysk6hBeaQ, accessed on 12 March 2021.

this book is not a substantiation to a theoretical principle; it is its own theory, seeking articulation in terms that are close to the skin. In that sense, there is no distinction we make between thought and experience, expressed so well by T.S. Eliot when he says of the poet John Donne, 'A thought to Donne was an experience, it modified his sensibility' (Eliot 1970: 307). The difficulty of defining experience is evident in the way Raymond Williams struggles with it, an entry he added in *Keywords*, ten years after the first edition. In the section on 'empiricism', Williams delineates the twin and inseparable roles of 'experiment' and 'experience' that form the basis of observation. The idea of a test or trial (so evident in Gandhi's autobiography, for instance) as a mode of knowledge makes experience untheoretical by itself. However, it is only when experience ceases to be a 'present participle' and becomes 'a consciousness of an effect' (1985: 116) that it acquires the meaning we mobilise in this book. Williams makes a very small entry on experience and sums it up as (1) knowledge gathered from past events, whether by conscious observation or by consideration and reflections; and (2) a particular kind of consciousness, which can in some contexts be distinguished from 'reason' or 'knowledge' (ibid.: 126). It is the word 'distinguish' that we need to focus on. Does the distinction between two kinds of experience operate in language or do they have an empirical basis—as if to say the mind and body or heart and reason could be divided, or assume that experience produced over time does not mediate through new experiences of the body or the mind? It seems to me that the distinction is constructed as a boundary to not let the messiness of life enter into classrooms—our academic writing and positions that secure for us a mystifying role as intellectuals. The embodiment of knowledge is rendered illegitimate by such distinguishing, and for my purposes, I prefer to think of Shah Abdul Latif, the Sindhi poet, who says,

Par aad o sad u, varu vaaeea jo je laheen
Huaa ag ehee gadu, budhan mein ba thiyaa

The echo and the call are the same.
In the beginning they were one.
In listening they became two.
(Tolani 2020: 18)

Experience is its own knowledge; it can inform reason. It is a difficult category to work with because it is ongoing and eludes borders. It may even appear so true as to be banal, and we are likely to miss the process of knowledge-formation. Social sciences treat experience as a transition to a more generalisable principle; however, literature is haunted by it, beckoning us to its ungraspable quality and untranslatability. The problem in theorising experience, says Sarukkai, lies precisely in the fact that it is so matter-of-fact and immediate (2012: 46). Drawing from both Indian and Western phenomenological traditions, Sarukkai asserts that descriptions of the properties of the world are, primarily and fundamentally, descriptions of our experiences of the world. The rupture between the subject and the object is historically produced, leading to disembodied ideas. Indian dictionaries define experience, not by opposition to knowledge, but by seeing its close relation with experiment, rather as perceptual knowledge. One of the earliest and most detailed dictionaries in Gujarati, produced under Gandhi's leadership, has an interesting entry on the word *anubhav* (the most common Indian word for experience) (Saarth 2012: 29). It defines it as *pratyaksh gyan* (perceptual knowledge) but also adds *jaate pote janvu te* (the one known by the self). Knowledge and subjectivity are inseparable, the latter not in abeyance for the production of the former. The second word is *veetak*—to experience yourself or to witness or test it yourself (*jaate aajmaish kari ne jovu*). *Veetak* is what you have gone through, *jo aap pe beeti ho* (in Hindi), suggestive of the relation between *veet* and *beet* in Gujarati and Hindi respectively. If I were to push the distinction between *anubhav* and *veetak* in the context of the Gujarati dictionary, the former (*anubhav*) is knowledge gained through experience and formed by experiencing. On the other hand, *veetak* are things that happen to you. The latter has a sense of the passive receptacle, not implying that there is a witnessing involved. Perhaps this sense of *baat/veet* makes the latter idea of experience stay with 'life' than with legitimate 'knowledge'. The *saarth jodnikosh* provides a range of suffixes to suggest experience as a condition for knowledge: hence *anubhav gamya* (the one that can be experienced); *anubhav janya* (the one that is born of experience); *anubhav sidh* (*pratyaksh gyan*); *anubhav mulak* (the one whose basis is experiencing) and *anubhav anand* or pleasure born of experience. In

Sindhi, on the other hand, the word *anubhav* (pronounced as *anbhav*) must have entered the lexicon after Partition, only to be heard in spoken Sindhi sometimes among Indian Sindhis. However, the well-known dictionary from the period prior to Partition lists Perso-Arabic uses and provides both experience and experiment as cognates of each other—*tajurbo* and *aajmudo*—experience and experiment (Mewaram 2000: 60). The title of Gandhi's autobiography, *Satya na Prayogo* or *My Experiments with Truth*, inhere the dual meaning of experiment and experience. But what of experience that makes your cheeks burn, that denounces humanity, that surfaces on the body even when words are not spoken or heard? Yengde's question at the end of the following passage may perhaps help us understand experience in more than one sense of the word:

> I recall an incident with my maternal grandmother, Sarubai Maay, who was a maid in the house of a Bania.... One day, as a curious ten year old, I insisted and followed her to see where she worked [despite her reluctance]. She was mortified upon learning that I was there, watching her clean a toilet. I suddenly got the urge to pee.
>
> I successfully used the toilet and my grandma almost pulled me outside so that she could flush away the evidence. As she did this, a woman with an eye of suspicion glanced at me from behind the door of the house. The malkin cursed my grandma with the kind of contempt one has towards a person who has murdered their family members. I did not understand the nature of the curse words, nor their meaning, but as a ten year old I recognised the negativity. The malkin did not stop there but also directed her rage towards me. I felt very vulnerable and insecure, I crouched, trying to hide my face,
>
> The incident brought home to me my beingness as a Dalit.... I was lesser than the bathroom that was receptacle of shit. I did not know what I was to imagine. Is there a lexicon that fathers the experiences of such an unexplainable act? I am yet to find it. (Yengde 2019: 17)

If there are many sites of subjectivity, how do we theorise experience? And what of experiences that are trenchantly gendered and caste-based? Does theory around identity politics suffice or should we look for the smaller frames—the minutiae of everydayness, textures of sense and sounds? Gopal Guru and Sundar Sarukkai urge us to move resolutely from disembodied ideas which order experience. In contrast, they argue for the primacy of experience, from which theory not only follows but also cannot exist without this foundation. The literary realm provides the richest spectrum of experiences, both direct and mediated. How does experience order theory in this realm, and what is to ask that question whilst leaving room for creative articulations that disrupt neat linear relationships between, say, authenticity of experience and its powerful or unconvincing outcome in literature? For us, students and teachers of literature, the challenges are complex: Guru and Sarukkai's exhortation to theorise the social sciences out of experience can only be more emphatic or put under pressure when we come to literature. We will have opportunities to discuss this at various places in this book. Sarukkai mentions that the 'I' is ontological but 'mine' is epistemological; however, either way, there is no experience without self, nor can we know the self without experience. What made my mother not go from 'I' to 'mine'—did the possession of her story as entirely her own seem excessive to her? Ironically, the one from whom your life can not be separated is also the one not named. Such rules governing intimacy are oxymoronic but experientially true. I have found trailing sentences, half-spoken words guiding me at home and in the 'field' to truths that are too heavy for words to carry. These are neither instances of linguistic incompetence on the part of speakers nor are they about linguistic competence on my part; they are, rather, instances of listening with close attention to words, spoken and unspoken.

Thus language, experience and translation are all packed into embodied moments. What does it mean to stay with experience, examine slowly the contours of language—now hiding, now revealing—an ungraspable element that eludes academic sovereignty and analysis? Is that residue material the untranslated? Was the conceptual impossibility of the self outside conjugality already evident in my mother's pronoun for a husband, who despite being supposedly intimate must not be named? How does my simplistically understood 'agency'-marked feminism make me migrate to this experience, translate them into her language and recognise in that vocabulary elements that would shape me too in ways which I can neither own up nor abandon? Does the language have the means to capture this experience? By making translation uneasy, this book, and in particular, this essay, seeks no question nor answer. It only demonstrates that a haunting survives the concluded acts of translation. In that sense, this book is about leftovers. It looks at impulses of life that escape language, the lived-ness that eludes summarisation. And if, sometimes, writers manage to communicate that somewhat, there are residues in acts of translation. This may be because experience is ineffable or that it is so intertwined with linguistic discourses of particular languages. In one of the chapters in this book, I discuss the slipping away of a character like Bhavaanbhagat—an old man who is both spiritual and politically observant—attuned to otherworldliness by recognising what is transient, maya-like and illusory but also aware of the self-image of the Dalit community in the village that needs revision to acquire a political voice. The particular quality of that life can only be known by proximity with him; in the world of English is a pale shadow of this force. How do we pin down that 'slipping away' caused by a constellation of factors, perhaps—language; the universe of the novel and its people; the English language; or discourses of modernity that do not allow his 'experience' of a spiritual-politics to be captured in simultaneity?

The Limits of Textual Knowledge

To the one learning from life, textual knowledge is a hindrance. So, for instance, the Dalit poet/sant Chokha Mela, like Akho quoted earlier, or even Kabir, Akkamahadevi and Guru Nanak would dismiss lessons reified and codified in texts. The scepticism about *gyan* (still, earnestly) is ubiquitous across India's medieval poetry.

आम्हा न कळे ज्ञान न कळे पुराण
वेदांचं वचन नकळे आम्हा
आगमची आडी निगमाचा भेद
शास्त्राचा संवाद न कळे आम्हा
योग याग तप अष्टांग साधन
न कळे ची दान व्रत तप
चोखा म्हणे माझा भोळा भाव देवा
गाईन केशवा नाम तुझे

(https://www.marathimati.net/aamha-na-kale-dnyan/)

I don't know of the divine knowledge or the Purana
Nor do Vedic words mean much to me.
I can't tell the Agama riddles from the Nigama secrets
Nor do Shastric discourses mean much to me.
I don't know of the yogic practices or its *ashtang* stages
Nor do I understand fasts and penances.
Chokha says
I am but simple and naïve, Lord.
I merely sing your name, Keshava.[5]

Our perception of Chokha Mela's devotion may obfuscate the rejection of textual knowledge that characterises many bhakti traditions of India. The primacy of experience he conveys has come to be associated with the simplicity of mystical faith rather than an epistemological position regarding experience. However, I also want to extend examples beyond the 'devotional' to what are seen as 'folk' or 'pre-modern' narratives. For instance, in a discussion on the translation of oral tales from Rajasthan, the translator Vishesh Kothari shared an excerpt from *Baatan ri Fulwari*, a compendium of oral stories heard, edited, compiled by Vijay Dan Detha. Vishesh Kothari brought to my class the 'original' (if oral tales can be considered one) and his translation *Timeless Tales from Marwar* (Detha and Kothari 2020). The 'original' excerpt was from a story that Detha had chosen to call '*Jhupdi ro Gyan*' which in English translation is titled 'The Learning of Toil'. An old woman foxes the king and his Brahmin companion on certain truths of life entirely through her experience of being a tiller and labourer and of having learnt the lessons of life through experience. The widely regarded King Bhoj and his subordinate Magh Pandit go on an excursion to discover true knowledge and meet an old woman on the way. The old woman or *dokri* (how she is referred to in Marwari) answers each of their questions in what appears as a series of quirky responses.

The raja asked her, 'Ma, where does this road go?' She smiled before she answered. Her toothless smile lit up her face like starlight. Then, she raised her head to look at the raja and said, 'Beta, this road will stay where it is. But the travellers who walk on it come and go.' Then she

5 Unless indicated otherwise, translations are mine.

asked them, 'Beta, who are you?' 'We are travellers of the road.' She said, 'Ni, beta. The travellers of the road are two others!' This time, it was the pandit who asked, 'And who are they?' 'One, the sun, and the other, the moon. They move across the sky, night and day. Don't stop for a second. They are the travellers. But tell me, who are you?' They said, 'We are guests.' She said, 'Ni, beta. The guests are two others. They are youth and wealth. They never stop for long. They are guests. But who are you?' 'We are pardesis.' 'Ni, beta. The pardesis are two others. They are the wind and the jeev. The jeev leaves and no one sees it go....'

This *dokri* had challenged all the assumptions the two men had come with, including what constitutes knowledge. Knowledge was not situated at a fixed destination but took place as a sudden encounter, on the way to a destination that did not exist. What made the dokri's life experience wisdom (her form of knowledge) was that she was of a labouring caste. She had understood what indeed was transient (beauty and age); what was short-lived (life itself) and what indeed moved the most (time). She had understood that true renunciation came not from arrogance of renouncing or that the illusion of knowing was what characterised an intellectual. When the identities of the king and the pandit are revealed to her, she then turned to look at the raja and said,

> You are Raja Bhoj and this is the Magh Pandit. Beta, why did you feed me all this nonsense? Have I lived off the crumbs of the raj durbar and wasted all these years? I see with my eyes, hear with my ears and think for myself. Those who live off the crumbs of the court do not think, hear or see themselves. But beta, those who live off their own toil cannot afford to do so. Only those who eat for free can afford such folly.

By now, the pandit was annoyed with the old woman. He said, 'This is all just clever wordplay. I will ask her a question, and we will get to know her wisdom only if she can answer.' The old woman started laughing and said,

> Whatever for? Whom must I prove my wisdom to? Those who must prove their learning to others have some selfish need to do so. I am content as I am. Even then, ask if you must. If I know, I will tell you. If I don't, I won't hesitate to say I don't know. This poor human being—how much can one know of this endless universe? Only the illusion of knowing....

This powerful account of knowledge and its institutionalised forms that exist among the powerful such as the king and the upper castes whilst the subalterns' knowledge is relegated to nonsense or stories at best captures the asymmetry of our world most. It is also significant that the dokri is a woman, and her 'knowledge' is consigned to an anecdote. In a manner symptomatic of this asymmetry, the dokri's story appears as a shorter and pared-down version in the English translation; a flavour rather than the main theme reproduced with all the dignity and centrality it deserved.

As upper-caste and elite readers and translators, we also mimic the illusory provenance of 'knowledge' and pare down the English translation to an edible size. We are no different from the king and his Brahmin companion for we have no room for wisdom, and we do not see that as a theory of life. Despite claiming to be followers of literature, we also have little time for the storyteller. Walter Benjamin reminds us that

> the storyteller in his living immediacy is by no means a present force. He has already become something remote from us and something that is getting even more distant.... [T]here is embarrassment all around when the wish to hear a story is expressed. It is as if something that seemed inalienable to us, the securest among our possessions, were taken from us: the ability to exchange experiences. One reason for this phenomenon is obvious: experience has fallen in value. (1999: 83–84)

Carlos Ginzburg's work *The Cheese and the Worms* exemplifies this abjection of experience. In the book, Ginzburg (1992) examines the life of Italian miller Menocchio who was tried for heresy in 1583 and eventually executed, owing to his beliefs about how the world was formed. Menocchio believed that the universe was formed out of the chaos of earth, water, fire and air mixed together—just as cheese is churned out of milk and worms appear in it. While he was immensely literate for an ordinary miller and was able to cite around a dozen books during his trial to justify his thoughts, his ideas around the creation of the cosmos were rooted in his experience and labour. This form of expressing his knowledge was seen as a disruption to the church's hegemonic conceptions of the cosmos. What is it about experience that is so immediately threatening that it has to be constantly doubted and relegated to the thresholds? I suspect it has something to do with not just the experiences but also the wisdom of the lives of those fixed to the margins.

For instance, what is the relationship between knowledge generated through experience and wisdom? Patricia Hill Collins cites Carolyn Chase, a 31-year-old inner-city Black woman, who notes, 'My aunt used to say, "A heap see, but a few know"' (1989: 758). This saying depicts two types of knowing—knowledge and wisdom—and taps the first dimension of an Afrocentric feminist epistemology. Living life as Black women requires wisdom since knowledge about the dynamics of race, gender and class subordination has been essential to their survival. African-American women give such wisdom high credence in assessing knowledge. Collins foregrounds the relation with material reality as a key to this experience-formation. The unpaid and paid work that Black women perform, the types of communities in which they live and the kinds of relationships they have with others suggest that African-American women, as a group, experience a different world than those who are not Black and women. These experiences stimulate a distinctive Black feminist consciousness concerning a particular material reality. Quoting an elderly domestic worker Rosa Wakefield, Collins shows how the standpoints of the powerful and those who serve them diverge. In Rosa Wakefield's words, 'If you eats these dinners and don't cook 'em, if you wears these clothes and don't buy or iron them, then you might start thinking that the good fairy or some spirit did all that.... Black folks don't have no time to be thinking like that.... But when you don't have anything else to do, you can think like that. It's bad for your mind, though' (ibid.: 748).

Both Collins and the *dokri*'s accounts point to a life of labour that generates materiality in the form of knowledge; and the self's relation with the many textures of lived experience. If *anubhav* is the collection of what-has-been-experienced (*veetak*) and wisdom the praxis of that experience—the one that gives the dokri the confidence to speak the truth graphically and figuratively so that it doesn't hurt—of leaving the reader/listener with the ambivalence of whether they knew that she knew. Her conviction that truth can only be told when it is not linked to forms of transactions stems from her experience but is also a testimony to her wisdom in how she has maintained a detached view of truth-telling. Meanwhile, Indian idioms about the experience of seeing life or gaining wisdom overlap, so that *dhoop mein baal safed nahin kiye* (I didn't become grey by sun rays falling on my head) or someone 'who has seen many Diwalis' become indirect ways of referring to experience and wisdom simultaneously, or the latter arising from a reflexive relationship with the former. One of the reasons why we might miss experience as an epistemological site is its lack of legibility, or rather what we consider legible. Like the *dokri*'s wisdom, experiential knowledge does not come with a fixed location or announcement. The burden of unravelling it lies with the translator-seeker, who must take note of the signs underneath the texts. In making such utterances brought into another language, the basic act of translation, we need to know when to be literal and when not to be.

Kwame Appiah discusses proverbs from the Twi-language (now known as Akaan) in Ghana. Uncovering them requires 'thick translation'—based on judgments of whether everyday language requires a literal or metaphoric translation (Appiah 2000). Our languages seldom use references to *anubhav* in everyday context; but contain a sense of 'having seen the world', or 'having witnessed ups and downs' or 'drank water from many wells' and so on. This displacement of experience from its direct reference to figurative expressions is suggestive of the difficulty of its legibility and definition as also perhaps its 'translation' as 'experience'. Thus, referents of experience by being non-named, often done through displacement and euphemisms, centre a void at the heart of this book.

Samskara: Theory and Experience

Experience is not comfortable, not for those who seek refuge in textual authority. My narrative around the text *Samskara* is built from the discursive role of experience in the novel; as also the experience of teaching it during the pandemic. Does experience become threatening? To some it does, and this is what reminds me of a novel that comes with renewed meanings today, its translation to new meanings extended beyond my earlier readings. One of the finest and most acclaimed translations in Indian literature has been A.K. Ramanujan's translation of U.R. Ananthamurthy's *Samskara* (1978). Translated from the Kannada,

Samskara set a benchmark for many of us who took to translating texts. That being said, this judgment is not based on a Kannada reading of the book. It was made by the attention that A.K. Ramanujan paid to the discourse of translation in all his writings. The Afterword in the book troubled the title *Samskara* as an untranslatable term that carries the polysemy of astounding variety in the Hindu context. Ramanujan provides us with the dictionary meanings of samskara, but only to juxtapose them with an afterword that demonstrates the untranslatability of samskara. Both things together assert the possibility and the impossibility of translation, leaving the reader with an entry into and the spillages of the word, samskara. If samskara is an inherited value, how can that ever be made to transfer, travel, translate and become someone else's? In other words, how can what sticks to the word and body as original meaning be made to drop, cease and fall?

The novel begins with the 'problem' of Naranappa's death. Related to Pranescharya by blood, Naranappa is everything that Pranescharya is not. He drinks and smokes, sleeps with women of any caste, eats meat with Muslims—in short, he lives an un-Brahminic life. The sharp contrast between him and Pranescharya (our chief protagonist) is made sharp and stark; setting up as if it were a virtuous and austere life on the one hand and its performative rejection on the other. Virtue clings to Pranescharya the way vice does to Naranappa. As long as both live, they can co-exist defining each other by opposition. However, Naranappa's dead body seeks more intimacy than his life. It needs cremation, his *antim samskara*. Much like the bodies in numerous hospitals in India today—begging to be recognised, owned up, touched and cremated or buried. They seek from us a relationship. Is everybody alike or does caste make even corpses Brahminic?—this is one of the central questions of samskara. The rotting corpse that nobody wishes to touch and cremate releases a plague in the Agrahara, contaminating a community that has spent its life focused exclusively on protecting itself from contamination. Were the souls contaminated already so that they needed to produce an external locus of pollution? This too is resonant with the times we are living in. The virus load is almost always elsewhere; in the body of the Dalit, the Muslim, the poor. In fact, very much like 'real' life, the virus was carried into the lives of the poor by the elite. What would it mean for all the Brahmins of the Agrahara to accept that in all of us lies a Naranappa, that we are all asymptomatic carriers of pollution? Would it shake the foundation of the caste system, that recognition? It perhaps would, for both the behaviour of the rich upper-caste in India today and the community of the Agrahara have this in common—the hygiene of one relies on the rejection of the other, the physical distance only an added layer of a social distance that has had a long inning in Indian society. The polluted, unhygienic upper-caste is made clean by Chandri, the Dalit woman Naranappa had lived with. It is she who makes Naranappa's Brahmin rotting corpse casteless by giving him a final release. A pivotal incident in all my earlier readings and many others has been Pranescharya's sexual encounter with Chandri—an experience that both 'pollutes' and enriches him, enabling him to undertake a difficult journey both in and out. The novel begins that section of Pranescharya's self-exploration with the following lines:

> Experience is risk, assault. A thing not done before, a joining in the dark of the jungle. He'd thought experience was fulfillment of what one wanted, but now it seemed like it was the unseen, the unpredicted, thrust into our life like breasts, entering it. (Ananthamurthy 1978: 82)

However, this pivotal incident, this assault was also made possible by Praneshacharya's inability to find answers in the textual archive.[6] Why were Vedas not able to answer a question about a real-life situation despite all the provisions the shastras have about exceptions granted to Brahmin men? Had Naranappa sought absolution as a living man, he would have been granted one, but the Vedas don't have an answer for an unrepentant Brahmin like him. We could backdate the moment of breakdown to the limits of the Vedas, which do not help Praneshcharya with the answer to Naranappa's samskara. I see *Samskara* now as a novel about the limits of *gyanmarg*, of theory, of textual knowledge.

6 I had asked this question in class; and it was Nitya Pawar, a student, who drew my attention to this point. My thanks to her.

The latitude that holy books provide to the privileged Brahmin men is not enough for Naranappa for he seeks not a solution or absolution but a critique of theory and knowledge itself. Pranescharya learns some life skills that neither he has learnt nor imparted to his community from Putta, a talkative stranger he meets whilst walking away from the Agrahara. It is from the experience of being with the world that he would now have to theorise.

In any case, once the sexual encounter has happened, Pranescharya needs as much to hide from the community as from his own self. The anxiety makes him walk and as he does, he is joined by someone called Putta. The novel has often prepared us for Pranescharya's alter-egos, people who define him as opposition. After leaving the Agrahara, Pranescharya is in a new companionship/opposition that has been thrust upon him like experience. In this redefined relationship with samskara, it is not Pranescharya but Putta, who draws my attention. Navigating through the carnival of life, straddling both the world of upper caste (for he is the son of an upper-caste man) and so-called lower caste (through his mother), Putta, a half-Brahmin half-Malera, walks through the fair of life. Pranescharya does not meet him but runs into him, organically, or rather Putta thrusts himself upon Pranescharya. Pranescharya simply cannot get rid of Putta, who insists on joining him wherever he goes. 'Putta of the Maleras stuck to Pranescharya like a sin of the past' (1978: 106).

This is one of the most profound lessons of *Samskara*—stepping out of the Agrahara as a space is also a stepping out of the gated life that monitored the coming and going in the life of a Brahmin. The sociality of the outside world impinges upon Pranescharya through well-meaning and interruptive ways; for that is how life asserts its presence, 'contaminating' the unpolluted but not with the desire to contaminate. Both Putta and Pranescharya walk together. Both the defining moment that made Pranescharya leave the Agrahara and start walking and the act of walking with Putta are important to the discussion below—they are a combination of experience (as an episode) and experience (ongoing and sensory).

I wish to dwell upon this moment of walking and think of walking as a form of conversation with the world, as a readiness to abandon sanitisation produced through caste and class, as a form of meditation and exploration that is used both by a mendicant and picaresque traveller, yet a privilege not accessible to all who may want it. Pranescharya seeks interiority through walking for it is his moment with the self, of turning over the questions he fled from. By not fleeing and choosing to walk, Pranescharya wishes to see what he has been fleeing from. This contemplation expressed through physical action is constantly challenged for its physicality. Pranescharya is made to stop, change routes and 'enjoy' the company of someone he had never met before. The 'slowing down' he seeks allows him to see he had had opposites—Mahabali, Naranappa and so on—but his truth cannot only be a response to opposition. What is the autonomy of what he considered the truth? These questions are played out in the interiority; but they are constantly disrupted by sounds and voices, especially Putta's voice. Actions don't need opposites; they only need a slowing down. Putta, on the other hand, rightly called Prattling Putta, wants conversation for it reduces the burden of walking. This central difference between the motivations of two accidental travellers found next to each other captures in the last section of the novel its most dynamic messaging: our worlds of the inside and outside are permeable and that caste 'purity' is not just against others but the self, rather against life. But despite all their conversations throughout their walk, their differences cannot entirely disappear. And how would they? Reconfigured, or approximated perhaps, like translation.

At a certain juncture in the novel, Pranescharya and Putta arrive at a temple and Putta must stay outside, he cannot go in. This exemplifies this rupture in Samskara, Putta holding both the hybridity of his identity as well as its limits.

> Putta said, 'You go in and eat your temple dinner.'
>
> 'Why don't you come along?' invited Praneshacharya. All of a sudden, he'd felt panic at the thought of being seen, alone, unaccompanied, by the rows of brahmins sitting down for the feast in the temple hall...
>
> 'What are you talking about? Did you forget that I am not Brahmin but a Malera?' said Putta, to which the Acharya said, 'Never mind, come along.'
>
> 'What, are you joking? This place is full of people who know me...' (1978: 127)

Caste is sociality, so Putta cannot hide the Malera side to himself. What is interesting though is for the first time, the verb 'forget' is used with caste. How did Pranescharya 'forget' that Putta could not go in? Unlike the Brahmins of the Agrahara, Putta was born of a mixed caste. Is that what caused a momentary forgetting in Pranescharya? It may also be worth asking if it's precisely this mixed-ness that produces Putta's view of the world—as one in which boundaries both exist and don't. Don't we find this nuance in mixed characters such as Vidura and Yuyutsu too in the Mahabharata, as people positioned to see the doubleness of lineage? Meanwhile, only Putta could have said one of the most profound and non-textual things in the novel, 'On the whole, I like people.' His own experiences of having moved in and out of various social circles allow him a certain multifacetedness, despite knowing its limits.

> 'You must be wondering why I'm prattling so much. You must have thought "What a leech" I'll tell you why. Though you don't talk much, you too need people, conversation. You're a meek person, quite a suffering type,' said Putta, wiping the water off his face. 'Am I right or wrong, you tell me. I can tell from the face, who's that type. Why should I hide anything? I hope you didn't get the impression I'm a low class fellow. I told you I am a Malera, didn't I? My father was a high class Brahmin. He took care of my mother whom he lived with, better than his lawfully wedded wife. He even performed a sacred thread ceremony for me.' (112)

The walk with Putta demonstrated the inevitability of the social in what Pranescharya desired as a solitary experience. To my mind, Putta persists as a character of life; half this and half that; quotidian and irritating; warm and helpful—essentially a life force that draws us into the fair of senses and encounters. While Ramanujan's translation has been hailed as a benchmark of literary translation and his exposition of samskara provided in the history of literary translation one of the finest examples of untranslatability, Putta remained somewhat marginal. In an interview with Susheela Puneetha, U.R. Ananthamurthy mentions the following:

> I had sent my novel to Adiga and others and they said it seemed incomplete. I sat down to rework it and I heard footsteps. It was a magical moment and Putta came in. My novel was transformed

> completely after his entry.... The structure of this novel came to me magically. I was caught by it unawares.[7]

It is surprising though that Ramanujan, and also the general scholarship on *Samskara,* have not paid attention to this character. Putta lingers for me as an exemplar of that quality of life, which is both necessary, inevitable and highly interruptive. Perhaps that is an experience of a kind. Through Putta's experience of life, Pranescharya learns how his barricaded life had rendered 'purity' but no lessons of human life, and how nuanced it was on the ground. Putta is a necessary interruption in the stillness of life—a walking that is necessary but not devoid of strange encounters that make us both active and passive (like in my mother's case) agents and non-agents at the same time. Pranescharya could have 'chosen' to do away with Putta or embrace a life of desire. But the allure and exasperation that characterises Pranescharya's coming 'into' the world of senses blur not just the interior and exterior but also the desirable and the inevitable forces of life. The 'exposure' to life through Putta at the time of the epidemic was also a reminder of the inevitability of social proximity, of remembering that carriers of contagion may well be inside and not outside.

Really speaking, teaching *Samskara* through Ramanujan's own writings and para-textual material helps fill many gaps. But does *Samskara* really reach its audiences if they are situated in a different class, time and location? Revolving around the existential and social dilemmas of the lead character Pranescharya, *Samskara* is both modern and traditional. However, one may see how its meanings continue to falter despite itself.

The memory of *Samskara* from previous years had stayed as a haunting novel about moral decay in a highly codified Brahminic community. Its social and existential moorings intertwined in the mind and the enduring figure had been that of Pranescharya. Texts speak different languages when their contexts are re-oriented. When that happens, it raises fresh questions of translation, for how can it not, if

7 I am thankful to Vighnesh Hampipura for this reference.

the original meanings don't stay in the same place? Teaching *Samskara* against the coronavirus pandemic diffused some of its distance. The descriptions of Brahmins falling off from life like dead mice were disturbing to go through with young students who have been battling many forms of anxieties. The gallery view of my Zoom class showed faces pinched with worry; for *Samskara* was not out there, back then, but in the here and now. Its 'obscure' Brahminic rituals in a Kannada-speaking Agrahara from the point of view of a predominantly North Indian class would have made it comfortable at another time. *Samskara* had become more relatable. It is after all a failure of social distancing. Pranescharya's efforts to protect himself from pollution, his own 'self' from his senses, his community members from waywardness effected through caste mixture—all of it come to nought. Sensuality and physical intimacy, hitherto policed through Sanskrit verses and injunctions of the shastras, are now lain open like a community transmission of a disease.

Experiences can be distant and remote, and sometimes suddenly proximate for they have been provided that one link, one analogy that makes literature life on some days. The lingering after-effects that make texts come back to us with renewed meanings are those incomplete acts of translation that could not match the ungraspability of experience. We 'refer back to life and lived experience, back to the I' as Heidegger describes experience (1971: 35). Even long after books have been sold and told, stories consumed and sealed, we linger over the residues of translation—its leftovers.

2

Language and Incomplete Travels

I: What is the Japanese word for 'language'?
J: (after further hesitation): It is 'Koto ba'.

—Heidegger (1971: 45)

Is our vulnerability to language a consequence of our being constituted within its terms?

—Butler (1997: 1)

If one of the most common ways to injure is through words, it is also through words that inclusion and healing are claimed. But the question is which words, whose words and which language? We are not only constituted within linguistic terms but also the specific terms of a historically named language. Hence we increasingly notice that attempts to both 'interpellate' and include are made by making messages available in multiple languages. Commendable though such efforts might be, they are sometimes bereft of reflection on how messages derive meaning from the will to converse. For instance, a well-known campaign in India, *Mann ki Baat* is available in over 17 languages. A procedural democratic act is achieved by translating *Mann ki Baat* into multiple languages. However, translation alone does not ensure a democratic function; it needs to first recognise the context of power. The missing or reluctant addressee; the obfuscation of the matters at hand; the complete disregard for the ethics of conversation make this a monologue that is efficiently relayed in multiple languages. Its 'availability' masks its monologic messaging, for even though it remains '*mann ki baat*'—as in coming from the heart—it is devoid of a connection. *Mann* is intimate but made public; it is not clear whose *mann* (mind/heart/consciousness) is the message about. On the other hand, less comprehensible words from a song may travel from heart to heart, like *dil ki baat*—less planned and less by fiat. Language travels through trust, intimacy and sociality, even when it is taciturn. The sheer availability of a linguistic translation in many languages does not ensure translation. Really speaking, one of the most profound acts of translation is to understand what language might mean to people; what are the terms of the interlocutors—what joys and sorrows, belonging and ambivalence, distance and proximity are generated through language. The affect of language is imperceptible, hidden even to the self. This essay is written around such affect; what it is to be in a language; what changes in us from one language to another; and how shifting the terms of self may require using a different set of words.

In the ruminations that follow, the backdrop of being in a multilingual environment in India is very crucial. Equally crucial is the fact that most of us, readers of this book, and English teachers, end up using English while other languages in us sit unofficially—impinging, infiltrating and made illegitimate. We seldom congratulate our students on their eloquence in the languages they come with but are quick to point out their inaccurate English. Thinking of these relationships of language with self and experience, how do we, as teachers who teach literature and study it with students, navigate this in a multilingual environment and ensure that our literary classrooms do not mimic the imperialistic functions of English? One way of doing it is self-examination, involving our own journey with languages that form us—the ones we travel with and the ones we leave behind. There has been a considerable body of scholarship on the politics and colonial genesis of the English language. There are also fantastic studies about how our own linguistic worlds play in relationship with English.[1] However, I had in mind an

1 To name but a few, see Svati Joshi ed. *Rethinking English* (1991); Rajeshwari Sunder Rajan ed. *The Lie of the Land* (1992); Susie Tharu ed. *Subject to Change* (1994) from the 1990s when the 'crisis in English studies in India' launched self-reflexive questions in the disciplines. Also, see Shefali Chandra's *The Sexual Life of English* based upon archival material around girls' education in colonial India (2012). An excellent ethnographic account of writers and spaces in India in tandem with language politics is Rashmi Sadana, *English Heart, Hindi Homeland* (2012). Aamir Mufti's *Forget English!* (2016) is a significant book that interrogates the assumed dominance of English as a literary vehicle. For a relationship between translation and multilingualism, especially as a complication of the idea of 'source', see Kothari ed. *A Multilingual Nation* (2017).

auto-ethnographic account of multilingual teachers and students, like some of us, who are constituted multiply by divergent affective worlds, and a significant part of the experience remains outside the pale of our professional life. Apart from diffusing the one-ness of the English language; or vernacularising it through infiltration (an exercise evident now in many creative works), it may also help to enhance the stakes of languages we come with. With English, sometimes we need only scratch the surface to see how inadequate it is to account for the many-sidedness of life. That being said, the location of historically named languages such as English or Hindi and the affects they produce for us is of interest to me; but, simultaneously, I am also intrigued by the idea of the syntax of the self, the languages that travel with, interrupt and inform people. I believe that the most profound role of language is manifest in the idea of self-fashioning, in ways that it gets mobilised in acquiring a new vocabulary for the self. This essay is not only about being in many languages but also staying with the idea of language—of words, traces of memory and power, the interactions of caste and class and desires to leave hurting words behind embracing new ones. Most of all, this essay foregrounds the necessity of not looking at languages as isolated affects, but rather noting that these very affects are interlaced with experience. The essay is not a linguistic exposition but an embodied relationship of a translator with language/s.

To this aim, I want to first begin with my experience of my 'mother-tongue'—a language with little or no significance in India save for a vanishing tribe of Sindhi-speaking generations of yesteryears. The following section articulates the hegemonic allure of certain languages, recasting the self with not just new words but even a shift in the smallest pronunciations. Adopting a new language or travelling to new syllables within the same language may allow one a certain degree of refashioning and moving away from one's ascribed experiences but only for so long. The third section elaborates on the complicated relationships with English, a foreign or 'foster tongue' co-existing with the mother tongue, or in other instances, where the mother tongue is cast off by sheer will. Languages, the ones we inherit as well as the ones we reach out to, do not operate in a vacuum. Language is both a dwelling and travel, a limit and an aspiration, a decision as much as an impulse, both being and becoming.

Sindhi: My Cracked Bowl

I remember my mother in her georgette sarees waiting to pick me up at the bus stand after my school. She stood there with her arms stretched out, calling out to me in Sindhi, '*Ach putta*'; my cheeks would turn hot with embarrassment as if an unpleasant and intimate part of my life had been exposed. I thought she should have just kept quiet if she didn't know how to speak English. I was the first in my family to go to an 'English medium' school, and I studied with Gujarati children who came from more well-to-do backgrounds. Their mothers waited in stiff starched cotton sarees, and my mother's presence stood out as an oddity, as a reminder of my distinctness from the rest of my classmates as the language itself. I wonder if not having English was the problem or if having Sindhi was.

That episode had laid buried, never completely gone, but it was unearthed with an immediate force when I watched the film, *English Vinglish* (2013, dir. Gauri Shinde). Writing off her mother for not knowing English is another cruel daughter in the film. However, this mother learns some English which she speaks more as 'Vinglish', generously Indian in accent and syntax. In one of the final scenes in the movie, she musters a whole speech in English as a wedding toast and it comes as a dramatic moment of revelation, sending shockwaves in her family. Gender and language intertwine to make this a tour de force, for Shashi, the timid one, has managed to learn English on her own in a foreign country. It was her best-kept secret. In the process, she has also learnt that her underrated 'activity' of making and selling sweets is entrepreneurial. The family is floored, and all's well in the world. Meanwhile, I realise now that I was both the daughter and the mother. The daughter, ashamed of the mother as well as the mother, determined to learn English under challenging circumstances. If that is indeed the case, how do I think of one language as meaning one thing? And how do I not think of language as being the most central motif of self-fashioning? Meanwhile, in all the languages I speak and know, language itself is gendered. It is so not only because the 19th-century construction of nation made language a biological entity as it pre-existed for nations to get formed but also because languages were feminised as mothers.[2] In a subsequent chapter, I discuss what the gendering language does in the most quotidian contexts. We need to disentangle the biologism of languages that make them an always-there phenomenon from the everyday forms of interpellation of subjectivity they do, making gender, caste and races, even accents its indexical outcomes. Meanwhile, I am less sure each day of what language *means* by and to itself but more and more convinced that we haven't even begun to understand its force in forming the selves and socialities we live with. It is these myriad questions, I invite you to see and join, and allow me to think aloud.

Language sits intimately with the body as the skin itself. Our relationships with languages endure, endear, disturb and even wound our ways of being of the world. In the early 1950s and 1960s, when my parents were raising me and my four siblings, Sindhi schools had come up in Gujarat. As a linguistic minority that was included in the Eighth Schedule in 1965, there were funds for starting schools with this medium of instruction.[3] It is one such school that my siblings were sent to. The teachers were identified and referred to by parents and others like them on the basis of regions they came from, back in Sindh, by then in Pakistan. English had not yet happened. I happened first, the youngest child in the family. We moved out of a chawl to a posher locality in Ahmedabad, again a Sindhi region but the children of this area had started going to English medium schools. As a child of that mobility in the lives of my parents, I was sent to one. This one decision my parents made with their fifth child set me off on a separate path—a lonelier and privileged one. I was alienated and special.

Growing up, I felt my own multiple selves and socialities fragmented in the multiple languages I carried with me—I spoke Sindhi at home, in the Sorbajee compound vegetable market, in the ex-refugee colony of Vadaj and with my extended family. I would then switch over to Hindi in my gossip with Marwari girls in school and to Gujarati with the Jain girls

2 For an excellent account of the construction of 'mother-tongues', see Yildiz (2011) and on the feminisation of languages in India, see Sarangi (2009).

3 For a detailed account on Sindhi's struggle to be included in the Eighth Schedule, to little avail, in making it sustain as a living language but also paradoxically to repurpose the identity of Partition Sindhis, see Kothari (2011).

in college, and then English in the classroom. These languages carried my life-worlds, sometimes in continuation, at others in opposition to each other, simultaneously hiding and revealing parts of me, leaving imprints along the way of one on the other. Their relationships were sometimes seamless, at peace with one another; at other times jagged, jutting out like exposed columns from our homes, places we might have moved away from but still carry within ourselves.

G.N. Devy once said to me in his characteristic aphoristic manner, 'Because we see with eyes, we can't see the eyes.' The pair of eyes that become the object are not the ones that we see. Language is like that. We live in it and look out through the walls, windows and *jharokha*s to see what it enables us to. But on some days, we also build new walls and break down some old ones. In that relation of being inside the language and also intervening in it, lies something called translation. Languages are embodied—I do not think of the translator's task as one of finding discrete synonyms in one language to substitute another, but rather to sit with the discomfort of the untranslatability of certain affects, to know that to translate a word is to translate an experience and that a complete translation in this sphere is not possible or even desirable.

In an essay called 'Traveling Languages? Land, Languaging and Translation', Alison Phipps proposes a new understanding of language and translation as one grounded in the land and our relationship with it (2011). She signals a departure from the preferred pairing of language and culture, which sees languages as culturally constructed and mediated and somehow apart from the physical world we live in. Rather, she suggests that we inhabit languages in a very similar way to 'landscapes', that is, when we learn and use languages, we embody them and experience them physically, a process she calls languaging. Building on the concept of languaging, Phipps argues that translation can also be examined as a 'sensory activity' born of our relationship with the world around us which is formed through sight, sound, touch, taste and smell. In fact, this dimension of language, or rather languages, is almost in its entirety missing in the otherwise brilliant book on *Experience, Caste and the Everyday Social*. The authors Guru and Sarukkai (2019) argue that it is a sense of belongingness that creates the sense of the social, and this social is accessed through our sensory experiences. Extending these arguments, I think of language and translation as both ways of belonging to the world and making sense of it. Many languages may sit inside us, sometimes restlessly, in contention with one another. Sometimes, we reach out to them as natural reflexes of the senses; like blinking at the sudden sensation of dust, we may switch over to English in situations where we suddenly feel the need to assert power, demarcate our bodies from the others around us. Or much like touch that collapses the distinction between the self and the other, speaking in our 'mother tongues' around family and old friends can foster intimacies. Language provides the scope for a recall and continuation of our own selves. And yet, languages themselves require recall as much as we do.

In this sense, languages are like people. They require legitimacy and respect from the rest of the world. They notice a lack of respect and shrink their existence and withdraw into small corners of rooms. Language is a universe if we are willing to make it one, but people can survive, or even flourish without speaking their language. However, the language may not survive. Something like that happened to the Sindhi language. A marker of identity from the Constitution's point of view, a Sindhi in India is the one who speaks this language. Interestingly, the province of Sindh in today's Pakistan was the first province in British India to be drawn according to a linguistic criterion in 1935. The time when I was growing up in Ahmedabad in the 1970s and studying in an English-medium school coincided with Zulfikar Ali Bhutto's government in Pakistan aiming to make Sindhi compulsory for administrative services in the province. Bhutto rode the tide of Sindhi nationalism and subsumed Sindhi identity under Pakistan's nation-building project, referring to Shah Abdul Latif, not as a 'Sindhi' but as a 'Pakistani national poet' (Jaffrelot 2015: 130). In India, the Sindhi language has held no such political currency per se. Its number of speakers has been shrinking at an abysmal rate. I am told by a Sindhi writer in Gujarat, confidentially, that the state textbook board publishes Sindhi textbooks every year which are not needed at all. Discontinuing the project would mean admitting the state's inability to keep alive the language of the linguistic minority.

Meanwhile, nationalists in Pakistan were at least, up until the 1980s, articulating the demand for a 'Sindhu Desh', but on the Indian side of the border, the community collaborated in the disuse of the language. It is the first and heaviest price the community paid by almost losing it. It is pointless asking how that situation could have been saved. I remember when I was beginning to work on my book *The Burden of Refuge* (2009) and began taking lessons in the script, my sister Mala had said, '*Chari thee aaheen chha, atto khuto tai? Asaan khe Sindhi sikhi chha miliyo.*' Translated this means, 'Have you gone mad, run out of flour in your kitchen? What did we gain by learning Sindhi?' My siblings went to Shri Abichandani High School at Lal Darwaja in Ahmedabad. They also learnt Persian, as did some others who may have gone on to learn English too. My siblings do not see their multilingual universe as a source of richness, rather they feel that their lives did not take off because they didn't learn English. Their relationship with Sindhi is one of stasis, whereas they see mine as one of growth because I speak English. This is a relatively less discussed aspect of languages in South Asia. They are a repository of treasure, or we see them as such when they are not prison houses and we are not bound only and entirely to them. But in cases where one finds no resonance, let alone an economy to their language, it almost feels like a solo burden. The figure of Ovid comes to my mind from David Malouf's *An Imaginary Life*. The Roman poet exiled in Tomis is the only one who speaks Latin. He forms a relationship with a young boy with whom he communicates in an unknown language. However, when Ovid grows into a man, the child disappears.

> Some time when my own body began to change and I discovered the first signs of manhood upon me, the child left and did not reappear, though I dreamt of it often enough in those early years, and have done so since. I have forgotten the language we used, and if he were to reappear, perhaps we could no longer communicate.... Or the language he used on whatever occasion it was had already passed my understanding and could not be translated into daily speech. (1999: 3)

Ovid's exile is not only one of dislocation from one's familiar geography but also a rupture of language.

At this point, let's ask what it is to possess and lose a language? It is not an object after all. Accounts of life-and-death situations in the 'last person speaking x language in the Andamans' do not, to my mind, capture the story. Who was that last old woman talking to? Who was being spoken to? The Sindhi language, like any other, is a living, breathing history and a present; it is the repository of who we are and where we come from, and embedded in the idea of language is the sense of self and community. What remains of this linguistic universe is a small sliver, its signification reductive and resting upon a set of 'things' (names of dishes, festivals, clothing, etc.) rather than emotions; symbols and banalities rather than entire philosophies of the world. Language is a dwelling and one that does not always require a physical habitat but sometimes creates its own continuity.

Despite being a language that is increasingly being sidelined in India, it was Sindhi that came to me first and facilitated my path of learning new languages. And how do I even begin to think of it as incidental to my life, its consignment to the domestic notwithstanding? In fact, the older I grow, the more I discover how embedded it is in me for it is the voice of keeping family together; it is the voice of being strong, of being patient, of learning the fortitude of life's troubles and tribulations. My father saying his clothes were worn and tattered and it was time to get out of them conveyed his waning relationship with life and his readiness for death. In Sindhi, the words, *kapda faati paya aahin, kithe kithe subhaan* (how many stitches can I put on a tattered piece of clothing) haunt me as a philosophy of death. My mother's words, *avval khair* (God willing) precede quietly my English words when I appear to make definite plans. Telling the story of my Sindhi anchors me in this unplanned narrative today; it provides a way of making sense of the world. Language becomes so incidental, instrumental, a matter-of-fact 'thing' on some days and a deep engagement with the self on some other days. This conundrum of language, as one on the surface and one that lies embedded in the self, almost like a shadow-play, makes it one of the most daunting subjects to tackle.

Incomplete Travels

If languages take us elsewhere, they also fuel the dream of being elsewhere. Literature and acts of translation deepen for us the role of language, showing us how selves are forged out of languages. Learning new words provides opportunities to see new dreams to Fateema Lokhandwala in the Gujarati novel *Vad* by Ila Arab Mehta (2011). Titled *Fence* in English (Mehta 2015), the novel is the story of Fateema, a lower-caste rural Muslim girl who studies in the first school in her region in Saurashtra. She invests in her education with the commitment of a hungry soul who looks desperately to change the circumstances of her life so that she could jump the fences of life in poverty and indignity. It is through words that Fateema experiences her aspirations. Words uttered by her upper-caste teachers and an upper-caste friend beckon the fantasy of being elsewhere. They fascinate her, especially when they were literary or poetic, almost *tatsam*, 'pure' words derived from Sanskrit. The Gujarati word *ramniya* played on her lips. She had learnt it from Gaekwad sir. In the first government school of a village in a princely state before Independence, all kinds of children found themselves next to each other. Of these, Fateema, a learner of the first generation and a first child also found a chance to educate herself. She heard words like *ramniya* beautiful and alluring and felt thankful to life. As an educated teacher in urban Gujarat, she looks at new buildings to buy a house of her own. She wishes to live in a mixed locality and not be relegated to a Muslim ghetto. The sight of new buildings reminds her of the word *ramniya*. It is this *tatsam* Gujarati that Fateema would use to fashion herself and remind the rest that she was like them. 'Sonkamal. Golden Lotus. Fateema loved the name, it had the tone of a fantasy. She longingly looks at all the new buildings or ones under construction' (ibid.: 2).

Her fantasy is to buy a house. However, the fantasy had an architecture to it. Fateema wanted a house that was not in a Muslim locality. It was defined by the negative, but it would give her a neighbourhood that reminds her she was a citizen first, then a Muslim. This ordinary wish does not come to pass in the novel *Fence*. Fateema's *tapasya* or penance is not over. Another word she loved. She got that from her Jain friend Chandan. Chandan's mother observed fasts, as her *tapasya*, and 'our studies are also a form of *tapasya*,' Chandan said to Fateema. The word stayed and so did the penance.

Language brings the promise of 'hiding' or 'passing' but not for too long. It competes with the sensory excess to fashion a different self and it is this struggle between hiding and being exposed which characterises experiences of those who don't want to be who they are. As a poor, rural, Muslim girl from Saurashtra, Fateema enters the world of literacy and literature through shapely polysyllabic Gujarati words that she learns from her Brahmin teachers. Imagining herself to be a citizen of this language, she wishes to fly out of home and make her place in this world. Her language fools people who almost forget she's Muslim for she doesn't sound like one. But she is one, her eloquent vocabulary notwithstanding, she must be reminded what her place is and cannot be given a house in a colony of Hindus and Jains. Fateema is fooled by words for when she is given a contract for a building called Chand-Tara instead of Moonrise apartments, she knows that her dream of living in a mixed locality and not a ghetto has turned into ash.

'Extricate yourself, in so far as you can, from the vocabulary that doesn't suit you, that doesn't get you the life you want. Think of the language you prefer, think of language as a pleasure and not a penance, as a celebration and not a sacrifice,' remarks the psychoanalyst Adam Phillips (2015: 9). To stop using certain words may also be an exercise in being and becoming. Fateema teaches her non-literate mother not to say '*hu*' but say '*shu*' as proper Gujaratis do. Words could be of the 'same' language or they could involve abandoning one language to use another. Or perhaps learning a new language entirely to forge a different self.

Reinvention is also about choosing to claim a language denied to you as the Dalit writer Kumud Pawde does. In an excerpt titled 'The Story of My Sanskrit,' Pawde shows how she became an object of condescending curiosity for being a low-caste woman and a Sanskrit scholar at the same time (1994). Pawde chose to make the language her own and reject its historic ties to being the language of upper-caste Brahmins in India.

> That a woman from a caste that is the lowest of the low should learn Sanskrit, and not only that, also teach it—is a dreadful anomaly to a traditional mind. And an individual in whose personality these anomalies are accumulated becomes an object of attraction—an attraction blended of mixed acceptance and rejection. (Pawde 1994: 110)

Fateema Lokhandwala and Kumud Pawde both adopt words that are not immediately available to them. Fateema wants to learn the standardised Gujarati that she believes will enable her to leap over the fences of poverty. Kumud Pawde, in her account, writes of how she first felt the wish to learn Sanskrit as a child after a Brahmin woman turned her away from her son's thread ceremony. Pawde felt that there must have been some connection between the Sanskrit Vedas and her that she was barred from even listening to the verses being chanted.

It would be easy to bracket their initiatives as one of only resistance, of learning the oppressor's vocabulary to fight back. But we must rather look at these two accounts in terms of the ambiguities they hold. Fateema's Gujarati is one that allows her aspirations and hopes of assimilation, not necessarily one of questioning the status quo. Kumud Pawde, despite knowing that the language she wishes to master is the very script of her oppression, still pursues it with immense passion. Both Lokhandwala and Pawde's negotiations with the immediate hegemonic languages in their surroundings promise a travel of sorts, though not necessarily a destination.

Language has both expanse and limits; it offers possibilities to both of them; but their accounts also show the afterlives of marginalisation. Pawde writes, '... although I try to forget my caste, it is impossible to forget. And then I remember an expression I heard somewhere, "What comes by birth, but can't be cast off by dying—that is caste"' (1994: 112).

Language's promises are interrupted by experience, which carries the most unsummarisable quality of life by now being interruptive, now enhancing. These transactions with words and the multiple operations of analogy-making, synonym-making and conversions of meanings—all remain uneasy and incomplete forms of translations.

These meaning-making exercises often need to refer back to the idea of experience to reveal a repository of possibilities, or lack of them.

To enter these languages with these experiences of oppression is to still remain at the threshold, arriving close but never quite. Or as Neerav Patel's writing in the next section explores, certain languages carry life-worlds and logics of these very marginalisations. Patel rejects the local hegemonic language in favour of the coloniser's language, despite it coming with its own complicated history.

Foster Tongues

If languages come with histories the same way people do, they enact their scripts on bodies, often leaving us with a sense of split-ness or duality depending on our relationships with them. Sometimes, the languages do not speak to one another. One language may sit dormant under the weight of another, but still find outlets to persist. Sujata Bhatt's poem, *Search for My Tongue*, illustrates how despite possessing abundant words, the ineffability of translating this experience persists.

> You ask me what I mean
> By saying I have lost my tongue.
> I ask you, what would you do
> If you had two tongues in your mouth,
> And lost the first one, the mother tongue,
> And could not really know the other,
> The foreign tongue.
> You could not use them both together
> Even if you thought that way.
> And if you lived in a place you had to
> Speak a foreign tongue,
> Your mother would rot,
> Rot and die in your mouth
> Until you had to spit it out.
> I thought I spit it out
> But overnight while I dream,
>
> Muney hutoo ke aakhee jeebh aakhee bhasha
> May thonnky nakhi chhay

Parantoo ratrray svupnama mari bhasha pachi aavay chay
Foolnee jaim mari bhasha nmari jeebh
Modhama kheelay chay
Foolnee jaim mari bhasha mari jeebh
Modhama pakay chay

It grows back, a stump of a shoot
Grows longer, grows moist, grows strong veins,
It ties the other tongue in knots,
The bud opens, the bud opens in my mouth
It pushes the other tongue aside.
Every time I think I've forgotten,
I think I've lost the mother tongue,
It blossoms out of my mouth. (Bhatt n.d.)

The first impulse of the poem above is one of translation. Its script appears odd, forming in the middle of a seamless English, interrupting a well-ironed out narrative. It is recognisably Gujarati for another translator-reader but may well be non-sense noise for the one who doesn't know. What the poem does is to put the burden of unravelling upon the 'foreigner', inviting her to understand through translation and identify the untranslatable loss in the poem. Is it possible for an 'other' to know what it is to lose a tongue? The addressee is a foreigner, not by race or location but by being distant from this experience. Unlike Ovid's experience, the 'loss' of the mother tongue is not complete. Ovid's secret tongue came to exist only around another person, whereas Bhatt's Gujarati holds an entire sociality of meanings, regardless of whether she is around people who speak it. It is perhaps these meanings that serve as a reminder of the language itself; it has only been nudged out by another tongue, a foreign tongue, which continues to be one's own and yet not one's own. Inhabiting this space between these two languages evokes anxiety even in Bhatt's sleep. The restlessness of languages is something that persists with or without her being consciously aware of it.

Where Bhatt senses unease with regard to the possibility of losing her mother tongue, Neerav Patel holds an entirely different position. Patel and Bhatt both refer to Gujarati as their mother tongue; yet, these are not the same languages or even the same relationships with these languages. Rather than pondering upon the loss of his mother tongue to a foreign tongue, Patel has argued that he'd much rather adopt his 'foster tongue' English because it does not offer legitimacy to caste and hence allows for a degree of freedom. The difference in both their relationships with their mother tongues is one of experience. Patel's account does not echo the romanticisation of the mother tongue; rather, it is something he'd consciously prefer to turn away from.

In his words,

> At the outskirts of Ahmedabad, my village Bhuvaldi is one of the 26 villages inhabited by the untouchable community of Rohits, to which I belong. In addition to following their caste occupation [of removing dead animals and skinning them], my parents also cultivated the land, and that is how they looked after our family. Their ancestors had followed the same occupation. This made the sphere of their social life and livelihood limited to a radius of about 25 kilometres. The mother tongue they had inherited, the language they acquired through a highly limited social sphere, and one shaped by the communities that their hereditary occupation brought them in touch with—Muslim leather traders from Mirzapur, the Marwadi cobblers of Madhupur, the Vora Muslim goldsmiths of Manek Chowk, the thakurs, hot-headed neighbours and landowners, the barbers and others—combined to make my 'mother-tongue'. How this 'mother-tongue' was vastly different from the 'Gujarati' of the upper-caste is something I wish to explain through an example.... When I was in the first grade studying in a school in my village, a lady teacher tried teaching me the sound and letter of 'gh'. But I found it very confusing. She would give an example of 'ghari'. I learnt much later, almost in college, that 'ghari' is the name of a sweet eaten by the upper-castes. Imagine if dalit children even today were taught the sound of 'p' by 'pasta' and not 'patang' (kite), would it not be confusing? (in Kothari 2013: 65)

Patel echoes Kancha Ilaiah in illustrating how the language of artisans, pastoralists, Dalits and other labour groups is formed through production and the materiality of everyday life (Ilaiah 2009). What constituted Patel's vocabulary through occupation, oral traditions, trade and labour were not enough for him to relate to standard Gujarati. Hence, when Patel was being taught the sound 'gh' of an expensive sweet, *ghari*, made of dry fruits and ghee, he found himself outside the imagination of that object.

Although the distance may appear to be one of class, it is difficult in Patel's memory and experience to separate it from caste. Patel's example underscores two things: first, standard Indian languages are carved out of the reality and convenience of hegemonic sections of society so that they neither reflect nor make provisions for the marginalised sections. Second, the marginalised groups' efforts involved in learning such standard registers are as arduous as their attempt to learn English. With this, Patel erodes an oft-assumed myth—that cultural and linguistic translations between 'Indian languages' are easier than those from an Indian language into English. While this may be theoretically true, Patel aims to show the many languages that exist in even what is officially the 'same' language.

For many years now, the Gujarati Lekhak Mandal, a literary circle in Gujarat, has engaged itself in a series of debates about the lack of phonetic consistency in the Gujarati language. Finding the rules of Gujarati spellings cumbersome and awkward, a group of writers are campaigning for an alignment of the written language with spoken Gujarati, which to them must be privileged as a more dynamic and living part of the language. One of the arguments this group posited concerns the less educated, rural and underprivileged groups whose Gujarati must not be deemed 'inaccurate' (read, inferior to) by the speakers and writers of 'standard' Gujarati. In 2012, the Gujarati Lekhak Mandal invited responses to the question, 'Who (all) can claim Gujarati?' for its journal (Jani 2012). Implicit in this question was not only the written/spoken dichotomy but questions of power, legitimacy and representation. Are the lives of the dispossessed, linguistic and religious minorities reflected in Gujarati literature? The question was meant to provoke Gujarati writers into thinking about the politics of language, and its inclusion as well as exclusion through standardisation. It was in the context of this question that Neerav Patel puts forth the hierarchical relationship between his own and the standardised Gujarati:

> My innocent gujarati has taught me fine things of which one is endurance. But it did not tell us the reasons how caste and class were

> the basis of oppression perpetrated upon the deprived and dalits. It did not tell us that in order to eradicate that injustice you needed a new awakening, knowledge and struggle. How would that poor thing teach us this? Living as it does in the shadow of oppressors, how would that mother-tongue of mine know that they had cast a web of oppression and hidden it deftly in their language? By forming words such as superstition, destiny, God, bhajan, rebirth and other-world, they had made it helpless, blind and fatalistic. I am grateful to the other tongue which became my foster language; it is this English that provided scientific thought and showed a way out of oppression and torture. (in Kothari 2013: 65)

Neerav Patel's relationship with his Gujarati is painful; bereft of the celebration that upper-castes might do on Matrubhasha Divas. How was he to valorise the commonsense of caste discrimination in its idioms and songs? And how was he to think of language in a unitary fashion? The English language, on the other hand, allowed him possibilities of re-invention by not allowing a seamless translation of the 'commonsense' everyday caste-based expressions into its context. Neerav Patel wrote in Gujarati and remained engaged with English by sometimes translating his Gujarati writing, at any rate, by reading in English and allowing its Enlightenment-led rationality to provide him with succour.

Many questions about make-over have come to play out in the body of English. We turn to a very powerful passage in Yashica Dutt's book *Coming Out as Dalit* (2019). A young writer who navigated her caste identity by making it 'unknown' to herself and others, Dutt 'came out' as Dalit after the suicide of Rohit Vemula. Upon reading his letter, which he wrote just before his death, Dutt says the following:

> I read it once. Twice. And then once more. I had never read anything written by a Dalit before! I had certainly never read anything written by a Dalit in English—the language I had hoped would help me escape my own Dalit identity. The language I had stubbornly practiced since I was five. Flawless English was supposed to bring me to the same level as my upper-caste classmates in school and college. I leaned on it when the carcass of my Dalitness became too heavy. Later, writing in this language became my career. It was very likely that English was Rohith's crutch too. He was probably still honing it so he could stand tall against

> those he had decided to take on—those who perhaps equated his Dalitness with an inherent sub-humanness. (xiv)

> … I wrote DALIT in a bold size 24 Georgia font. Underneath I defined the word in English and Hindi as 'one who has been oppressed.' In that moment, I stopped being ashamed. (xvii)

In several interviews after her book was released, Dutt has mentioned that it was Vemula's letter written in 2015, after he had been suspended from Hyderabad Central University, that propelled her to write this memoir. 'Coming out' is a phrase often associated with queerness in the Western imagination; it puts immense weight on a singular moment of rupture where a person announces their queerness to their world—be it friends, colleagues or family. It assumes that prior to this moment, this person was 'passing' something which they have chosen to reveal. Dutt uses the same phrasing in the title of her book and writes of how for the longest time, she negated her Dalit identity with her middle-class upbringing and English. Dutt writes of her constant attempts at 'hiding' by adopting upper-caste practices, English being her stronghold. I have argued that English represents agency and mobility to many Dalit writers despite not containing the symbolic markers to articulate caste; or, perhaps, as in Neerav Patel's case, precisely because of this (Kothari 2013).

What are these relations with languages that are neither fully volitional nor entirely imposed, tugging at us, torturing, making us a home but reminding us how much we need to break away from these homes? Yogesh Maitreya's poem below, however, articulates the impossibility of breaking away.

Ontology of Our Language

Naturally, when the placenta is cut
The child is separated from mother
However this isn't the case with us

We are never separated from our mother
Only those who fed on surplus

Grow up, separated from mother
We grow up inheriting the sound of her pain
The sound which never reached the fate
Of a language on paper

Our handsome Bodhisattva taught us:
Not talking to one's mother is a horrible form of
Alienation from our existence

Therefore we understood:

Mother tongue is essentially the sound
We inherit when inside her abdomen
Language is a just a suitable rendition
Of that sound

My grandfather had a hammer
My father had the steering wheel
I have a pen
But we have been writing the same language
The language of our mother
Missing from the history of our existence
(Maitreya 2019)

The 'language of our mother' is finally neither Gujarati nor Marathi. It is the unspoken and unarticulated history of pain inherited like language, quietly. Maitreya is not speaking of language linguistically but rather as the inherited scars of experience. The Dalit struggle from the hammer to the wheel to the pen may modify some circumstances of life but not 'separate' them from suffering. The hauntings of experience are heard from Neerav Patel to Yogesh Maitreya, both poets who write in English. Patel's 'Gujarati' and Maitreya's unnamed language in the poem, a repository of pain, do not make it to the scheduled list of Indian languages. The limits of *Mann ki Baat* are most evident here, where a translation of the speech cannot hold space for the marginalisation of several experiences that do not conform to the 'positive' message of the campaign. This is also precisely because these languages only translate words and not the unspoken words of a dialogue that did not happen. They lay bare the circulations of power by treating its terms as default, we need only scratch the surface of its taken-for-grantedness. Language as a dwelling offers temperate shelters to those whose experiences (of power) find resonance in its meanings. For others, the very same language may be a source of claustrophobia, the walls caving in on them; the necessity of travel beckoning as an urgency. The assumed democratic nature of words and their meanings hide the inequities of experience.

To sum up, this reflective essay has not aimed to offer a conclusive theorisation of language as a dwelling, its travels, its shifts and stasis. Rather, it sees languages as fragmented as our own selves. I haven't tried to make a case for multilingualism as much as thinking through the spaces between languages, where the untranslatable self sits most resolutely. If speaking multiple languages hold the myriad articulations of one's personhood, one must also think of the in-between junctures as both—the untranslatability of language as well as the untranslatability of the self. Some translations may be possible analogously, but all meanings that are built experientially do not transfer. In its dualisms, its travel, its both lack and abandon, it is not even entirely desirable that language be able to hold all meanings as Toni Morisson's Nobel Prize acceptance speech reminds us:

> It (language) arcs toward the place where meaning may lie. When a President of the United States thought about the graveyard his country had become, and said, 'The world will little note nor long remember what we say here. But it will never forget what they did here,' his simple words are exhilarating in their life-sustaining properties because they refused to encapsulate the reality of 600,000 dead men in a cataclysmic race war. Refusing to monumentalize, disdaining the 'final word', the precise 'summing up', acknowledging their 'poor power to add or detract', his words signal deference to the uncapturability of the life it mourns. It is the deference that moves her, that recognition that language can never live up to life once and for all. Nor should it. Language can never 'pin down' slavery, genocide or war. Nor should it yearn for the arrogance to be able to do so. Its force, its felicity is in its reach toward the ineffable. (Morrison n.d.)

This incompleteness of language, its failure to explicate the self, experience and the world, is perhaps one of its greatest strengths. According to Morrison, language in its lack of finality, in its incompleteness in itself, can summon hope of a future that holds better promises than one's current circumstances may offer. This is the hope with which many of the people cited in this essay, reach out to new languages or newer forms of languages. It does not fulfil its promise but the impulse remains. It is this urge to grasp new words, to adopt new vocabularies of the self, to resist the commonsensical nature of violence in intimately known words that I keep returning to.

Language is both, a sense of 'being' and a move towards 'becoming'. It holds one captive to experience, offers an exit out of this mode of life, and yet does not necessarily arrive at a destination. Language or multiple relationships with languages then become ways to account for experiences that are default in one language, but not so in others. And it is in these untranslatabilities that language travels as far as it can, making meanings, sedimenting them and yet falling short; pushing one to think of a language as one that does not transcend experience, but rather is embodied by it, not the other way round.

3

Scripting Caste: Pedagogies of Translation

The architecture of syllabi implicitly carries ideologies of knowledge, both conscious and unconscious. For instance, a course titled 'Indian Literature' I teach at my university is an elective course. However, it generates an expectation of a normative framework; almost as if all its ingredients have an always-already certainty to them. The discursive qualifier 'Indian' appears in the title as a mere description and it is in the labour of pedagogy that it may be deconstructed. On the other hand, elective courses such as 'Partition' and 'Dalit' literature appear curated—making overt, as it were, the ideologies underlying their selection. Really speaking, such expectations and boundaries are held together tightly, rather resolutely, to make convenient the leaking and spilling effects of questions that we know do not keep such borders in place. And even after decades of teaching, I find no architecture of a course that is foolproof, staying within the threshold marked out for it. Think for instance how conversations of 'communalism' and 'caste' get divided between courses on Partition and Dalit literature; almost as if to say forms of neuroses that 'other' the Dalit and the Muslim are entirely separate. This essay has emerged from an attempt to rescue a Dalit story from a course on Dalit literature (which I have now ceased to teach) and bring it into the framework of pedagogies used in the course on Indian literature. In doing so, I voice the nature of multilingual operations carried in the body of writing and allow them to uncover the elliptical nature of caste. More as we proceed, for I need to go back to a particular moment.

I was teaching Rabindranath Tagore's novel *Gora* (1924/1954) in 2019. The protagonist Gora, a member of a well-to-do Brahmin family in the early 20th century, undertakes a journey to the surrounding villages. Torn and assailed by questions of a life of authenticity in the midst of colonialism, Gora is a troubled soul. Animated by the same restiveness that characterised many real and fictional figures of his time, he also hopes to find a 'real' India in its villages. In doing so, Gora encounters for the first time, poverty, destitution and lack of both will and resources in the life of the poor. However, he is not able to see these as structural consequences of caste. Interestingly, it is also the first time he encounters caste. This is where the nub lies; Gora is himself a privileged product of upper-caste (foster) parents. He is born to Irish parents, a truth he has been protected from all his life. Nonetheless, his staunch Hindu foster father refuses to touch him. Moreover, Gora himself on his way to becoming a pure and staunch Hindu, refuses to accept food from his (foster) mother Anandamoyi for she has a Christian maid. This means that notions of touching and not touching, of pollution and purity, were very much a part of Gora's life. It is the caste homogeneity and blindness that makes Gora not see his own insertion in a system that he throws an outward gaze at. However, upon coming to the chapters describing Gora experiences repulsion in the barber's house and is duly shocked by the pettiness of the Brahmin Madhav Chatterjee. It is difficult not to notice his phobic and externalised relationship with caste.

> The barber was surprised to see Gora, return alone. The first thing Gora did was to take the barber's drinking vessel and after carefully cleaning it, fill it with water from the well. After drinking he said: 'If you have any rice and dal in the house please let me have some to cook.' (Tagore 1954: 136)

That Gora acts like a saviour Brahmin from this point onwards is not surprising. What occurred to me during class was the similarity between my own location as a teacher of two different courses on Dalit and Indian literature. It was almost as though caste was relegated to the former; and the latter, Indian literature, had turned into a course on reading texts by situating them in the specificities of their bhasha contexts. I was as short-sighted as Gora. In trying to make caste explicit in one course (Dalit literature), I was drawing the boundaries around Indian literature's Agrahara, deeming this literary segment to be outside of caste, confining and projecting caste exclusively onto

Dalit literature. During that period, my ambivalent feelings were legitimised by new studies and conversations (Jaaware 2012; Guru 2009; Kawade 2019).

After much thought, I designed a course called 'Scripting Caste' where Gora figures now. However, this also raised a question on the ethics of teaching literary texts embedded in specific linguistic and caste traditions of India. While I don't have clear answers to this, I brought into the Indian literature course a story by Neerav Patel that I translated for an anthology of Gujarati short stories (Kothari 2022). It seemed to me that the acts of translation had to be taken from the outside to inside the classroom. This means that the engagement with the text as an amalgam of different bhashas or languages (even linguistic registers) need not happen away from the students. It was in foregrounding those as a pedagogic method that the challenges of teaching and learning Indian literature and its relation to caste locations could be demonstrated. This also means that texts needed to be read together rather than taught and a leisurely dwelling upon the small work of language and translation could be the chief form of uncovering the elliptical layers of caste-regional-linguistic interactions. It is in that spirit that I offer the following experiment in pedagogy. Based on a view that our scripts of selves are inseparable from caste, this course foregrounds my location, and why I see what I do, and also encourages the students to do so. It does this task through language and acts of translation.

Pedagogy is work-in-progress, and only to a lesser extent, a set of tried and tested tenets. A literature class in particular has the potential to unfreeze established methods; for shifting demographics of a classroom press themselves upon how and what is being taught. Stories also allow non-intimidating entry points, bringing to the fore points of view that are at once cerebral and emotive. But what is to read in ways that are internal to self and subjectivity of both the reader and the text? This exercise is to respond from terms internal to the worldview and logic of a text. The word 'internal' assumes perhaps the presence of external—foreign, evoking the Indian prefix 'para' from outside—*paragaami* (of another village), *pardesi* (foreigner), etc. It generates an expectation of a nativist swadeshi mode of reading, which is not the intention; however, the intention is certainly one of listening to texts without drowning them out with voices that don't belong to them. The epistemic violence involved in hijacking the life-world by ready frameworks is not foreign to academia. This essay makes an attempt to listen to texts in their range of linguistic registers and develop out of a mode of multilingual close reading. It allows the language to do its own unveiling, halt at little things—use of certain words, senses of touch, sight, smell, etc. and textures of place and dwelling, stillness and movement. In facilitating this reading, the teacher–translator claims not to occupy a position of defining meanings, but rather speak after, do *anuvaad* and make the story speak for itself.

This exercise also employs translation as a mode of reading and is a shift away from 'consuming' literature in translation. The small work of language we set out to do does not externalise and outsource the Dalit experience to a body; but includes in this reading the gaze of the reader, the locations of her meanings. It effects a move away from questions of identity politics and representation and instead draws attention to the invisible performances and effects of language. This essay grapples with remaindered material in translation. It rummages through that pile of leftovers to see how translation is understood in a fallacious manner, as an activity that is concluded.

Written by Gujarat's most well-known anti-caste writer Neerav Patel, the story 'Creamy Layer' is arguably the last one Patel wrote before his death in 2019 (2019).[1] Its poignancy lies in the absent presence of upper-caste norms that define not a relationship evidently with an upper-caste person outside but torn halves of the 'same' self. The story troubles the questions of agency evident in Mr Vaghela's life when we are first introduced to him. A well-to-do Dalit man living in Mumbai who seems to have 'fitted' enough to be allowed a blending into the 'casteless' city dwellers. However, this blending has put pressure when the costs involved become clear. Mr Vaghela makes a physical move away from the city to meet his community in the village, and the journey becomes a testament to his acts of deliberate forgetting. The story has quiet but disturbing encounters with the self.

1 See my tribute to Neerav Patel, 2019.

Creamy Layer[2]

Mr Vaghela and Mrs Vaghela lived in Mumbai.

This statement in English only means what it says, that is, a certain couple lived in Mumbai. It is a 'straightforward' translation into English from Gujarati. Now if you are Gujarati-speaking, you might know that Vaghela is a Gujarati surname. This means that the address of this simple sentence is both to the region and its audience. This embedded address in this simple sentence is neither remarkable nor unique. It would be true to say, 'Mr and Mrs Chakraborty lived in Delhi.' However, if we go a step further or deeper, a Gujarati-speaking person may also know that Vaghela is a Rajput surname. Gujarat had a Vaghela dynasty in the 13th century. This dimension of a warrior caste in that simple English sentence encoded in the name 'Vaghela' makes itself available all at once to a linguistically marked reader. In the case of Chakrabortys, a Bengali speaker would know that the couple is Brahmin. However, if we push the Gujarati example more, it is likely that some Gujarati-speaking readers would also remain 'open' to seeing whether Vaghelas are Rajputs or members of a caste lower in the hierarchy but use a Rajput name to escape the stigma of their own. Thus, caste has been made both overt and elliptic in Gujarati.

Meanwhile, what has happened in the English sentence then? Does the marker of caste become a sign without signification, and does it rely abundantly on the reader's ability to decode all the layers, including the overt ones in Gujarati? In other words, has the English sentence managed to inhere this knowledge or does it reside in the mode of 'reading' which is located, situated in particularisms of region and language? The Gujarati reader would read the city (Mumbai) with all its associations with urban modernity, capital, anonymity and cosmopolitanism along with caste. The English reader will only 'read' the modernity of the Mumbai city, inhabited by a particular 'ethnic' name. We may also ask who this 'English' reader is and if an English translation can have indexicality of Gujarati—certainly not of the

2 R. Kothari. 2022. *The Greatest Gujarati Stories Ever Told.* Aleph Publishing.

region and in some sense, an indeterminate location of language too. There may be a native English reader, a diasporic Indian reader reading in English or any reader (Indian or otherwise) reading it in English; in such as case, the signs of caste, as well as associations of 'Mumbai', may vary but perhaps seldom come together in their immediacy as they do in the Gujarati sentence. While the examples I provided are from the context of caste, there may be many other elliptical forms of 'knowing' that are integrated into the way a bhasha speaker would read. Language then is available in its spoken and unspoken forms to the addressee of a bhasha text while the English text may require an effort or facilitation for its embedded forms of knowledge to open up. The corollary to this premise is deciding the nature of facilitation, that is, theoretical tools, available to us. We will return to this question after carrying out an exercise of 'reading' in this essay. This act of reading is not guided by a predetermined framework, but one that listens to the text multilingually, comparatively, as a sign in the socio-literary system.

Meanwhile, Patel lived in the city of Ahmedabad, and the village he left behind was Bhuvaldi in the Daskroi taluka of Ahmedabad. A member of an untouchable community (whose occupation has been tanning and skinning), Patel had managed to leave behind that past and become a bank officer. Deeply saddened and furious at persisting caste violence, Patel spent his time writing stories, articles and poems.

The story 'Creamy Layer' turns its gaze at a self which is riddled by the need to move away and feels loathsomeness at having moved away from the community. The title 'Creamy layer' is *originally* in English. It is not regionally marked but transregionally available in India—a term used for those among the Other Backward Class (OBC) who have done well for themselves—socially as well as financially. Despite being an English phrase, it is hard to find it in the English language outside India, we are more likely to find usages of 'cream' to refer to the upper echelons of class. The adjective 'creamy' and the noun 'layer' combine to make a peculiar Indianism. The term came into common parlance after the central government implemented the Mandal Commission report's recommendation for providing reservations for people who were marked out as OBCs. This was challenged by several petitions to the Supreme Court, but the ruling was upheld in 1992 in the Indira Sawhney case. Yet, the court mentioned that a 'creamy layer' amongst the OBCs must be ascertained based on economic criteria and be excluded from availing these reservations. In 2018, the Supreme Court applied the term 'creamy layer' to reservations for Dalits and Adivasis too, and this has been contested since because economic mobility does not ameliorate the social marginalisations.

We must also note that the term 'creamy layer' is controversial, especially when used by the upper-castes like this reader. All these meanings work behind the title of Patel's story but do not add up to a label; rather, they help trouble the relationship between experience and labels. Patel's metonymic gesture made in a language associated with modernity becomes clearer as we go further into the story. While the Vaghelas are 'modern' in the upper-middle-class sense, the schisms of their life become evident in the story soon.

> It's no joke to manage a wedding single-handedly in this **cosmopolitan** city of Mumbai, away from all loved ones back home. And really speaking, things like clothes, **jewelery, party plot, catering, decoration, music party, beautician,** guest accommodation and myriad such things get done in a wink, fatafat, as you keep tearing leaves from a chequebook one after another. That's all it takes. But it was the so-called small **formality** of scripting the kankotri or the wedding invitation that left the Vaghela couple most confused. After a lot of back and forth, they finally decided on two kankotris, with different designs and different texts—one in Gujarati, the other one in English. One for people from the caste group, another for rest of the world. Haansh, they felt relieved! (Kothari 2022: 139; emphasis mine)

The words in bold hope to draw the reader's attention to their being present in English in the original before the English translation. The first word is 'cosmopolitan' and it applies to the city of Mumbai, a paradise for fresh beginnings. And that's one thing being in the wrong caste does not allow you to do easily—fresh beginnings. In his brilliant study, *An Ambiguous Journey to the City*, Nandy reminds us of the metaphors around the village and the city that came to be cohered in the 19th century. For our purpose, it is important to remember his lines:

> A Dalit, landless, agricultural worker or a rural artisan seeking escape from the daily grind and violence of a caste society has reasons to value the impersonal melting pot of a metropolitan city. He is ever willing to defy the pastoralist's or the environmentalist's negative vision of the city ... to lose oneself in the city is to widen one's freedom in a way not possible by migrating to another village, however distant from home. (Nandy 2007: 12)

On the face of it, the Vaghelas appear to have found possibilities for a new life in the city. They have entered perhaps the urban middle class. The story shows the sign system—money, English language, purchasing power, education, employment—that is not based on the caste system. The Vaghelas 'perform' their middle class, tear cheque leaves, *fatafat*—in a wink. This capacity for buying the good life but making it seem hectic and manageable also consolidates their membership in the class they belong or aspire to. The language here both performs and reveals this membership. The cosmopolitanism of the city is in relation to those living in the city, who don't know where the Vaghelas come from. Simultaneously, it is also about those who needed to be left behind to come to the city. This dual referentiality is made evident in the Vaghelas' dilemma about who exactly is their addressee when the wedding cards needed to be readied. A momentary confusion, a *formality*, but one that marks a pause in the hectic enumeration of commodities and services that could easily be bought. What was the 'back and forth' about? We are not told, but we are made familiar with the smooth resolution achieved by the mechanics of bilingualism, a classic solution to asymmetrical constituencies. The 'caste' group or *jnatila* does not particularly specify which caste, in a way that the name Vaghela does. All that the caste group reference does is specify the language in which that connection is made available. Gujarati is the language of connection of the cosmopolitan Vaghelas with their loved ones and their caste group. Another complex operation is carried out through language—the affective tie to the community is psychological and social, and its comfort from afar is caught in the phrase 'loved ones,' while sociality is caught in the phrase 'caste group'. This is the Gujarati-speaking world for which *kankotri* (wedding invitation) needs to be in Gujarati. Who then is the English *kankotri* for? The passage below makes the relationship between English, Sanskrit and caste location clear.

> Shalini looked smart and sweet in her air hostess uniform. The kankotri received much appreciation from her colleagues. Captain Chopra apparently said to her, 'Oh such elegant language!' while the flight purser Swaman Deshpande said, 'What an abstract art you chose for Ganesha! And that saptapadi shloka in italics …' One would have thought the recipients of kankotri considered themselves lucky, such was the nature of the pleasure they conveyed. As for Shalini she felt a surge of pride when she was told how cultured and tasteful [her] parents were. However, her utmost joy came from the kisses her co-pilot Kulin Joshi showered upon her. It was comparable to little else. Would she, Miss Shalini Vaghela, now be known as Mrs. Shalini Joshi! 'Arre, how can anything be missing from a wedding at Bapu's place, hanh?' One of the clerks, remarked with sarcasm in his Kathiawadi accent. Shalini was too lost in some fantasy world to notice. (Kothari 2022: 139)

Mr and Mrs Vaghela's daughter Shalini takes the *kankotri* in English to her colleagues in the airline where she works. We come to know from them that the card has a shloka in Sanskrit and the rest in English. As upper-caste readers, we are aware of what this card contains; the 'look' is familiar. The font, the abstract Ganesh, the economy and elegance of language and probably a matte-finish paper gesture towards an aesthetic considered 'tasteful' by Shalini's colleagues. Their names such as Chopra, Deshpande and Joshi mark their upper-caste location and the languages of the verbal and non-verbal communication in the card draw us into this recognition. It's time to ask whether we continue to be linguistically marked readers at this stage. Until we come to the last line of this paragraph, when one of the clerks 'throws' a remark in Shalini's direction, we could be 'Indian' audiences with some familiarity with upper-caste surnames. However, the clerk's comment is a departure, not so much in terms of caste, in fact far from it. It is a departure in terms of the elliptical nature of a caste slur that only a Gujarati-knowing reader would pick up. The clerk mobilises the ambivalence around the name 'Vaghela' by saying 'Arre, how can anything be missing from a wedding at Bapu's place, hanh?' A Rajput is referred to as Bapu in Gujarat, a term of both hilarity and deference, depending upon the context.

By referring to Shalini's family as Bapu's family, the clerk is 'testing' her or rather mocking her and showing that he knows the irony of what he is saying. This little mischief can go missing from the reading of a non-Gujarati reader. It would also then not reveal to the reader that firstly Shalini herself does not know who she is; but more importantly, there's always someone reminding you of your caste, in that, caste is as much being who you are, as being seen as who you are. It teeters on the privilege of announcement and the fear of being discovered. Words and intonation are mobilised to remind Shalini of her origins, that her class-passing cannot hide her caste. It is significant to note once again how language both hides and reveals. For instance, in Baburao Bagul's famous story, *Jevha Me Jaat Chorli Hoti*, the protagonist's language does the hiding for him, or it might be fairer to say that the protagonist's Hindi obfuscates the legibility of caste for the upper-caste employers he meets in Surat. Until his caste is suspected or revealed, the protagonist refers to having 'stolen' the caste in Marathi:

> माझ्यावर जात चोरीची जी आपत्ती आली होती, तिची आठवण झाली म्हणजे अंत : करणाचे अग्निकुंड होते. डोके दुःखाने दुभंगून जाते. अन मग वाटू लागते, या दुर्देवी देशात माणसाने दलीत जातीत जन्म घेऊ नये.
> (Bagul 2000: 78)

> When the difficulties visited upon me after I concealed my caste comes to mind, memory ignites furnace in my heart. My head begins to ache as if it is about to burn; in this luck-forsaken country, human beings should not be born as Dalits. (Bagul 2018: 116)

Jerry Pinto's use of the word 'concealed' or 'hid' (in the title 'When I Hid My Caste') displaces the obfuscation and ascribes it to an agency that Marathi does not have. The verb *chorli* or to steal (in English) is closer to avoidance, a slinking away than planned perfidy. Does Bagul 'steal' the upper-caste by speaking with eloquence and erudition or does not he simply not reveal his caste, and his eloquence makes the passing easier?[3] However, let us come back to Shalini whose existence triggers action in the story, although it's difficult to say whether she heard the comment and ignored it, 'stole' the upper-caste or 'hid' the one she had.

3 I am thankful to Prashant Ingole for our discussion on this.

We are told that Shalini is too busy to notice. How do we deconstruct this 'innocence' and distinguish it from the alleged 'innocence' of the upper-caste who claims not to know her caste, thereby suggesting that caste does not matter? How do we compare forms of protection between an upper-caste parent's lack of communication with the child on how her privileges are a product of this social capital with the Vaghela couples' protection of Shalini's identity? Would the latter have been possible had the Vaghela couple not been living in Mumbai? Lurking behind these questions is also the shadow of modernity. The upper-caste's dream of being modern is made through a deliberate forgetfulness in which many other actors collude. Shalini's aspiration to be modern or that of her parents for her to be modern rests on the precarity of her finding out or for others to 'remind' her what they have chosen to be natural modernity in their case. This offhand remark relies upon the recognition of irony in the reading that a Gujarati reader would do. The paragraph involves a play of three languages—Sanskrit, Gujarati and English—and all of them have divergent purposes in 'identifying' and 'marking' the profiles of the actors involved. This, what I prefer to call the small work of language, is the texture of 'Indian literature'—an archive formed through multiple languages producing a self and society in non-summarisable ways. From the membership in Brahminic networks through the Sanskrit shloka to the use of English, the Vaghelas' *kankotri* ends up being a linguistic sign of desire and mobility, of inclusion and forgetting.

In the discussion that follows, we will see how the Gujarati *kankotri* has trouble fitting into the audiences, unlike the English one. Armed with the *kankotris*, the Vaghela couple takes a flight out of Mumbai to go to Gujarat and a taxi all the way from Ahmedabad airport to their 'native village'. Members from the extended family surround them and the Vaghela couple becomes anthropological objects, much like Dalit subjects do in 'our' writings and theorisation. Since the extended family is that of Mr Vaghela, he, in particular, feels/is judged. Is he the one telling us this tale? Perhaps. He is probably hurting the most.

> They were so unrecognizably well-dressed that they looked pardesi, a couple from elsewhere.... Taunts and reprimands came from all

> directions, 'Oh ho ho, bhai, finally you remembered your ancestral land, hanh? Your old man joyfully came for every new year and every year made an offering to our Goddess during navratri, and Ramapir's proud and colourful flag furled thanks to his efforts.... But you are a big sahib man, what with your studies-vudies and all. Bringing up your beloved daughter in Mumbai ... and you forgot all about people in the family. Does it even mean anything to you, tell us, this family and relatives, mean something? Nothing. (Kothari 2022: 140)

The gaze falling upon Mr Vaghela becomes evident if we shift ours as readers to the ones who are 'reading' the Vaghela couple—the members of the clan. Huddling together in the *vas* (quarter) of the village, elders and youngsters, men and women have gathered around to see the Vaghela come after a considerably long time. They must have looked *pardesi* (which could include both foreigner as well as outsider) for they have been away through both, time and space. The *pardesi* is also distant—somewhat inaccessible, either by our not being able to reach him/her or by his not coming to us—not merging and not allowing anyone to forget that he is different. The gaze falling on the 'unrecognisably' different clothes produces this sensory social. The prefix 'par' in Indian languages effects myriad forms of othering, for instance, *parpranti* (from another region), *paraswa* (foreign, as opposed to *nijaswa* or one's own), *pardharmi* (of another religion), *pargami* (of another village) and so on. Where is alienation located here? If the gaze holders, Mr Vaghela's extended family and community members (*jnatila*), find Mr Vaghela looking like a *pardesi*, do they feel distant from him or is this Mr Vaghela's projection onto them of what he feels as disaffection and alienation?

As we go further, the community members greeting, reprimanding and chiding also bring up symbolic memories to the fore which only reinforce the *pardesi*-ness of Mr Vaghela. He gets addressed directly by 'Oh ho bhai ...' These words of wonderment, envy, resentment produce mixed responses without any direct words. Mr Vaghela has let down not only his community but also his ancestors and forbears. Did he do that by not going to the village, by turning away from a cesspool of poverty and caste-ascribed roles or also by turning away from the traditions perpetuated by his ancestors? Is it possible to give up one without the other, the story asks. Let's note the loaded significance of goddesses and Ramapir, icons specific to marginalised communities in Gujarat and parts of Rajasthan. While the Goddess of Navratri cuts across many castes and classes with varying iconography, the reference to Ramapir is particularly emblematic of the Meghwals and other tanning communities in western India.[4] Were these gods abandoned because, as the next line says, Mr Vaghela has become a big sahib with these 'studies-vudies' and thereby pointing to an ideological difference that middle-class, educated and politicised Dalits may have come to have with religious practices? D.R. Nagaraj notes that '… Dalit movement rejected the traditional Hindu world and thus dismissed untouchable pasts entirely' but adds further that 'rebels too require cultural memory' (Nagaraj 2010: 4). This 'banished world of gods and goddesses' (5) was very much part of Neerav Patel's life.

Patel remained a staunch critic of the institution of religion and subscribed to an Enlightenment-stamped modernity. Whether the genesis of Patel's particular modernity lay in Ambedkar, in addition to other ideological predilections, is difficult to say. It may also lead us to collapse the story with the author's biography, which while being an instructive exercise, has its limits. Meanwhile, the rupture with the community has been encoded in what Mr Vaghela has not managed to—to keep in touch. The mundane idiom 'keep in touch' in English is seldom about touch; its physicality has long been evacuated. However, it is, as Aniket Jaaware, shows us, the pathology that characterises relations with both the human and subhuman (2018). The city-dwelling Vaghela is implicated as part of the not-touching group. In the paragraph that follows, the divide becomes evident not only in the village-dwelling community and city-dwelling Vaghelas through the lack of 'touch' by the latter but also in the rejection of Mr Vaghela's new god—Ambedkar.

> The paternal cousins had quite an attitude. They were not very literate, but the youngest one had been pushed to go to school with the lure of a mid-day meal. He had learnt to put letters together, somewhat haltingly. With arduous effort he managed to read out the kankotri to everyone.

4 In this context, see Dominique Sila-Khan's (1997) work on Ramdev Pir.

> On hearing of their own names among some two hundred hosts they felt pleased: Dhulabhai Punjabhai Vaghela, Kalidas Punjabhai Vaghela…. But the mota-bhabhi turned the kankotri over, up and down, and snapped: 'What Bhai, you forgot to put our kuldevi chavanda on it? It is through her blessings that our clan survives. You have become such savarna that you put aside our own mother? You put the picture of your kind of coat-pant wearing God, but abandoned our ever-present mother goddess, haan bhai?' With a broom over her shoulder, she muttered on her way to the village, 'Go get your daughter married to rich ones, our presence will not bring any glory to your aangan.'
>
> Instead of the image of the kuldevi and a kankotri starting with 'With the grace of Chavanda ma …' the Vaghela couple had chosen to put the image of Babasaheb Ambedkar, a sign of new awakening. One would have thought they had committed a heinous crime! They didn't realize that such a gaping chasm lay between them and the community…. (Kothari 2022: 140)

The literacy of the 'younger one' is but an accident, it wasn't expected. He went to school to have 'mid-day meals'—a comment that could easily escape our notice. However, it fleetingly touches on the emancipatory project of education for those who need to both survive materially as well as emancipate. While the education would have been minimal, it was enough for the moment for someone to decipher the distance formed in the community. The legibility of the *kankotri* is simultaneous with the 'reading' that unfolds. If the English *kankotri* was so aligned with the symbolic world of its recipients, the Gujarati *kankotri* exemplifies how one distance made the other's proximity possible. Initially, the 'mirroring' of their own selves made the extended community pleased, but mota-bhabhi, who probably could not read the letters, 'read' the visual signs. The accusation in her words is unmistakable:

> What Bhai, you forgot to put our kuldevi chavanda on it? It is through her blessings that our clan survives. You have become such savarna that you put aside our own mother? You put the picture of your kind of coat-pant wearing God, but abandoned our ever-present mother goddess, haan bhai? (140)

Totems of faith and collective identity of a social group have been replaced by another god that the community does not recognise.

Would this have happened in Maharashtra, where Ambedkar has his largest following? Should we read this as a comment about how far Dalit communities are from Ambedkarite ideology in the villages of Gujarat or how distant is Ambedkarite self-identification distant from the ground realities of another region or place? Mota-bhabhi's accusatory tone has an interpretation of betrayal in this distance. Mr Vaghela is judged for what Nandy would call 'deculturation' with respect to gods and goddesses (2001). Tragically, in another circle, he may be judged for pursuing them. Meanwhile, the Vaghela couple tries its best to pacify the angry relatives, the humans and gods had both been abandoned.

> They joined hands and beseeched everybody to grant them forgiveness. Just then the youngest bhabhi, who stood with a veil drawn over her head, and eyes lowered, began to speak, 'We can barely manage two meals a day, how do we get the fare to come to Mumbai, tell us. Here, our children wear clothes from discarded rags and if we weren't seeking leftover food from homes, we wouldn't have known how to feed them. Wouldn't we stand out in the presence of you all big-big people? It's not so much about us, but you will feel ashamed of us.'
>
> Precisely. That's why the Vaghela couple had planned two different kankotris, two different menus, two different receptions. Appearing to be thinking through a solution, Mr. Vaghela took out money from his wallet, 'Take this, please don't worry about anything. Buy good clothes for all, women and children. But please do come. Be large-hearted, forgive our mistakes and honour us by being there.'
>
> People were pacified, and it seemed things were on track. The youngest daughter-in-law came with a glass of water from a cloth-covered pot lying beyond the door. Mrs Vaghela saw this unhygienic water and blurted, 'No, no. We have our water with us.' She took out a bottle of Bisleri from her bag and gave it to her husband. Meanwhile a young girl from the neighbourhood turned up. 'Here, have this tea. It's made entirely of milk. Especially made for your kind of people.' Mr. Vaghela could not take his eyes off the creamy layer on the surface of his tea. Ever so quietly, and veiling his discomfort, he picked the cream with the tip of his finger and flicked it away. (141)

Guru and Sarukkai tell us that 'We experience the social as if we experience the world through our bodily senses. Thus, it is possible to talk of a social sight, social touch, social smell, social taste, and social hearing. In the same way, it is possible to talk of a social self for the social and a "life" of the social' (Guru and Sarukkai 2019: Introduction). The Vaghela couple's most challenging moment is when they see, touch, smell things that repulse them; putting them outside the sociality of the community. Patel deftly constructs an upper-caste *swatchhta*—'cleanliness' that sustains its existence by seeing dirt elsewhere, outside in the body of the Dalit. The feel and sight of the cloth-covered pot—what might have appeared to Mrs Vaghela as a potential for diseases—appears fleetingly to be replaced immediately by Bisleri. The immediacy of 'solutions'—Gujarati *kankotri*, money, Bisleri—is subtle manoeuvring by which Patel comments on the Vaghelas, as well-meaning people who would want little to do with the sensory life of the Dalits. The loathing is directed as much towards the outside as inside, rejecting parts of a past from which it must have been so difficult to break away. The psychological stakes of the story build through the sight and touch of a cup of tea with a creamy layer on top. An object made with cognisance of how the Vaghelas needed to be marked out for a 'special' tea, it appears as a signifier that has ruptured with its signification. The tea appears excessive—sweet and thick and with a layer of cream on the top that Mr Vaghela removes with a flick, almost not touching. Where does this excess lie and how does it appear so repulsive to the senses? In the subsequent section, the story continues with more encounters with the world of poverty and deprivation that Mr Vaghela has left behind but is conveyed in each context with considerable complexity. There's one more development further ahead in the story. Chastised and frustrated, the Vaghela couple now turns to the relatives of Mrs Vaghela and hopes that their interaction with that part of the family is better.

> They halted at a grand building next to the banks of Sabarmati river. The building bore its grand name appropriately, 'Kailashdham'. The Vaghela couple went past its beautiful lawns towards the end of the estate where the servants' quarters lay. Just then pall bearers alighted from an ambulance chanting 'Ram Bolo bhai Ram,' carrying a dead body with them. Instead of greeting his relatives, the mama rushed towards the electric crematorium. This is the mama they had come to invite for his customary role of mameru during Shalini's wedding. The

Vaghela couple had made a special trip from Mumbai to persuade him to come. Considering the situation, they decided to be patient and wait.

'Look at this bhai, the wretched fever has taken over the bloody city … not a moment's rest have I had. The Munshipalty people are not giving leave either. You chose to come at such a bad time…' Mr. Vaghela pushed away the awkward situation by changing tacks, 'Where are the sons and their wives? Nobody is to be seen.'

'Bhai, to each his own dhandho. People have to fill their bellies, no? Can you do that without slogging? The eldest son's wife is a sweeper with civil hospital. The eldest son works in a morgue. The little ones have spread themselves a sheet to collect a few coins in charity people toss after dead people. If you have time with you, the younger son is not far away. He has proper employment. You can meet him until your mama comes back.' Mami put forth a proposal after an elaborate account of her family.

The Vaghela couple wished to escape the stifling and modern crematorium, so they accepted the proposal promptly. They took directions from mami and got back into the taxi. Whoever they asked for directions on the way was amused, 'You want to go to the Mayor's bungalow?' Why would a mayor live in a poor *basti* of Dalits? They reached their destination to find indeed a well built structure that looked like corporate building. It announced itself confidently with large letters, 'Sulabh International.' And below that in smaller letters it said, 'Pay and use Sublabh Toilet.' Right at the centre of the posh foyer stood a young man flaunting the entitlement of an owner. The Vaghela couple went directly up to him. The young boy nonchalantly gave the rates, 'One rupee for urinating, two for the rest.' When he noticed that those were his relatives he felt sheepish, but immediately recovered his confidence by ordering someone, 'Go get two kadak-meethi cups of tea, and two pouches of water also.' The Vaghela couple kept using their respective kerchieves to protect themselves from the assaulting stench around them. They kept refusing to have tea etc. but the young manager of Sulabh Shauchalaya will not take no for an answer. Cups of tea were served on his table. (141–142)

The *kadak-meethi cha* in Gujarat is associated with the life of labour; the more upwardly mobile in Gujarat, as elsewhere, drink tea that is not cooked thoroughly and is also mildly sweet with less milk. The memory of taste triggers off in the Vaghela couple both shades of affection and unappetising flavours, creating an allure of an identity that they have come to resist. The encounter with death on the occasion of giving a wedding invitation is also quite symbolic of the impossibility of unadulterated joy in the lives of the Vaghelas. From amidst death and toilets, opportunities for employment and life get created, reminding both the Vaghela relatives and us of the inescapability of Dalit lives. Both going away and coming back in the case of the Vaghelas become rife with difficulties; the unchanging nature of their relatives' lives is a marker of how little they can change about their own without severing themselves completely. When Mr and Mrs Vaghela race back home, somewhat disturbed by the events of the day and impatient to re-live their 'normal' life, they are greeted at home by their daughter Shalini. Oblivious of what had transpired during the day, she is happy to know that her parents' extended family may come to the wedding. Mr Vaghela asks her to make tea and hastens to add, 'no creamy layer' on it, please. He had been served what is called *aakha doodh nee cha* (tea with only milk and no water) at every home during the day—a special tea for privileged guests. The revulsion in those words towards special tea but served amidst squalid surroundings in an atmosphere of blame and guilt, blurs the lines of loathsomeness felt towards the self and the community.

As we bring our reading of the story to a close, it is time to ask what the stakes of the small work of language are. Language performs the role of 'separating' the worlds of the protagonist and the world he has left behind, and in that sense, the forms of otherness lie on the inside, rejecting and loathing parts of the self, the price a middle-class person pays for having 'arrived'. The attempt to read along and with is to see whether language prepares us for representational asymmetries and if language enables us to see the social in which otherness is constructed not through obvious markers. Caste is encoded in every example of Indian literature. And only sometimes does it announce itself. How does language make caste both elliptic and overt? How does it mark modernity as both an affliction and liberation, especially in relation to community and caste social? Modernity attaches itself to becoming something else, someone else and this spill-over of desire also resides in language. In wanting to be someone else is also the break of what one is, and this simultaneity of both rupture and desire characterises myriad articulations in Indian literature. If modernity falsely promises an unmarked language, where does it exactly play out? Does caste reside in the subcutaneous layer of anonymous modernity, and how does translation mimic the ellipsis of caste then?

A subset of the question on language is also one of translation. The bilingual wedding invitations, the use of English as markers of a 'creamy layer' life and the dialectical differences between the Gujarati spoken by the Vaghelas and the rest of the community make language an important character in the story. Language performs the function of transformation and becomes suggestive of a good life, but it also makes implicit that the Vaghelas are alienated, privileged and ruptured. On the other hand, the language of the community remains untouched by possibilities of re-invention, making stasis the norm. As upper-caste readers, we could be easily allured into thinking we are exonerated by the story as one that is sometimes about strife within and that we could not be responsible. But it is precisely the hegemonic structure we perpetuate that makes it inevitable and desirable for the Vaghelas to break away from the roots. The sense of shame experienced by the Vaghelas has to do with us—even if the language seems to be telling the Dalit story. We need to look for what makes for the ordinariness of this rupture, and we are likely to find ourselves mirrored there, invisible forces who contribute to such schisms. We run the danger of feeling too comfortable with this phenomenon and externalising it as something about 'them,' about 'Dalits' and the lack of homogeneity. The liberal, politically woke vocabulary positions us as sensitive readers but has yet to create a mechanism by which the gaze can turn back on our 'selves'. Does the upper-caste risk such sharp forms of rejection by going away, physically and metaphorically? I am reminded of the eleventh chapter titled 'Outcaste in M.K. Gandhi's Autobiography', which has the following conversation:

> 'In the opinion of the caste, your proposal to go to England is not proper. Our religion forbids voyages abroad. We have also heard that it is not possible to live there without compromising out religion. One is obliged to eat and drink with Europeans!'
>
> To which I replied: 'I do not think it is at all against our religion to go to England. I intend going there for further studies. And I have solemnly promised to my mother to abstain from three things you fear most. I am sure the vow will keep me safe.'

> 'But we tell you,' rejoined the Sheth, 'that it is *not* possible to keep our religion there. You know my relations with your father and you ought to listen to my advice.'
>
> 'I know those relations,' said I. 'And you are as an elder to me. But I am helpless in this matter. I cannot alter my resolve to go to England. My father's friend and adviser, who is a learned Brahman, sees no objection to my going to England, and my mother and brother have also given me their permission.'
>
> 'But will you disregard the orders of the caste?'
>
> 'I am really helpless. I think the caste should not interfere in the matter.' (Gandhi 2018: 106)

Gandhi's decision to cross the sea (hence court pollution) was questioned by his caste council and he was threatened to be ostracised from the community. A nonchalant Gandhi walked away from the caste council announcing to them that it didn't matter to him. The ex-communication or social ostracism of the upper castes has been much written about and individuals lauded for their courage and conviction. We may also recall Pranescharya in Ananthamurthy's novel *Samskara,* who walks out and away from the Agrahara after his purity has been 'tainted'. The existential iconoclasm associated with the upper-caste heroes' movement is not available to Mr Vaghela, who remains between the pressure of assimilation and alienation. Mr Vaghela is neither ostracised nor lauded. He is reminded of how his self-fashioning has come at a cost and has been possible by not others' rejection of him but his own rejection of a part of his life and self. For those who occupy the 'creamy layer', the nature of caste-produced misery changes and morphs into new schisms. The challenge does not lie only from the upper-caste other but forms of otherness that cause a tumultuous relation with the self. Nagaraj notes that 'the working of the caste system has always tried to create mental states of self-doubt, self denial, and self-hatred among lower caste individuals in the modern context, and generally these attitudes are collectivized' (2010). This civil war inside Mr Vaghela stems from themes of shame and humiliation for which others, the upper castes, are responsible. It is some of those themes that we shall turn to subsequently.

4

Elsewhere: Language, Gender, Translation

> If writing itself is a translation of thoughts and ideas in the metaphorical sense then when women have to use this language, they are obliged to 'translate' this male discourse in the real sense in order to share their experience.
>
> —Kamala (2009: xiii)

On the face of it, what can gender and translation have in common? Nothing really. The former is about everything and the latter a mere linguistic activity of transferring one set of things from one language into another. As some people remind us, translation is as secondary as the woman herself. What does it take to transfer meanings? It's a quiet in-house activity that makes some people happy and brings them a little something—joy, money, whatever. It's a hobby, not a real job. The real thing is the 'original'; translation is a mere copy of that, a parasite that depends on it. These reductive and much-repeated views don't help us open any questions. In fact, they close them, and merely contesting them does not help. The hegemonic symmetry is too neat and sterile. It is non-generative by restricting itself to binaries of men and women, and their respective forms of labour. I am hoping that in this thinking-aloud essay, we go beyond this impasse, this stasis.

On the basis of myriad examples in this essay, I hope to show that gender is the jaggedness in the bridge translation is meant to create. It is the rocky part of the bridge where you are likely to fall and sink, but you may somehow also manage to bypass, should you so will it. How do we then trace this tight embrace that language and gender create? I suggest we look at language hidden in plain sight, in the quotidian modes of living—the very spaces we occupy in the everyday. I believe that we need a simultaneous gaze, at both the spoken and the unspoken; the linguistically available as well as the implicit assumptions of gender. It is possible that in some cases of literary, textual as well as everyday instances, the linguistic difference is marked, drawing attention to itself.

Words are thrown at women in real life and in stories. And when women who translate also notice this, they throw them back, baring them of any euphemism. Feminist writers in Quebec did it particularly and starting in the late 1970s. A famous example in this regard goes as follows: '*Ce soir j 'entre dans l'histoire sans relever ma jupe*', in French rendered into 'This evening I'm entering history without pulling up my skirt', by a 'traditional' translator and 'This evening I'm entering history without opening my legs'. The latter, termed a feminist mode of translation, lays bare and makes explicit what is implicit. It signals 'the repossession of the word by women, and the naming of the life of the body as experienced by women' (Godard 1984: 14, also see Flotow 1991). One may ask whether the latter is faithful, but the judgment rests upon the object to which women translators may be required to be faithful—patriarchal language? Or to the project at hand? From my point of view, the relationships between gender and translation remain restricted for three reasons in the French-Canadian and Anglophone contexts. First, the translations in question are occurring in a professional sphere; translation becomes a cognitive and conscious action that is undertaken to fulfil a definitive purpose. Second, it is operating in a realm that attempts to make language intelligible, overt and explicit. And finally, translation is understood in relation to the text in its most physical sense.

In contrast to this, the sheer range of South Asian languages produces a range of linguistic contexts of class, caste and gender, especially in the varying contexts of domesticity. These stratifications lay their imprint on and are shaped by language in innumerable ways. Everyday translation in this multilingual terrain is not a professional cognitive act but rather often an involuntary switching. Language and personhood are intricately tied. There are multiple languages of the self that circulate between families, colleagues, homes, workspaces and the travel in between. Languages in the South Asian context are always in transit. Translation, for this reason, operates not in the neutral plane of diversity, but rather in the uneven, unequal relations between languages that often produce competing narratives of the self and the world.

It is language that provides me with the template of knowledge. Its instability; its real-ness; its emotive charge; its instrumentalisation and more importantly its presence along one or the other border—all of this has helped me understand the regions; the communities; the anxieties of places. The indexical accents, syllabic differences in words as you go from one region to another, and echoes of places you leave behind or aspirations of places you want to go to—all these have helped understanding the world indexically and metaphorically. In doing so, I have also noticed how gender boundary is the most difficult one to transgress. Language creates both intimacy and distance, much like family, it pulls one close to the source of anguish yet establishes a boundary sometimes. This tussle, its translations or lack of perhaps, is what constitutes being gendered.[1]

Translating Many Gods in One Body

In a Kannada poem titled 'Dhanyavaadagalu', the poet Lalita Siddabasavayya addresses god and says, 'We are translating you … in all the languages of this earth … simultaneously everywhere in all the unpublished writings of all the mothers' (trans. Kamalakar Bhat, unpublished) A powerful image appears before my eyes; one that has no cultural or political relativism but a universal phenomenon without a universal language. Its universalism is produced by its relation to an unseen power that drives all the women of the entire world to follow an unseen original, a scripted document. We could use women as a provisional category, to expand it and include all forms of performativity

1 While it is the everyday I focus upon, it is important to pause here and cite the interventions that feminist scholarship has already made in the arena of gendered concepts. For instance, J. Devika demonstrates in an important article how feminists in Kerala have been translating concepts largely produced in first-world contexts into the local language. This has involved multiple efforts such as coining new words, importing some, re-orienting and redefining some. An example of what is euphemistically called 'eveteasing' (which I discuss in a subsequent section) when re-named as 'sexual harassment', signals a feminist act of translation (Devika 2008: 183).

and not only the assigned female gender. At the same time, a distinct female body, a reproductive body is important to the poet. For we are told in the next stanza,

> God,
> We don't know its script
> In the caressing by our palms
> In the tight folds of our arms
> In the low cradle formed by our thighs
> In our milk-filled breasts
> Prior to that, in the flesh and blood of our wombs
> We keep translating you
> Close to the source
> Committed to your motifs.
> ('Thanks' trans. Kamalakar Bhat, unpublished)

The 'bearing' of the 'original' is the task of the women translators, we are told.[2] They sustain it in their wombs without possessing it fully. For they know they must continue to not be egoistic and claim full possession. They have it in the body but only for keepsake. They must translate but also keep 'close to the source'. In this onerous task they take upon themselves, they are the privileged ones, the chosen ones undertaking God's agenda. Or are they by being women short-changed and made to be of secondary assistance to a male father figure of the god? I am reminded once again of Chamberlain who remarks that the metaphoric of translation betray a mimicking of the 'patrilineal kinship system where paternity—not maternity—legitimizes an offspring' (2000: 315). Does the maleness of god lie in the grammar, or rather in the nature of

2 It would be interesting to examine the adjectives around female authorship and confirm if the perspective that collapses the woman and translator impinges upon reviewers' comments on works by women. In Gujarati, for instance, it is more common to see claims of capturing the zeitgeist or effecting a turning point conveyed through words like *yugparivartan* used for male authors. Women authors, notes Bindu Bhatt (a renowned author from Gujarat) are reviewed with words like *laagni* (emotions), *vedna* (pathos) and not meant to turn the tide, a prerogative reserved for male authors. I found Bhatt's use of the word *anusaran* (to follow) very telling, in that, women are perceived as doing *anusaran* while the male authors are supposed to have set the norm. The prefix *anu* means after and used in translation also, as in *anuvaad* or speak after (Bhatt, personal communication).

this relation, by the performance of power? It's also interesting to think that the mothers translate without knowing the script, as if to say, that translation is not the writ of literacy. Perhaps not knowing the script makes the translators stay close to the source, not daring to go astray. The last stanza of the poem recapitulates the question I asked earlier—if this is a privilege or non-consensual labour. And we are told, I think, somewhat ironically: God, do not make us greedy/Alert us time and again against corrupting the original/Let us not ask for any gain from this translation/May all rights always remain with you/God/Thank you for choosing only us/As your translators (Bhat, unpublished).

The paradox of privilege and compulsion in the poem is as much of interest to me as the perception of reproduction-as-derivation. Only women could be chosen to translate—to take on the most important and trustworthy job. But only women could be told to do the most important job and stay within the boundaries of a text, the *maryada* or limits of life; for only women and translators would be construed 'greedy' if they asked for more. This poem raises very significant questions about translation, labour and gender, and especially the paradox that underlies prerogative and coercion. In doing this, the poem troubles the collapsing of marginality—both of women and translators.[3]

My interest lies in experience and language and how they might produce sites of gender relations, which are not in isolation from caste and class. The sites may or may not lie in texts or the assigned bodies and sex of the translators and authors, but ways in which language bears implicitness of gender, inviting us to 'read' through translation what lies hidden in plain sight. In doing so, I draw attention to vignettes from multilingual sites and hope to demonstrate that questions of gender and translation are before and beyond the paradigms of translation studies, and it is those we need to study to nuance the existing positions on how to do feminist translation, which may simply be about how to listen

3 Lori Chamberlain remarks how the 'opposition between productive and reproductive work' may be read as the 'distinction between writing and translating—marking, that is the one to original and "masculine," and the other to be derivative and "feminine"' (Chamberlain 2000: 314). Echoes of this argument are to be heard in several subsequent writings on translation but also with extensions of what a feminist translator can do, what is the nature of the relationship feminist translators can bring to bear upon a text.

as a feminist. Feminism is homework, as Sara Ahmed writes, 'because we have much to work out from not being at home in a world' (2017: 236). Questions of language, gender and translation trouble these very conceptions of the home, the world and the complicated relationships it produces with the self.

This essay grounds gender-mediating language and language-mediating gender, and both produce a certain kind of translation affect. It observes this through multiple sites of reading language, both as specific historically named languages and also language in its role of constructing gendered subjectivities. In doing this, the essay not only effects translation as a consequence but also as a form of understanding. The exercise helps us in seeing the phrase 'gender and translation' beyond the intertwining of marginality; rather, it opens up everyday situations and literary examples to the scrutiny of a translation gaze.

Vignette 1

'*Anya sum payo aahe?*' Is my brother still sleeping, I was being asked by my father. The question had the possibility of a volcanic eruption. With heart drumming in my chest, I went to my brother's room. His anger was more physical than my father's but back then, I didn't know if the feeling of fear was any different. I was supposed to return to my father and tell him what he already suspected. 'He's about to get up, it looks like,' I replied in Sindhi of course. By not lying, I had been truthful to my father but by hoping that my brother would wake up soon, I was giving him a chance to do so before all hell broke loose. This was not an unusual instance and also a deeply experienced schism in my house between my father and brother. My *bhabhi*, mother, sisters and I watched with trepidation when their differences widened or shrunk. We anticipated the consequences that would have on us, who waited and served. '*Putta, marda tah gusso kanda aahein*,' my mother would remind me, 'men do express anger'. In fact, I just added 'express' to what is more like 'men do anger' in Sindhi. English somehow made anger into a feeling that needs expression rather than an act the way my mother implied. My language carries these itchy scars.

Elena Basile reminds us of trauma underneath almost-healed scabs. Where do we map the *skin* of language(s), she asks (Basile 2012: 151). Quite often, translation for hurting bodies like those of women is a reconfiguration of these wounds on the body of language. We bear different languages in our bodies. Sindhi, the language my mother taught me, is the language in which men's and women's roles were normalised the most. It was the language of guilt—one in which I learnt the duties of a daughter-in-law to be, '*Sas saan ihan na galaybo aa*' (You can't speak like this with your mother-in-law) or '*Chhokri vaat khole ta ghar kharab thee vanye*' (When a woman is loose-tongued, she brings the entire house down). I refused to translate this into English—into my life—for English made my mother's words seem archaic and regressive. It was the language of that judgment on her. I oscillated between the guilt of Sindhi and the indignation of English. Mediating between Sindhi and English is Gujarati—a source language of the texts, the kitchen language of my joint family but rife with power relations of a different kind. In the state of Gujarat and a family with Gujarati in-laws, my 'mother tongue' Sindhi remains in the same place, inside me. It was to Gujarati I first turned, learnt, translated (into English) and established legitimacy. I moved from a mother tongue to a husband tongue, from a stateless minority language to the official language of the state, seamlessly assimilating into a more hegemonic culture. My food was re-named so that *bassar jee koki* became *kanda-na-thepla* to help the Gujarati household appreciate my difference on their own terms. These politics of language and translation between unequal segments of a 'joint' family were an early insight into the subject. Sindhi was a strange language, with its origins in a hoary Pakistan and its association with people who seem difficult to fit into the Gujarati Vaishnav's notion of a normal Hindu. The effort to translate this non-textuality was enormous and seemed unnecessary for a while. Hence, Gujarati became my language of 'source' from which emanated new legitimate meanings. The fact that I was a daughter-in-law with a minority language entering into a house with a minority language positioned both me and my language in specific ways, relegating both of us to a private unspoken world. This is one of the most fundamental dyads of translation—a minoritisation of expression produced through a collusion of the self, body and language.

Perhaps by being its outsider, I heard its outsideness most strongly and words like 'those people' or many other forms of non-named references to the poor, the illiterate, the Dalits and the Muslims made themselves heard to me. It is in my language matrix, a language of normalising otherness, just as Sindhi is the language of normalising patriarchy. Sindhi drew boundaries for me and my sisters. It was a language of borders. I would learn later though that it was a transborder language, spoken here and there, in Pakistan. It was an opening-out language, making me feel welcome in Karachi, where I could flaunt a language I had hidden in Gujarat. It found hospitality, not in its close-neighbour Gujarati but in its splintered self in Pakistan. Compulsively mediating and translating, I heard and reproduced meanings from both sides of the border. The everyday patriarchy of the language got suspended for a while; I had become an adult who could curate parts of the language when I liked. It now stays within me as a language that both opens out and closes, depending on the nature of my subject position. Contradictory, almost oppositional tendencies, characterise Sindhi's relation with me. A part of me wants to ignore its 'commonsense' and not translate, and another part of me warms up to it as the only memory of pre-Partition days. Sindhi also became my site of resistance to Gujarati, my husband tongue; my in-laws' tongue and the language of the state that divides the world between Hindus and Muslims, between vegetarians and non-vegetarians. It adopted me, by ignoring my Sindhiness, and of course, I also collaborated in that convenient amnesia for many years. Translating from Gujarati consolidated that position; it became evidence of my loyalty to both, my in-laws and their language. The gendered perception of my good behaviour came to play around the text than in the text. Because I spoke the language well, I proved my loyalty to Gujarati. My gender came not just in the body or one particular domestic script, but rather in the space between and around these multiple languages. The precise site of where one becomes a gendered subject is not easy to locate. Hence the elsewhere.

Vignette 2

Jeni dal bagdi, ehno daahdo bagdyo. If your dal is ruined, so is your day, I was told; the *tuver* or *toor* dal of an upper-caste Gujarati family—sweet and filled with *kokum*, peanuts and *khajur*—the kind that is served in a *vara*, a community meal. I was being indoctrinated into the Gujarati family. '*Amne dal wagar to chalej naheen*,' my mother-in-law said. The cooker would be filled with dal in the morning, and as I woke up to that whistle, I knew the script for my life was written already. I was scripted to have dal twice a day and only of one particular kind. Its life began before mine did. It was the reason why I was where I was, a Sindhi in a Gujarati household, a quasi-Muslim child of a community known for its aggressive business tactics and so hated by the Gujaratis for more than reason than one. How could I dare say I don't like the dal, wasn't I grateful enough already to be accepted? My resistance if any existed in English, for the vocabulary to resist came only from my education in English. The Sindhi language in me reminded me of my mother's voice, '*Putta saavran mein sambhalein haljein*' (Beta, be careful when you deal with the in-laws). And to have escaped my own illiterate, debt-ridden home? And imagine such anger towards dal. '*Har chhokri khe aidjust [adjust] karan gurje*,' my mother said. She had said this to all her daughters, every girl should adjust. I focused on her peculiar English word and wondered what it was to aid and also to be just and let the dal go. Where I fashioned my English as resistance, my mother perhaps saw in it a scope for authority, the validation of an ideal she wanted me to abide by. The word, 'adjust', seemingly out in a sentence in Sindhi was in fact exactly in its right place. It stayed in my life for years and years and years. Language, with its small 'adjustments', leaves imprints that linger beyond one's imagination. The adjustment stuck to me, only in that form, that pulse and that sanctimonious authority. *Aamaj hoye.* That's the way it is. I began removing jaggery from my portion and then my portion from the food altogether. Sometimes silence itself is a language, not just one but many at the same time. My silence was one of 'aidjusting', being upset and yet making my way through the household. My mother-in-law's '*Aamaj hoye*' was the innocuous polite work of generating norms that she was familiar with.[4] Gujarati came with its specific historicity, it stabilised a very particular set of temporal inter-generational habits, structures that I was to abide by. Transactions through language (sometimes called translations) are made on the basis of power. A dominant language and patriarchal power reinforce each other's strength and at times, a minority language and experience of being dominated go together.

The quiet and polite assertions of language are the most compelling. The norms offer no justification for their exclusions. While a lot of writing about feminism has offered important critiques to the patriarchal state through an emphasis on agency, language's normalising effect lays bare and yet hides in plain sight the incapacity of agency to address gendered divisions. Gender remains the unnamed other, subsumed under the norm that requires no utterance. *Aamaj hoye*.

Vignette 3

Let me give you another example of 'elsewhereness'. The following is a text exchange between me and Abhijit Kothari, my husband. The two of us had collaborated on translating a trilogy of historical fiction in Gujarati by the famous K.M. Munshi; Munshi is Gujarat's most popular, successful storyteller and also the architect of the conceptual term about Gujarat's regional pride, *Gujarat nee Asmita*.[5]

> Abhijit: Manjari died. I had tears in my eyes.
> Rita: Who Manjari?
> Abhijit: Kaak's Manjari, who else?

---

4 The mother figure has emerged in my examples as the carrier of normative assertions. Is she the originator of these articulations or being faithful to norms laid out for her, and in turn passing them on for me to do the *anusaran*, the follow-up? The matter can only be speculated upon. It is possible that ambivalences surrounded both my mother and mother-in-law, but their use of language did not allow these chinks to show.

5 For more details on the writer, his significance and discursive views around his ideological positions, see Kothari and Kothari (2021).

Kaak and Manjari's romance characterises for many in Gujarat the most predominant memory of Munshi's fiction. It figures in the second and third parts of Munshi's trilogy. A relationship formed through a chequered history, this was perhaps the first instance of a stormy and romantic couplehood in Gujarati fiction. Hence when Manjari died in the last novel of the trilogy, it evoked for many readers a highly charged response. At a time when we (Abhijit and I) would have been translating the chapter in which Manjari dies, I was away in Delhi, adjusting to a new life. Abhijit and I used to translate together. One of us would read out and suggest a rough translation while the other would key in, and we discussed possible options. It was difficult to say who did what, and a question that came up every time the book would be discussed on panels was how did we divide the work between us? Had we admitted that he was better at scenes of actions, and I was at the more poetic and affective, we ran into the danger of stereotypes of masculine and feminine strengths. And really speaking, it may well have to do with the kinds of reading we had done and internalised. Without stopping to think of these distinctive strengths, we moved on and almost completed two and a half novels of the trilogy together. While some portion of the third novel was yet to be over, I moved away from home. The text message reminded me of how distant I felt from the woman protagonist whose death my male collaborator had conveyed. The distance could be explained by my physical distance from the text, and for some weeks, from the project of translating Munshi, which Abhijit was carrying on valiantly in my absence. Or did he experience Kaak's loss and was in fact relating to the husband even if the sentiment was occasioned by the death of Manjari?

I wish to mark this moment (through the aforesaid example) as one that is not about a woman-translator relating to a woman character (which as you see is not happening!) or rather the affinity a male translator felt towards the woman character (which as you see is happening!). The moment is to suggest how irrelevant it would be to restrict this discussion on translation by thinking of the male–female binary or even bodies as a starting point. Our performed gender and its alloyed chemistries may have, would have lent more complexity to our relationship with the task of translation. However, its effects may not be manifest in the text, and perhaps we need not even look for them there. It seems to me that this relationality, rather than the beginning and endpoints of texts and people, invites further reflection. So, the question of what might be the relation between gender and translation may be less fruitful if focused on how bodies are gendered. I suggest we explore different questions that fall under the arena and then assume a core that defines or resolves it. Thus, our being male and female translators in relation to a celebrated text by a celebrated male author with a strong woman character in it provided no easy symmetries of gender and identification. What got generated that day was my guilt at not only doing my share but feeling so disconnected. Or was it guilt at being away from home? Did translation then become a proxy, as it usually does, a stand-in for something else? I hope to be able to explore this surrogacy in translation, of being elsewhere. And before I move away from K.M. Munshi, a powerful name in Gujarat, I must also draw your attention to another instance outside the text, not in the activity of translation but around its feminised labour. In two recent interviews in Gujarat, I was told in Gujarati, '*Tame Munshi sahib ne translate karya, e Gujarat taraf tamari moti service kehvaye*.' You have translated Munshi Sahib and that's commendable service towards Gujarat. Not having heard these words or any word while translating a Dalit person or woman's writing, I was struck by being at the service of this powerful male writer. The use of the word 'service' immediately evoked notions of translators' servitude to texts, tyrannical notions of the original and inflated egos of writers, and of course selfless nationalism in general. We seldom think of gendered labour, the relation that we women translators have to the extolled male writers. Is the labour of translation gendered then? Is its syntax drawn from imagery of service, servitude and duty like women's or child labour, as such arduous work but processed as a duty. I asked myself what made this particular instance feel like I was 'serving' Munshi while the translation of Macwan's Dalit novel, *Angalilyat* and women's writing did not feel like one? Abhijit, on the other hand, responded to these questions by saying how Munshi was part of his staple reading through childhood. The feminisation of my labour occurred elsewhere, in the perceived hierarchy, not in the nature of the text. Munshi's fiction, by being ideologically conservative, generated unease about my own role and politics in translating it. It did so by being xenophobic. It was an unease that both Abhijit and I carried, while also attending to its formative influence in Gujarat and hence the need to bring that to the discussion. Munshi's women were feisty, setting terms of engagement and are perhaps the first set of women in the history of Gujarati literature to do so. That did not make me particularly identify with the women. Dalit and women's writings escaped the notice of Gujarati journalism and the literary world; drawing neither appreciation nor censure, the labour remained invisible rather than feminised. What is brought over once again is a dialectical relationship that both translation and gender are a part of in the larger cultural and political structure, and the foregrounding of that relationship becomes evident in surprising and non-uniform ways, but almost always played out in the body of language.

Commitments to feminist and anti-caste modes require us to pay attention to utterances and see them for what they are—intentional, non-intentional, symbolic, normal, literary or literal, but contextual and implicit even when they appear obvious, in fact, especially when they appear obvious. How do we, for instance, think of the colloquial untranslatables such as *khandaan*, *karpu*, *izzat*—words of honour, boundary, lineage, family that create an artillery against female-assigned bodies who transgress, overreach; carry desires held illegitimate by their class and caste? And how does English interact with these languages, bringing the promise of agency and modernity? If we examine how English interacts with regional languages on this issue, we notice two things. The commonsense about and normalisation of molestation, rape, discrimination is part of the linguistic repository in 'our' languages—terms such as *karpu* (Tamil), *maryada* (Indo-Aryan languages) or *izzat* and *aabru* (Urdu), which translate as chastity, boundaries/protocol, honour, etc. sustain unequal gender relations. The calling out and the legal terms are oftentimes in English. They draw from a transnational vocabulary of feminist discourse and are then translated into the bhashas. Thus translation is both the object and mode of 'reading' gender discourses. In that vein, I am providing an excerpt from a story by Varsha Adalaja, an acclaimed writer in Gujarat.

Vignette 4

The story 'Nayana Rasikbhai Mehta' is an interaction and memory (Adalaja 2011). An upper-class Gujarati woman staying in a 'sea-facing' apartment in South Bombay goes to a police station. She is haunted by instances of violence, both physical and linguistic, perpetrated upon her by her mother-in-law and husband. She's had enough. The police inspector and his minions speak Marathi while she responds in Gujarati. The banality of the interaction is something like this:

Name?

N..a ..y..a..na

Full name?

Nayana ... Rasik Mehta

Hmm. Sarnamu?

What?

Address ... where you stay, kuthe rehvanu?

Jay Mahal, Marine Drive

Wow, near the sea, dariya samovar?

Yes, Saheb. Near the sea, dariya saame. [She matched the words with Gujarati to his Marathi]

Savant! This is that building, remember, where we had gone for a theft case ... what's its name now, kaaya naaunv?

Sea bird.

Yes. First-class building.

Saheb..my complaint.

One minute. Don't do ghai, shanti theva. What's the rush.

Jee.

The Marathi-speaking police inspector assumes that a woman from a 'good' family ... *khandaan*, living in a sea-facing apartment, would have come to complain about a servant. Language here performs class and gender relations more prominently, caste is more implicit.

The police officer returned to his desk. He yawned audibly as he sat down. He cracked his knuckles. Nayana read his name on the uniform. S.P. Jadhav. Her tongue moistened her dry lips and she stood up, erect. Jadhav opened the complaint book, ruffled its pages. He took a pen in hand.

'Alright Madam, so what time did the theft take place?'

'Saheb'

'How many do newspapers mention that don't hire servants without doing some due diligence. You should find out, na, if they have any criminal records. Ask police stations ...'

'Saheb, listen to me'.

'Do you have a foto and tencha gaanvacha address? His village address? No need to worry. How much did you lose? Did you bring a list with you? Wonderful. You don't want to tell me. Look, I am quite busy.'

She stammered.

'Saheb, there's been no theft.'

'So why aren't you telling me Madam? You lost your mangasutra in a local train then? Is your dog missing? Some roadside Romeo eaveteased you? I am a terror to those kinds, telling you.'

'Saheb. My husband hits me and my mother-in-law also ... with ...'

Her voice choked. She had meant to fall into the arms of her Rasik and lose herself in fantasies of companionship, how did she then come to be this condition?

Jadhav put his pen down. His lips curled. Sawant came and stood beside Jadhav.

'Jadhav, what is Madam's complaint?'

'Domestic violence,' he replied in English.

The English word makes it official. The homely advice that gave the inspector self-importance is suddenly rendered irrelevant; a legal term in English re-orients the nature of transaction. English names it and nails it—the phenomenon of 'domestic violence'. The inspector's Gujarati–Marathi saw as a mere inconvenience in the usual life of a woman. A linguistic–legal switch takes the matter out of the domain of persuasion and condescending advice to one of action. It has affected the socialilty of the entire interaction, almost as if someone had used a weapon in a perfectly normal situation. She becomes the third person, unpleasant, whining, petty. The inspector Jhadav says to this companion,

'Savant, you know how it is, this so-called "domestic violence". The husband must be peeved about something, yelled maybe, and Madam made a dash for the police station.'

She looked at both men with petrified eyes. Will they refuse to write her complaint? She immediately said, 'No ... no ... Saheb that's not how it is. You must listen to me.'

> *'Of course I am listening to you. I am.' He repeated in Marathi. 'How long have you been married?'*
>
> *'Seven years. But ...'*
>
> *Savant spoke in an incredulous voice, 'Seven years?! Long period that is. And you suddenly rushed to file a complaint today? Did he suddenly become cruel?'*
>
> *'See Madam, you seem to be from a respectable family. Khandaani ani sanskari ghar. You must be educated too, right? By doing this you are jeopardizing family honour, do you understand?' Jadhav continued.*
>
> *'But ... but will you at least hear me out?'*
>
> *'Woman, you listen to me. Have you informed your family that you are coming to a police-station?'*
>
> *'No, no ...'*
>
> *'Bas then. It's not too late. Go. Go home. Married life madhe sagda hote, all kinds of things happen.'*
>
> *'Utensils when next to each other will bang, you understood?'*
>
> (trans. Rita Kothari 2022, see Adalaja 2022)

What makes Nayana so illegible to the language of law? The incommensurability is evident through 'utterances' and homilies that the police inspector is used to dispensing, they are in his everyday language, which happens to be Marathi. It's possible that Nayana Rasik Mehta, if she had registered a complaint in Gujarat, would be hearing phrases like, '*Ben ghar maan be vaasan to khakhde*' or '*Badhu thaye, lagn jeevan maan, emaan dodta dodta fariyaad nodhanva na aav vanu hoye.*' This commonsense made through a domestic metaphor of utensils that will inevitably bang against each other is neither about the intention of the speaker nor an accidental use of words. Words flow effortlessly flattening out the individuated narrative, subsuming it all in the already-understood meanings of life. Once again, language performs sociality before it can be noticed for sustaining the status quo. The boundary-making words such as family (*khandaan*) have been thrown in casually; their associated meanings of restraint, adjustment, and acceptance are understood to a shared meaning. These are not the words the inspector would be using for a Dalit woman, who would be seen not only as having even less legitimacy but also as having less to lose in terms of honour.

Vignette 5

The address 'saheb,' for the police inspector in Nayana's story appears elsewhere, in a Dalit poem. However, both the speaker and the addressee are unnamed. The perpetrators are unnamed, but they are recognisable by symbolic markers of caste. The violence upon the speaking body is conveyed like a banal event of daily life—same people, same actions, and it is not a sudden episode of recognition or retribution. It is a poem, but not one. It is rather accidentally in verse what appears like a regular everyday business. This tone, this timelessness marks its difference from the moment of #MeToo it gestures itself to. The 'poem,' so to speak, is called 'Me too,' an English phrase of a specific moment, of a specific class, and caste but used for a context outside the discourse of #MeToo.[6]

વહેલી પરોઢે પાયખાનું પખાળવા આવું છું
ને રોજ કોઈ ઓળો
મને ઉપાડી જાય છે અવાવરુ ખૂણે,

મને જકડી લે છે જમીન સટોસટ,
મારા ઉપર સવાર થઈ જાય છે સૂવ્વરની જેમ,
મને કોચ્યા કરે છે,
હું બેશુદ્ધ ના થઈ જાઉં ત્યાં લગી!

મને કંઈ યાદ નથી, સાહેબ ...

કદાચ થોડું યાદ છે તો બસ એટલું જ કે
એના શરીરે સૂતરના તર્ણ તાંતણા જેવું હતું,
એના ગળે તુલસીની માળા જેવું હતું,
એના મોઢે વીછીના આંકડા જેવી વાંકડિયા મૂછો જેવું હતું,
એનો વાન ઉજળિયાત હતો,
એ હરે ... હરે ... જેવું કશું બબણતો હતો.

ઉતરીને એણે સીધી ગંગા ભણી દોટ મૂકી હતી ...

(Neerav Patel)

6 The Gujarati original 'Me too' is by Neerav Patel. It is an unpublished poem. The English translation is mine, also unpublished.

Every single morning
I come to do the toilets
And every day a shadow
Drags me away
To a desolate corner
It pins me tightly to the ground
It climbs upon me like a pig
And picks on parts of my body
Until I have turned impure

Saheb I honestly don't remember
All I recall is this:
its body had the sacred thread
its neck a tulsi mala
its face a handlebar moustache
And its body was fair, upper-caste-like
It muttered something like Hare, Hare
And it got off my body
And made a dash for the Ganga

In the first instance, I read the title 'Me too' in Neerav Patel's poem as an undocumented sexual molestation of a Dalit woman. Which it may well be. Really speaking, Gujarati does not provide a gendered pronoun for the speaker. It provides its caste markers more clearly—first through the occupation of a toilet cleaner, or night-soil carrier. Then there are caste markers of the body or the shadow that rapes, mutilates, makes impure the speaker, but makes a dash for the holy waters of the Ganga as if 'it' was made impure. It is easy and tempting and fully legitimate to read the speaker's body as that of a woman and an upper-caste male as one of a man. And yet the only gendered address is 'Saheb', who is being told of this continuous, everyday, invisible to the world form of rape. Who is the Saheb? A male police officer? Clearly a figure of authority to whom this is being told. Is this a form of complaint?

The first reference to caste emerges through the speaker's occupation, as one who cleans toilets at the crack of dawn. The 'shadow' that rapes the speaker acquires markers of caste in the second stanza—the sacred thread points to 'it' being a Brahmin; the tulsi mala, a Vaishnav; and the handle-bar moustache, male and Kshatriya. These metonymic references to the three upper–castes collapse into one person to make for his membership in an *ujaliyat* or upper caste that has historically fed upon the Dalit body. *Ujaliyat* also embraces allusion to class. Inserting the pronoun 'she' constructs for us an unremittingly familiar situation of a Dalit female body that is fed upon by a male body. And considering the poem is called 'Me too', it is only 'natural' to reproduce those terms, and set them up in opposition to the indignation of upper-class and upper-caste women at their sexual exploitation. On the other hand, withholding the pronoun, and withholding gender makes the poem a structural symbol so that all upper-castes collaborate through different layers of society to keep the Dalit pinned to the ground.

Any translation discussion around the poem would dwell on the difficulty of the implicit markers of caste and the 'meaning' of the poem would be confined to the oppression of Dalit women at the hands of upper-caste men. In doing so, there may also be an assumption that the English title of the poem 'Me too' moves smoothly between Gujarati and English. Generally speaking, we view translation as acquiring its legitimacy from linguistic differences, not sameness. However, it is precisely the 'sameness' that inheres to many political signals in this poem. And ironically that would seem not in need of translation. The campaign #MeToo that gripped the world of the media, arts and politics—rehearsed in English and enacted on social media—was produced by and addressed to situations of the urban privileged. By naming a relentlessly continuous situation of a Dalit woman that can neither name nor shame, Patel points out the irony of its ever-present banality in the lives of some. He draws attention to the amnesia regarding the bodies of Dalit women and the enshrining of the mostly upper-caste body in the #MeToo campaign. Gender, caste and language come together in this poem in a way that complicates the assumed syntax of translation, which is not about finding equivalences between languages, but between the unspoken violence in the Dalit universe and the speaking out of privileged women. The poem is also a harsh reminder of the fact that the phenomenon has *now* come to be named, which, particularly in the case of Dalit women, is relentlessly continuous and centuries-old.

The English word is not translated into Gujarati. On the other hand, some words exist in new coinages. For instance, languages have been forced to coin new Indian words forms of words, such as *dushkarma* for molestation. Someone said to me, 'Pehla aapne chhedkhani kehta' (Earlier we called it eve-teasing), but now we call it *dushkarma*. The equivalence between sexual molestation and *dushkarma* (evil/ wicked action) is far from perfect, and yet the term has been scaled up (somewhat)[7] from 'eve-teasing', an innocuous little act of the kind Krishna the God was known to have been doing with the *gopis*, the maidens. Why this word? I asked a senior journalist. 'I believe it's the influence of Hindi media.' By this, the journalist was referring to the way the Hindi word had entered into the lexicon of Gujarati journalism. The trace of a borrowed language irked him, as did the hegemony of Hindi journalism. The root question that Gujarati journalism could have found a word that created a better equivalence did not come up. In his mind at least. What is also interesting is what that endeavour might have led to—coinage of another word that also stuck out as things do when newness enters the world. How are we to read these inadequacies and excesses of words, slippage of a residual intention to make it milder than sexual molestation or to externalise the unacceptable by attributing it to a non-native origin? Is that a problem of language, culture, gender or translation? Let me illustrate the non-native dimension of #MeToo that I witnessed in Gujarati journalism and everyday conversation. The articles responded to the moment of anger and awakening among women who called out their sexual predators from the immediate and sometimes former past, only to rest upon generalities of understanding, fellow-feeling and excesses of over-reaction. The vocabulary stayed within the Gujarati text reluctantly, as it were, alien and unwanted, with its origins assumed to be elsewhere, Delhi, US, or at any rate, the English language. 'Me too Me too *karva jaiye*, so half the population will vanish. Whom are we going to live

7 Note that the 'sexual' activity is still not being named. Also note that the Hindi word for sexual molestation would also be *balaatkar*, which was also not being mentioned. In the world of comparative euphemisms, *dushkarma* may have appeared a more acceptable choice to the 'respectable' world of Gujarati journalism.

with?', my mother-in-law said. The language of assertion had seemed to her clearly as a language of pickiness, of wanting to eliminate most of humanity and dignity for self had translated for her as a desire for the genocide of well-meaning people! Inadvertently, she was admitting the endemic nature of sexual violence, however, the language released certain effects on her and me. From her point of view, the combinations of 'me' and 'too' must have appeared particularly selfish, not suggesting that sexual abuse happened to me as well, but that I too will demand attention. Or I too want it; give [attention] to me too.[8] The vocabulary of feminism, as perhaps that of an individual self, is the outcome of modern subjecthood. This is not to say that it did not exist in pre-modern India, but perhaps its forms remain illegible to us, demanding therefore translation both from English or retaining English as in me-too, and in any case translation of pre-modern frameworks to suit more contemporary needs. 'Oh so now translation can also be feminist', a wise friend remarked bemusedly when I mentioned that I had to write an essay on the relationship between gender and translation. I was arrested by 'now'. It was not merely an anodyne adverbial but an impatient temporal marker, never-ending evidence of women's greed. The admission of victimhood turned into a claim for attention. Another form of #MeToo.

This informal and reflective essay has grappled with various forms of untranslatability, lurking memories that outlived the task, for instance, the adoption and resistance to #MeToo in Gujarati—a coercive entry into an unwilling language/society or a commonsense in Indian languages that resist English—the language of the law, naming and blaming, affiliations to patriarchy that are manifest in languages we embrace and resist and so on. I have attempted to create an archive out of our surroundings, experiences that do not make it to translation theory; in multilingual lives within whose folds lie some of the most intricate lessons of gender and translation. In doing so, my attempt has also been to carve a more local, rooted and grounds-up approach to questions of translation theory in India, not one where the engagement

8 The language of demand or rights was being dismissed as ethically wrong, and in socio-individual terms seen as self-indulgent.

begins and ends with official translators and official texts, but one in which we observe as feminist translators that language is the first institution of patriarchy and that any act of translation must begin by seeing language not as a source and as a system of signs, but also a living text that requires attention. To sum up, the gendered politics of translation is complex and elusive; it resides neither at the translator nor the text-end of things, but elsewhere. It is generated in all these forms of relationality and manifests in both overt and covert ways.

5

The Illegibility of Shame

> Shame. Shame and self-contempt. Nausea. When people like me, they tell me it is in spite of my colour. When they dislike me, they point out that it is not because of my colour. Either way, I am locked into the infernal circle.
>
> —Fanon (2008: 96)

> Sharam, that's the word. For which this paltry 'shame' is a wholly inadequate translation.
>
> —Rushdie (1983)

Dinesh lives in a 'colony'. His neighbours are well-to-do upper-caste people. His caste is unknown amongst his neighbours and perhaps an assumption is made that he is an upper-caste person, like the rest of them. Dinesh has not 'corrected' this assumption, it's easier that way. His Brahmin neighbour Ramprasad Tiwari often visits his home and eats food or drinks tea, a practice impossible to imagine had he known that Dinesh was a Dalit. When Dinesh is made to bring a dead pig to make a sacrificial offering by his mother, he dreads being 'found out' by Ramprasad Tiwari. The story 'Bhaya' by Omprakash Valmiki (2020) builds upon this fear, an inchoate terror that resides in Dinesh's psyche making him jump at every footstep and knock at the door. As such, he is also mocked and shamed by the people at the Dalit *basti* where he has gone to buy the pig. Kalu the butcher remarks on his pathetic and absorptive imitative attempts to become like the 'Baman-Baniya' (Brahmin and Bania, the upper castes). Underlying the mockery amongst the Dalits and the fear of rejection in the colony is Dinesh's deep sense of shame. Towards the end of the story, after making the offering of the pig, Dinesh lives through nightmares in which he sees Tiwari laughing mercilessly and the male pig growling at him. The shame makes Dinesh incoherent and catatonic. Meanwhile, we can imagine how whole and put together Ramprasad Tiwari would have been. *He is whole, there is nothing wrong with him,* Ambedkar remarks (emphasis mine, 2014: 94). It is because the 'touchable Hindu' is assumed to be faultless, above any blame for causing this shame, the scourge of the untouchable. Ambedkar mentions that 'it is usual to hear all those who feel moved by the deplorable condition of the Untouchables unburden themselves by uttering the cry, 'We must do something for the Untouchables.' One seldom hears of the persons interested in the problem saying 'Let us do something to change the Untouchable Hindu' (2014: 3). To make Ramprasad Tiwari and his kind account for the shame Dinesh experiences, we need to understand both the incoherent state of shame Dinesh has been into and how Tiwari's language (and our own by extension) has no acknowledgement of this illegible shame.

In this essay, I attempt to encounter the usually quiet, ever-present, illegible and invisible-to-the-world state of shame that many subaltern bodies carry. I want us to think of 'shame' as a noun and not an action, and an inner life/death that eludes a direct correspondence to the events outside. This is not to say that the 'outside' events have no consequence for they may be the ones producing shame. Nor do I want to suggest that the inside and the outside of the body are binary. However, I am urging us to look before and beyond the regulating practices used in language that remind women, Dalits and similar subaltern bodies to behave themselves. Through salutary lessons of humiliation or normative and epistemic forms of control, hegemonic groups make sure that people, who are deemed to be inferior on grounds of sexuality, caste and gender remain within their limits, their *lakshman rekha*. Such a language invokes words like *aukaat* (status), *aabru* (status and standing), *maryada* (limits) and so on and does the act of shaming if boundaries are crossed. Think of the way lessons are conveyed through phrases like '*Tum apni aukaat mein raho*' (Remember what your station is) or '*Ghar ki izzat ko dhyaan mein rakho*' (Remember the prestige of the family before you). Dalit people are in particular reminded of *aukaat* where they belong and what they must not transgress. Orsini reminds us that in everyday confrontation and caste politics in contemporary India, *aukaat* always carries strong illocutionary force, that is, it is spoken as a warning, a threat, an abuse so as not to 'trespass' with the promise of retribution of punishment (Orsini 2022). Words like *lajja* and *haya* (Hindi-Urdu words for 'shame') are spoken in a platitudinous manner and reserved mostly for women who are seen as bearers of family/clan respectability. I am also thinking here of the very significant word *karpu* in Tamil that carries, like *lajja*, the burden of chastity, respectability and limits. However, regardless of gender and caste, most words in Indian languages for shame such as *lajja*, *haya* and *sharam* emphasise 'doing' or 'maintaining' shame and often occur in verb forms. In the case of Dalits, the lessons may be similar, but there is perhaps a greater dehumanisation of the self. The state of shame produced through forms of humiliation that makes an individual ill-at-ease with his/her body and self, the self-loathing and self-contempt that quietly and imperceptibly eat away at selfhood are implied in the use of the word 'shame' by Fanon (in the epigraph).

Imagine looking at shame inside—not in the social, performing as if it were the job of maintaining boundaries but a presence of loathsomeness one carries towards oneself. How is this presence to be noticed, named and translated into words if the ones holding them, like Dinesh, are invisible? Or rather the ones holding them are hyper-visibilised through the gaze that falls on the expressive and the overt but not the psychic trauma held within. This particular meaning of 'shame' appears to be absent from Indian languages. This raises certain questions for me: how does the discourse of humiliation speak with shame (especially from the point of view of the ones who are humiliated and made to experience shame), and how do we see both—shame and humiliation—as pressing concerns thrown up by subaltern narratives in the last two to three decades. What makes me notice that now? If words like *apmaan* appear adequate in capturing the feeling of being humiliated, how might we understand the illegibility of shame both linguistically and phenomenologically? In other words, how is that translation of shame as one's own interiority into language so uneasy?

It is important to qualify here that there have been plenty of scholars in the West who have written about shame—from psychologists to philosophers. But while they may have been able to see shame as distinct from humiliation, they still cannot explain this inexpressibility (breakdown of speech, non-verbal state of self-repulsion) of shame we see in our Indian contexts. Erik Erikson, one of the most pivotal psychologists to have approached shame, argues that shame is under-theorised because it is subsumed under guilt (1956: 227). While Freud thought of shame as a far more primitive emotion, the domain of women, children and savages and guilt as the proper adult emotion, Erikson contradicted him stating that shame was arguably a part of everyone's fear of being seen when one is not ready for it and consequently 'a rage turned against the self' (ibid.). Levinas writes of shame succinctly as something that 'arises when we are unable to make others forget our basic nudity' (2003: 64). The Biblical overtones are almost dissonant for our purpose in the Indian context. More meaningfully though, Levinas describes shame as when one does not only seek to hide oneself from the other but also himself, its deepest echoes are a personal matter where there is a binding of the 'I' to itself, the fact of being riveted to oneself. Agamben extends Levinas' articulation further and states that in shame, a person becomes a witness to their own disorder (1998: 106). Agamben turns shame into an ontological question where the person is bound to something they can neither escape nor assume—be it language, body or death. This binding makes the person a subject, yet forces them to witness the limit of their own subjectivity.

But despite naming shame as such, many of the readings (cited above) have abstracted and universalised shame without much account of how it rests in bodies differently, how it alters an experience of the world, what it does to the boundaries between the self and the other, how shame as an instinct is felt more deeply in certain bodies. These accounts either pinpoint shame as a psychic developmental structure or turn it into ontological questions of 'being'. As we see, it is also hard to separate shame from guilt in certain instances as Erikson has already argued or from humiliation in the scholarship produced in India (for instance, Guru 2009) as we will explore further in the essay. In the existing scholarship on shame, there seems to be a flight away from shame as an experience itself—either to locate its source in the outside world or to locate it so deeply in one's psyche or the nature of existence that it becomes invisible, even to oneself.

While this invisibility of shame even to oneself is something I will take note of, I will also argue that attempting to stay close to its illegibilities and untranslatabilities, rather than escaping them, allows us to understand shame to its deepest extent of experience. I undertake this exercise by discussing the work of two writers in detail—Daya Pawar (1978) and Dhrubo Jyoti (2018). They belong to divergent regional locations and two very different generations. Daya Pawar's autobiography *Baluta* was written in 1978 and published in its English translation by Jerry Pinto in 2015. It documents, among other things, Pawar's participation in the Dalit Panther Movement, an awakening to Ambedkar and the challenges of becoming an educated Mahar. Dhrubo Jyoti is a contemporary writer and activist; and although 'A Letter to My Lover(s)' employs the age-old epistolary method, it too provides a sense of a journey and a re-assignation of the terms of interaction between a Dalit and upper-caste person. I hope to show how shame (as compared to humiliation) is illegible and yet such 'literary' writings provide a glimpse into this inarticulate world. If our lessons in this essay emerge from and are restricted by particularities of experience in a few texts, it is not a limited outcome—rather, a choice to make an embodied listening to the particular.

We will also note in *Baluta*, the unevenness of translation where Pinto has had to make many leaps to translate a visceral feeling of shame in the body that is unnamed as such into a legible form in English. For instance, observe the absence of verbal language and the presence of physiological reactions in the following excerpt from Pawar's text we discuss in detail subsequently:

> With my heart in my eyes, I tell him how much I need this job. But the officer continues to make sport of me. My eyes begin to fill. When he tells me that in his opinion, I would never be fit for a clerk's job, my self-confidence is crushed. It feels as if I have left my breath behind in that office. I want to go somewhere to be alone so as to weep my shame and frustration. (Pawar 2015: 150)

The expressions of shame are often physiological. The blushing, the quickening of heartbeat, perspiration and changes in breathing temporarily inhibit speech or action (English 1975: 24). In fact, the Marathi original in the abovementioned passage captures this inarticulacy by not using the word shame at all, instead of saying, '*Kunhi paanhaar naheen ashaa ekaantat jaun radavas vaatat asat*' (Pawar 1978: 131). This translates as 'I wanted such solitude, away from everybody, so that I weep away.' How this sense of solitude came to be translated to shame is a translator's decision perhaps, but it again circles back to how this permeability of shame in the body that marks all experiences finds no precise resonance in Indian languages.

It is not just the elisions or absences in the Indian languages but also the Englishness of the word 'shame' that interests me. The texts we talk about (some in more detail than others) use the word either by the authors or translators. However, Indian languages evince huge undecidability on this issue and a repertoire of words such as *lajja*, *sharam*, *haya* and *maanam* do not make an equivalent to the word 'shame' in the special context of this essay. In the next section, we will delve more deeply into why this may be the case and attempt to discern shame as separate from narratives of humiliation.

Shame, Humiliations and Uneasy Translations

I believe that to delve into the questions of shame's untranslatability, we can first look at how it has been approached by scholars—however obliquely before we try to gauge the gaps. There has been a recent surge of interest in humiliation studies, especially owing to its political and moral force. In a series of essays on humiliation edited by Gopal Guru, Ashis Nandy argues that humiliation is only possible owing to the collaboration between the tormentor and the tormented. V. Geetha's essay sheds light on humiliation as an 'ontological wound' (after Cornel West) that Dalit bodies carry (Geetha 2009: 95). While the series makes the violence of humiliation explicit, a vocabulary of shame in the Indian context remains elusive. I also believe that humiliation is overt and legible, and hence draws attention apart from the promise it carries of a radical overhaul of power structures. It is also more urgent, given the violence it carries—think of Dalit men in villages being forbidden from growing moustaches or riding horses. These everyday experiential marginalisations confound humiliation and shame where the marginalised body is expected to stay within their limits. In these cases, humiliation may subsume shame and regard it as the afterlife of humiliation. Shame, I will argue, may definitely be caused owing to humiliation, but its hauntings can precede humiliation even, and act as armour against it. Unlike humiliation, which is made overt owing to it being episodic, as having crossed a limited situation of violence, shame has a certain intimacy with the body that is difficult to disentangle and name as such. As we have already briefly noted, there aren't separate terminologies in Indian languages for this state, feeling and abjection towards the self, however one may qualify this shame.

In an outstanding essay, Udaya Kumar argues for deepening our understanding of humiliation by looking at shame (2013). This argument is unique in its standing of starting with shame rather than the other way round. He remarks that

> shame is not identical to humiliation, and that while shame often has its source in one's low estimate of oneself, humiliation often has an external, and what the subjects see as an unjustified, origin. Humiliation is precisely that instance where shame can be produced in the subject not only without desiring it, but also without deserving it. (ibid.: 167)

In the instance about Dinesh from Valmiki's 'Bhaya' we discussed at the beginning of the essay, Tiwari does not need to humiliate Dinesh, but the latter feels unbearable shame anyway. In that sense shame occludes the possibility of feeling humiliated, rather it pre-empts the consequence of humiliation. It is this interior and phenomenological life of shame that interests me in this essay. There is a particular kind of shame—one that is dark and inside, accompanied by a tormenting voice that reminds you that the blemish lies with you. It's not legible to the world outside. Probably the 'world outside' exists as much inside too so that the structure that diminishes the self to this state of shame now exists in the mind as well.

It is not the dishonour or disgrace of the aristocracy—a fact or truth that is legible and overt and known to the one who is dishonoured as well as the world outside.[1] It is also not overt forms of insults and humiliation that characterise subaltern life narratives, which of course do exist. However simultaneous with recognisable forms of violence are also the quieter modes of shame. It is the inescapability of it but also the

1 I am thinking here, for instance, of a study called *Humiliation* by William Ian Miller (1993). As a scholar of heroic epics and sagas, Miller finds the ancient codes of honour re-worked in modern everyday life but passing in the name of humiliation. Miller thinks of humiliation and embarrassment interchangeably as emotions associated with loss of face in social interaction. To my mind, Miller's study can have an important conversation with notions of caste masculinity seen among Rajputs etc., in India.

intense need to disown it—a self that is intimate, not external but may feel foreign. There can be many contexts to this state of shame, but its presence in Dalit/trans and other forms of subaltern writing shows its deep connection with histories of humiliation by hegemonic groups. Shame, despite being internal to the self, carries an ancestry inherent in words like *aukaat* and *zaat*. The arresting of 'excess' in illocutionary phrases of the kind illustrated earlier needs more elaboration.

Who defines the excess? The one who does this is also the one shaming and humiliating; especially the latter if there isn't sufficient evidence of the former. The excess, or what is perceived as excess, is then punished through acts of humiliation. That being said, the tormentors become invisible and lodge themselves inside the psyche engendering a continuous sense of inadequacy. This inadequacy, what in my mother-tongue Sindhi would be called *ghat-tai* or in Gujarati *heenta* (sense of inferiority) also leads to anxiety to collaborate with the oppressor. While Nandy writes of breaking apart from the collaboration as the end to humiliation, it may not be possible for all bodies to do so. A recognition of this truth is perhaps the bedrock of humiliation. It's also possible that feelings of shame and humiliation both exist creating a tussle. Such psychic wounds, especially in the context of caste, are perhaps just about beginning to be studied.

By and large, Dalit life stories have been read as narratives of humiliation rather than shame (Kumar's article cited above being an exception). In a 2016 article titled '*Baluta* and *Joothan* amid Humiliation', Purnachandra Naik notes that the two Dalit autobiographies are 'moulded in the armature of anxiety, humiliation and discrimination' (2016: 19). Naik cites a series of instances in both the autobiographies that are traumatising and degrading—use of casteist slurs; food given as *joothan*; and forms of abuse that are both physical and psychological. The writing of the life stories, as also the acquisition of education, enables both the writers, according to Naik, to subvert the narratives and throw a challenging glance back at the oppressor. Gopal Guru has also documented the power of Dalit life stories in contesting power structures; however, Guru is circumspect about their power. In his preface to essays on humiliation, Guru also notes that in

> the realm of literary studies, particularly from Dalit literature, humiliation has been the recurrent concern, principally autobiographies, short stories, and poems, and not so much the novel which Dalit literature has so far failed to handle successfully'.[2] However, the theme of humiliation in the literary genre has operated through very powerful allegories, thus giving vent to the experience of humiliation through metaphors like poison break or *zoothan* or branded. Though Dalit writings proved an important medium of articulation, such a format could not unfold to us the many nuanced aspects of the experience of humiliation. They could not be the adequate substitute for the theory of humiliation. (Guru 2009/2011: x)

Guru's evaluation of literature as an inadequate site for theory is consistent with what I have discussed elsewhere in this book (see Chapter 1). The separation of experience and theory that Guru contests has its greatest chance of meeting in the literary realm that he is dismissive of. However, that's not very pertinent to the present discussion which actually wishes to draw attention to a serious consideration of shame and its dialectical relationship with humiliation. The essays compiled by Guru and especially his own introduction make a compelling case for seeing humiliation as a political, moral and generally a conceptual force which seeks reparation, redressal and revision of non-democratic structures. Shame appears in this discussion as a cognate, neighbouring term of humiliation, only to help define humiliation better.[3]

If I may hazard to say, most people have had some or the other 'experience' of humiliation. Even those who have enjoyed the privileges of being white, men—upper-caste, upper-class, urban—may claim to have been humiliated. Legitimate or not, we recount humiliation through particular episodes and see that as having, for want of a better

2 This comment is somewhat bewildering considering that the Gujarati novel, *Angaliyat* (The Stepchild), had appeared by this time, and it is a study of the weaver protagonists rebelling against the humiliation wreaked upon the community by the upper-caste Patels and Kshatriyas in Gujarat (Macwan 2003).

3 For instance, Bhikhu Parekh argues, rather problematically, that degrading does not lead to humiliation. Pornography and prostitution may degrade women but not lead to their humiliation. Sanjay Palshikar separates humiliation from shame, suggesting that the latter is a passive state and does not have a moral force (Palshikar 2009; Parekh 2009).

word, contributed to the experience of life. Mostly such episodes remain vivid, and their recounting is possible unless they have engendered shame and therefore remained buried and repressed, a subject we return to again. By and large, episodes of humiliation appear through a sensory detailing of how we felt, and its effect is produced by words spoken and heard. We may also want to think of forms of humiliation that collective movements (regardless of their legitimacy) invoke and attach timelessness to such claims. Nandy draws attention to how ethno-nationalists perceive humiliation as a potent weapon to inferiorise others on the basis of categories that may not have been historically present (2009). But such experiences of humiliation felt by certain bodies do not automatically translate to a deeply held sense of shame.

I return once again to Nandy's argument on humiliation being a collaboration between the tormentor and the tormented, though I have tried to show its limits in absolving the tormentor of their conduct; another way to look at this argument is that perhaps the tormentor begins to reside in one's own mind and it is this that needs to be dismissed. It might be difficult to ascertain what came first—was shame already present prior to humiliation? Is shame the anticipation of humiliation? Or does humiliation suddenly remind oneself of their station, severed from the world and completely exposed to it? These questions can perhaps be best answered in reading texts by those who know shame to be home, who feel its tight grip on one's own skin as the skin itself. It is to one such account that I turn now.

Baluta: Humiliation and Shame

> Sometimes Aai would come to the hostel to sell what she could. I never spoke to her in front of the other students. When the students had finished buying and she had left, I would run after her. I burn with shame as I tell you about how I would only speak to my mother in secret. For an education, I was willing to sever the umbilical cord. (Pawar 1978: 122)

At the time when Daya Pawar recounts this incident in his autobiography *Baluta*, it is a memory from the past. Pawar was in a boarding school then. He had struggled his way to high school and battled many situations of caste violence. However, by seeking refuge in books he had also managed to distance himself from the atmosphere that produced him. Myriad instances come to Pawar's mind of things and people whom he abandoned along the way, their faces haunting him on sleepless nights. Memories come to Pawar in fragments and his account in the present is equally fragmented. One of the most recurring lines in the autobiography is '*Tar kaaye sangto hoto?*' (So what was I saying?). It is this forgetfulness, says Pawar, that kept him alive. At the same time, Pawar also mentions how difficult it is to forget,

> I have tried my best to forget my past. But the past is stubborn, it will not be erased so easily. Many Dalits may see what I am doing here as someone picking through a pile of garbage. A scavenger's account of his life. But he who does not know his past cannot direct his future. (2015: 63)

Growing up amidst poverty and discrimination; encountering divergent forms of destitution in both the village and the city, at home and in school, the Mahar child Dagdu (later one of Maharashtra's most well-known writers and activists, Daya Pawar) narrates a life story that shook the Marathi literary world. The narrative mode of Pawar's life story takes place through a conversation with a part of his own self. The word 'conversation' glosses over the split-ness which characterises this narration of, to quote Du Bois, 'two souls warring in one dark body'. This also prepares us for the gaze that is both at the self from a part of the self but also co-terminus with a shaming and humiliating gaze from the outside.

The autobiography begins with a first-person narrator saying the following. 'Even now, when I meet him he is always alone'. The narratorial voice captures the desolation and loneliness of another splintered self and brings the reader immediately in touch with a war that goes inside Daya Pawar. The first-person narrator watches Daya Pawar giving a speech and also remarks to him later about why he continues to look unhappy despite being successful and an object of envy. Pawar replies to this other part of his self that he has lost his shepherd's cap, implying thereby through a parable that an integral part of his identity remains unseen, unavailable and perhaps discarded. Jennifer Biddle argues that shame has the function of splintering the self—on the one hand, one desires the recognition of the other and hence, abides by the rules of what is shameful and what is not, and on the other, one wishes for self-definition too. Shame ensures the failure of both simultaneously, which is what makes it such a potent force (1997). Yet, she largely takes this splintering to be a question of identity-making; Biddle sees shame as an interruption to the self, where the self still holds an interest in continuing the act that has been brought to light and belittled—the resistance to this belittling is what forms identity. But in Daya Pawar's account, the splintering of the self is not an episode but almost a continuous process. Unlike identity, experience may not always hold the scope of cohesiveness, a self that can be carved out in a neat unitary fashion. The splintered selves resist reconciliation precisely because shame is a bridge that hinders attempts at crossing over. The life story in some sense becomes a means to retrieve the shepherd's cap and, in the process, brings to the reader a highly layered and complex life beset by betrayals and friendships; love and violence; shame, humiliation and healing. The memory from the past has lingered, disrupting the temporality of grief that continues to be felt in fits and starts.

The above incident is one of the many events where Pawar conveys discomfort at both its location in the past and its persistent haunting in the present. From this tumultuous, jagged, half-said and half-forgotten narrative, many slivers of memory appear, but some bring shame with it. Like the one quoted above, Pawar uses the following words in Marathi, '*He saara saangatana matra maajhi malach laaj vaat-te*' (1978: 72). Jerry Pinto translates this as 'I burn with shame as I tell you …' (2015). The word *laaj*, as mentioned earlier, has a gendered history in Indian languages. Pawar's shame is deeper; it is also the shame of feeling ashamed of the mother. Meanwhile, it's possible that the aforementioned incident may have stayed with me for personal reasons, resonant with my own sense of shame at the family I came from and rejecting my parents in the particular context of school. I do not claim any similarity between my experience and the incidents in Daya Pawar but simply mean to gesture at a subjectivity that governed the choice of the above passage. As such, the affect of Daya Pawar's autobiography *Baluta* is hard to articulate; the quiet and ever-present turmoil in the mind and body makes me continue to grapple with it.

For the moment, let us continue to stay with the text and focus on a more empirical detail in the passage. Pawar refuses to talk to his mother 'in front of the other students'. The 'other students' were upper-castes, who humiliate him in several instances. Pawar's avoidance of his mother was perhaps his shield against an anticipated humiliation. Shame is then a 'protective mechanism' that helps one avoid vulnerability to humiliation. It allows Daya to maintain his relationship with his classmates and 'survive amongst them'.[4] It could have also emerged from his attempt to blend into the upper-caste universe of the school and the mother's presence would have disrupted that attempt. It is also possible that the 'other students' did not need to be physically present but were a presence in Pawar's mind, goading him, tormenting him to feel shame at his origins. The triumph of education in that case rests upon severing this umbilical cord. Should it though? In the Marathi text, Pawar posits this as a question to himself. It is equally important to note that the severance is expected of a Dalit student, not of the upper-caste boys who would have been able to proudly show off their parents. Udaya Kumar remarks that

> many Dalit self-narratives, in fact, highlight the disciplinary dimension of modernization, by focusing on the alienating experience of institutions such as the school and government offices. Even as they trace the emergence of the modern Dalit citizen, these autobiographies open up a critical space by presenting a complex account of the subject's inhabitation of the world. (2013: 165)

This means that the school or the educational space is casteless for those who project their caste prejudice onto the Dalit students.

For instance, why does acquiring an education involve severing the umbilical cord? What is the nature of education that requires Daya to do that, considering that the idea of education has been credited with resultant emancipation? It is quite possible that as teachers, we have gone and come out of classes without thinking of how many students would have lived with schism—of disowning, hiding the families they come from. Their shame produces the schism, but the fear of our humiliation

4 I am thankful to Aparna Vaidik for this insight.

of them also aids the production of this shame. Caste and class, shaming and humiliation (and most often they overlap) acquire their most rampant forms in educational institutions. The irony of Ambedkar's pictures and the tremendous isolation that schools engender for Dalit students is a story we know but seldom dwell upon. The hardest myth to give up on is the one produced by modernity, and the emancipatory role of education is its chief bulwark. Admittedly, Daya Pawar manages to educate himself and find employment; he acquires sufficient standing to be sometimes charged pejoratively as a 'Dalit Brahmin'. However, the knowledge of the shaming origin of Dagdu who then becomes Daya appears like a long shadow every now and then, sucking the confidence out of adult life by whiplashing it with memories of childhood. This schism characterises the memoir throughout; a self uncomfortably put away and one that makes its appearance to the world. The vignette of an unacknowledged mother in school is part of a flurry of images that haunt Dagdu/Daya. For Pawar, the school, in fact, is a painful reminder of the impossibility of reinvention; it is rather a testimony of caste. The poignancy of a son not seeing his mother or acknowledging his relation also has a critique of an education built upon severed ties.

In keeping with the discussions around theory and experience in this book, we might even want to think of the mother standing for experience and the school for theory. That is to say, the latter is supposedly casteless in principle, expunged out of context and manageable if mothers, experiences and selves could be put away. It is experience yet again that threatens the sanitisation of theory. Its excesses bring to the fore the impossibility of abstractions, universalisations and the very promises of theory as the explanations to the world.

The disjunction between experience and theory is oftentimes of this nature—that one must not see the other. And yet we do have Daya Pawar's memoir as we do of many African-American writers, who document the splintered lives they lived.[5] We study such memoirs, Pawar's for instance, in a literature class but do not allow it to touch

5 Meanwhile, for a persuasive analysis of how school experiences are different for different races, see a case study, 'Performing Blackness', by Abdi (2015).

the 'theory' class. The untouched theory is like Pawar's school, can only exist by marginalising truths, hiding parents.

When Pawar talks of his home, whether in Maharwada in the village or Kawakhana in the city of Mumbai, it is a cohesive world despite all ups and downs the family faces. Pawar's father was a generous and loving man who took to alcohol and womanising but left behind a legacy of mixed feelings in the son. The women of the house, Aai (the mother) and Aaji (the grandmother) showered unconditional love upon the child. In fact, Pawar makes several references to the closeness he felt with the mother and how the autobiography was inspired by her advice to tell at least one person everything about the self. Outside the home, humiliations of different kinds from the Maratha boys and other castes made life difficult; however, there was a cushion of acceptance at home. Also, members of the Mahar community stood by each other at times of crisis.

It is in the school that the dissonance between his life experience and modern subjecthood stands challenged the most, generating a sense of shame about origins. It was the figure of the mother who comes to embody through the gaze of the school as a symptom of origins that Pawar wishes to distance himself from. In this context, Daya's Mahar Marathi would also have further exposed his origins, blurring in the process both the mother and the tongue. Pawar mentions that he would often be humiliated for his Maharki or Mahar-inflected Marathi. In order to be like the oppressors who mock him, he tried to speak like them.

> In reality, I spoke better Marathi than they. For this, I was mocked. Slowly, I stopped playing with them. On the subject of language, then, some more memories. In the taluka school, we were mocked for using 'Mahardya' language. This cut to the bone. I would lash out in anger at the boys who insulted us. To prove how chaste my use of the language was, I would invariably use words like 'nahin' for 'no' or 'bazaar'. (1978: 45)

We examined in an earlier chapter how the syntax of self is sometimes inseparable from forms of language. In fact, language becomes the first enactment of assimilation and hiding. Language here does not restrict itself to verbal artefacts but also accents, diction and syllabic changes.

Frantz Fanon says,

> The black man entering France reacts against the myth of the Martinican who swallows his r's. He'll go to work on it and enter into an open conflict with it. He will make every effort not only to roll his r's, but also to make them stand out. On the lookout for the slightest reaction of others, listening to himself speak and not trusting his own tongue, an unfortunately lazy organ, he will lock himself in his room and read for hours—desperately working on his *diction*. (2008: 5)

This abandoning of origins and language is one of the hallmarks of subalternity in situations that delegitimise diversity even as they claim to be inclusive.[6] Meanwhile, Pawar's memoir gives us a searing account of the number of times Daya the boy felt ashamed and also the number of times there were humiliators around him in school, Maharwada, Kawakhana and all the places he lived as a child. Another memory leaps up and shame is suffused through it, anchoring itself now on the child-self of Pawar and now to the mother.

> When it was our turn to collect the Mahars' share of food, I would go with Aai. The Marathas were particularly proud of their generosity in giving their buttermilk to the Mahars. Although I knew of the saying 'When you're going to beg, why hide your bowl?' I was always ashamed of going. I took care not to be seen by my upper-caste school friends. (67)

Shame finds its targets in the symbols of origins: one's language, accent, colour of skin, food, home, parents, which is to say shame circulates. It cannot be demarcated as resting in the body or the aspects surrounding one's life; rather, it clings on to whatever lies exposed. Hence, the necessity of hiding.

Pawar mentions on several occasions how ashamed he felt of his father, especially of his alcoholism and sexual behaviour. At one point he says, 'Majhich mala sharam vaatavi, asse prakar dada tya veli karat'

6 Another and a similar image leaps up: In the Marathi film *Fandry* (2013, dir. Nagraj Manjule), the Dalit protagonist had to hide his family's occupation of catching and tanning pigs, whilst being at school. The story 'Bhaya' we began with has another modern institution—the housing colony.

(1978: 17), which Pinto translates as 'My father's behaviour in those days shamed me' (2015: 27). *Sharam*, according to Salman Rushdie, is inadequately translated into 'shame', and the question I mean to ask is what it means to shift the terms of the question itself and ask if shame, of the kind Pawar conveys, is better captured in this inadequate translation. What exactly is the source of this *sharam* or shame? Pawar continues, 'Here in school I was being taught, "Always speak the truth" and there, I was taking Dada's loot to sell at Chor Bazaar. The world I learned about at school seemed fraudulent compared to the world I lived in' (28). Once again, shame is generated by the distance theoretical knowledge has from a Dalit student's material circumstances. In that sense, the entire archive of knowledge we have learnt and taught carries this epistemological violence, whose effects we have not even stopped to consider. Meanwhile, to continue once again with Pawar's relationship with his parents, the following passage, after his father's death, is also a telling one:

> Aai now became the man of the house. All her life she worked hard. I was deeply moved to see her strength. She gave us more love and care than our father could have. She nursed us with the tenderness you might show to a blister on the palm of your hand. I sometimes wonder: if Dada had lived would I have become the person I am? Who knows whether I would have studied or not? Where are all those children who studied with me in the Maharwada? Aai's sacrifice gave me the impetus to push myself out of the abyss. Dada's ways were not ours. There was an unspoken agreement that we would never do any of the things he had done. (55)

Given how much weight the symbol of the mother carries, the transference of shame from the father to the mother—the former being far more absent than present—is understandable, albeit unfair. The figure of the mother also causes shame for the work she does, the truth of the origins of her presence reminds the son. And yet it is a feature of the experience of shame that finds new targets—all of which lead the experience of shame back to the self. Really speaking, the shame is not only at the mother but at the self for feeling that shame. This inner and invisible circuitous mode of shame is very hard to see and is a peculiar presence in the lives of those who have had to face multiple forms of rejection all their lives. This may partly be the reason that discussion on shame in the construction of South Asian caste-based identity has been scarce. In scholarship emerging from the European and Anglophone world, shame has usually appeared as a cognate of guilt.[7] As we have briefly mentioned what Erikson says in the essay,

> Shame is an emotion insufficiently studied, because in our civilization it is so early and easily absorbed by guilt. Shame supposes that one is completely exposed and conscious of being looked at: in one word, self-conscious. One is visible and not ready to be visible; which is why we dream of shame as a situation in which we are stared at in a condition of incomplete dress. Shame is early expressed in an impulse to bury one's face, or to sink, right then and there, into the ground. But this, I think, is essentially rage turned against the self. He who is ashamed would like to destroy the eyes of the world. Instead he must wish for his own invisibility.... Doubt is the brother of shame. (98)

This doubt also prevents a sense of indignation that humiliation and the claim to humiliation are based upon.

From Daya Pawar's account, we see shame's obstinacy, not only to one's own skin but also to everything associated with it. The splintering of the self, hiding one's mother and one's mother tongue are all symptomatic of a self that anticipates humiliation and works to safeguard oneself against it. Shame sits in the body but its anxieties constantly circulate with other affects—anger, guilt, resentment—neither of which are incidental to his experiences; they are rather the very foundations from which he writes to the world. The Marathi word

7 A recent book on shame (ed. Akhtar 2015) mentions how 'shame is a latecomer to the scene of psychoanalytic discourse which has been preoccupied with the affects of anxiety; guilt, and mourning' (Introduction, xix). Restricted largely to feelings of shame and guilt among children, psychoanalysts considered shame to be a feature of more primitive (read non-Western) societies. The recent upsurge of interest in shame is driven not by wanting to understand the linkage we make between shame and humiliation—rather between societies of shame and shamelessness or impunity. In Salman Akhtar's words again, 'The rise of narcissism in Western culture has perhaps necessitated the examination of hubris's underbelly where we encounter insecurity, inferiority, and shame.... The culture of shamelessness has paradoxically stimulated the study of shame' (xix).

for 'shame' cannot be found here, but its effects spill over throughout the narrative, marking its omnipresence. We now turn to another text—that of Dhrubo Jyoti, who writes in English and captures the term 'shame' with sharp precision as the first step to undo it.

Shame, Body, Gaze

> Before you, there was the Internet. It taught me love. It told me that it was easy to shed this body, this history, this shame. So I chose for myself a new body and a new name with an upper-caste surname. Hiding was my first lesson in queerness because caste wouldn't let me be queer. (Jyoti 2018: 19)

We now turn to one of the most exquisitely sad, shame-filled but also uplifting account of a different generation. The torment and the tormentor are even more blurred; they come in more well-meaning ways—not explicitly humiliating visibly but mildly condescending. The landscape is urban, the references metropolitan, the metaphors contemporary and the outsided-ness of a Dalit queer both establishes continuity and interrupts it. If Pawar is addressing his splintered self, which is eventually dispensed with, Jyoti speaks to us—upper-caste readers. The affirmation with which the reader is told that 'books are for you, written by you' sets the tone of a Dalit voice that is not waiting to be interpreted or understood by a non-Dalit to discover or recover. It does its speaking and tells how little you think of what you do. With this reader, Jyoti shares their letters to 'P'—a lover from Calcutta's upper-caste bhadralok—genteel, liberal and well-meaning. If P is bhadralok, the writer of the letters belongs to the 'un-genteel' section. The letters enact a simultaneous unseeing, a blindness on the part of the upper-caste lover and the relentless gaze experienced by the Dalit queer narrator. This dialectic of both being unseen and squirming at one's inadequacy under a gaze captures that element of shame which is to both hide and become desirable in the other's eyes.

Caste is interlaced with dysphoric sexuality making the threads even more difficult to disentangle. If the affect of *Baluta* is an unresolved, tumultuous self that moves between memories of shame and humiliation, Dhrubo Jyoti's 'Letters to P' written almost four decades later testifies to the mediation of caste in the experience of love and desire. This is one of the shortest accounts that manages to say so much that has not been said in South Asian literature so far. The note to the reader at the beginning reminds you and me that if we thought love was transcendental and unique, it is because we, upper-castes, wrote books about love for us and people like us. What of love that is wrenched out of survival and surnames, poverty, shame and caste? From this point, we find the narrator writing letters to P. The narrator says at some point to their upper-caste lover: 'Let me tell you something about myself. I always wanted to own a nice pair of shorts.' The anglicised upper-caste bhadralok wore full trousers in the sweltering heat, but the narrator's shorts could not do the covering for him. Neither wanting to subject their thighs and legs to the torture of full pants nor having the means to hide the callused and coarse skin laid bare by the old shorts, the narrator evokes an image of hiding and revealing. The gaze of the bhadralok on their callused skin and old shorts operates both from the outside and inside. In Du Bois' words, 'It is a peculiar sensation, this double consciousness, this sense of always looking at one's self through the eyes of others, of measuring one's soul by the tape of a world that looks on in amused contempt and pity' (2018: 4). As such, many of us (women) would know, experientially, what it is to be an object created through the other's gaze. Shame is at the bottom of this creation reminding us that we cannot reach that ideal self that's acceptable to others. The anger, instead of being directed at those who judge, acquires a relentless judgment towards the self. The shame of an urban Muslim in using certain forms of greeting if his Hindu friends are around; the one of a Dalit in admitting his/her distinct dialect and food when upper-castes are around; the self-doubt of a woman that lies at the base of a highly confident and combative self—all of these are yet to draw the attention they deserve. When Daya Pawar speaks his Mahar Marathi or talks to his mother, he feels watched and judged. He censors himself and sometimes lashes out. The two processes are not linear—being inadequate and then indignant.

Meanwhile, the niceness of the shorts lay in their ability to hide the legs: '... a haze of looking enviously at men and women and then nervously at my ankles and feet, too hideous and damaged to bare'. Shame is produced by this bareness perilously real and a recognition that this bareness is both intimate and foreign. It is in the relationship with another class and caste that 'callused skin' evokes recoil. Shame transfers from the self and home to the body; to the legs and feet that have no means of covering. The nakedness of the feet symbolises a shame itself that must be hidden. Kaufman speaks of the taboo on shame, especially in American societies, that forces people to behave as if shame does not exist in the self, as possessing it would be shameful by itself (Scheff 2003). But in South Asian contexts, shame is already deeply rooted in one's location; it does not even require the actuality of the other's gaze to be brought to light and then hidden away. The negotiations between hiding, acknowledging and revealing are not a separate set of acts but rather an everyday practice of survival. To be 'found out' is not an episodic risk but a wounding that dictates the self.

All memories of the callused skin and poverty are inseparable. Equally inseparable is the fact that the mother 'fled the city' during that period, 'the only link to my childhood, to my mother, and so they have remained as memories'. If the upper-caste lover has 'random things' from his childhood, the narrator carries their childhood in their shame, in their skin (8). In a complex manner, this shame is not entirely hidden. It is owned up and expressed but felt nonetheless. But how is caste to be hidden? In order to protect oneself from jabs and queries and supportive pats, the narrator hid the caste away. One way of hiding is to speak like the upper caste, and the narrator here crams up impeccable English. The word 'gay' occurred somewhere in this process. The hiding and revealing tussle were of both caste and queerness. English enabled an entry into a queer relationship but it was caste that broke hearts. It reminded us that 'we don't deserve happiness'. Meanwhile, the upper-caste love is casteless for he has a good caste, good queerness and good class. Unlike Pawar, Jyoti's narration voices the politics of schools and locations: 'You had studied for eleven years in the institution my mother didn't dare dream I could be admitted to until a month ago' (2018: 12). The mother's outsidedness to the school in both cases is the interruption of experience not allowed in the theoretically egalitarian school. If the spaces like Kawakhana in *Baluta* remain marked, the genteel sections of Kolkata also remained marked by their blindness to caste.

In Dhrubo Jyoti's experience, it is P's 'casteless' queerness that makes them constantly aware of their caste and brings shame to the surface to be tackled. Jyoti takes a similar recourse to language as Pawar did, 'Many years a lover told me that Will & Grace had taught him to embrace their sexuality, assured him that it was okay to be gay. I didn't have the words to tell him that it had shaped my sexuality too—by teaching me English' (2018: 9). While Pawar speaks a Marathi that his family wouldn't have, Jyoti embraces English to gain entry into queerness. They write, 'Even now I don't think I would have dared to love you if I didn't know English' (2018: 10). Their letters are a testimony to the codedness of desire and desirability that do not transcend the limits set by the upper-caste Calcutta universe, they recognise their own desires as coded too. 'I had been trained to know what good looks are (Brahmin), what good queerness is (English-speaking), and what attractive background is (urban rich)' (ibid.). It is precisely contact with these limits that makes one aware of one's own excesses of experience, of the shame surrounding it. An entry into this world can only be gained by learning its codes (English, the latest books and music, visiting the posher parts of the city) while simultaneously amputating one's own history or at least relegating it to a corner where it cannot be found. It is a paradox perhaps that the excess of experience holds the primary concerns for food, surname and survival, whereas the absence of this, in terms of living a life that is by default respectable in the society, allows for a leap into abstractions.[8] P's friends speak of dysphoria and recommend readings by Butler, Simone de Beauvoir and Chakravarti. Jyoti is grateful when they don't laugh at the mispronunciation of the term 'dysphoria' itself: 'I remember talking to your friends about queerness and they knew more about gender and sexuality than I knew

8 See Das' 'The Life of Concepts and How They Speak to Experience' (2018) for a similar debate around experience and theory.

about my own body' (2018: 14). While Jyoti gestures towards dysphoria in terms of failing the standards of femininity, the dysphoria is not only between the world and the body as it is perceived but also between theory and experience. Theory cannot hold space for the articulation of Jyoti acknowledging his mother's grief, 'Do you think she regrets that I'm no longer a man?' (2018: 8). Shame and grief both signal the threat of a rupture of a bond, a loss that not only demarcates the self from the other but also isolates it. Jyoti perhaps preempts the loneliness and holds back from telling P that they didn't know many of the things P talked about as their love wouldn't survive this truth. The relationship between caste and queerness in the text is not one of intersection, but rather one of splintering the self in order to gain companionship.

The shame is at once deeply rooted in one's history and also one that travels. Hiding parts of the self allows one to reach the threshold of a different universe but never completely enters it. Hiding the self and hiding one's shame at the self are no longer disparate acts; rather, the two become synonymous. Jyoti, until the end, writes how the lover cannot be claimed. 'Our people shouldn't have the temerity to ask your people where you spend time, or when you are coming home, or whether I mattered to you at all.' But it is only in naming the shame as it is that Jyoti is able to step away from it and formulate a queerness that is not transcendental but rooted in small everyday joys. Jyoti finds refuge in friendships, less exacting loves and new cities and writes this letter perhaps as half-testimony, half-catharsis, ultimately refusing to hide. 'My skin has memory' (2018: 25). It is only by acknowledging the fracture in the first place that they are able to reconcile the disparate elements of life.

Conclusion

The articulations of shame in Daya Pawar and Dhrubo Jyoti's texts are of a different nature from each other. There is an undecidability in Pawar's autobiography manifest in a tumult of emotions that gesture towards shame. However, they are not named as such. The Marathi text uses a range of words such as *laaj vaat-te*, *sharam vaat-te*, '... *mee khubach oshalaaycho*' (I felt embarrassed/diminished). It is only to be expected, some degree of incommensurability notwithstanding, that words like *laaj* and *sharam* would be translated as shame. However, even a phrase like '... *mee khubach oshalaaycho*' (I felt small/embarrassed, 48, 60) in Marathi appears as 'shame' in Pinto's translation. For instance, Pawar says, '*Tasa martyacha porga manhun karun dileli olakh ekun mi oshalaycho*' (1978: 60), and Pinto translates that as 'I was ashamed to be called Maruti's son…' (Pawar 2015: 80). Pinto may have done an astute reading by zoning in on the affect of *Baluta*; on the other hand, Pinto has also perhaps overdetermined his case. The undecidability of words communicates a deeper pathology in which shame remains hidden from the one experiencing it. In fact, it may be present even when Pawar is not using any word to indicate its presence. This tentativeness in Pawar's voice makes the life story a complex blend of a modern, politicised Dalit identity but also one laced with self-doubt.

On the other hand, in Dhrubo Jyoti's letters, we find the English word shame used as a way to denote a hidden state of psychic fragmentation. Jyoti knows that shame has come to inhabit their body and skin from the gaze of the upper castes; and it is this complex dialectic of the internalised gaze that the narrator struggles with and eventually sheds, perhaps. English has become the language of naming not only the experience but also draws attention to the system in which intimacy with an upper-caste person has lent no comfort but produced shame.

How is this particular state, beset by now-smouldering, now-cowering and hiding aspects of psychic life to be captured in words? And which words will suffice? The English word 'shame' has made its way from child psychology to contexts of racial and gender shaming and assisted in marking out a mental state that is perhaps recognisable in certain discourses. Was Pinto, while translating Daya Pawar's work, bringing the word from those discourses? Or is Pinto helping name what an Indian language names tentatively? I have less to say about the answers to these questions which, really speaking, may take us to the propriety of translation. However, it is gaps that open up and what they say about divergent linguistic worlds and the relationship between experiences and concepts that I would like to spend time on.

This brings me to Salman Rushdie's quote in the epigraph, 'Sharam, that's the word. For which this paltry "shame" is a wholly inadequate translation.' The question for me is not so much about a translation or the equivalence between 'shame' and *sharam*, but rather a sense of inadequacy in each of them in the contexts they appear. Rushdie's novel, titled *Shame*, is based on a brutalised South Asian society in which the prohibition to feel shame among powerful men leads to and sustains the making of a masculinist autocratic dictatorship. The emphasis on posturing made to the external world and conducting oneself without the embarrassment of an illegitimate social legacy make the Hindi-Urdu word *sharam* appropriate for Rushdie. Omar Khayyam's mother/s forbid him from feeling *sharam* and considering himself inferior. The opposite of shame is unfortunately shamelessness—a state determining Omar Khayyam's despotic actions. It's understandable that Rushdie should have found shame a 'paltry' word; the term *sharam*—tied to notions of societal honour, codes of conduct, a whole universe of hierarchies—cuts much deeper and puts the interior life in the social.

On the other hand, the experiential contexts of the texts discussed in this essay invert Rushdie's point. The narrators in both texts convey festering memories in the body, and the excess of hurt has turned inwards into a haunting. Shame has a more complex and less legible presence; it has not been invisibilised but is invisible even to the ones carrying it. Their very experiences are ones of constant awareness, of being hollowed out by the tormentor's gaze. *Sharam* in this context with its deeply social aspects cannot account for the interiority of feeling diminished. Rather, it is shame that comes closest to articulating a deep-seated sense of one's loss of the self.

Both the English term 'shame' and the Hindi-Urdu term *sharam* show tensions between experientiality realities and concepts. There may be many experiences which have no concise terms in which to articulate them; some of these are important to take note of because they can turn into virulent political rhetoric. About a year ago, the Rashtriya Swayamsevak Sangh chief Mohan Bhagwat made a comment about how the word 'lynching' does not even exist in India and all the fuss made over certain unfortunate and stray incidents were being given a foreign name and history that has little to do with 'our' culture.[9] The absence of the word was meant to signal the absence of a reality that has stood staring in our faces, not once or twice, but several times in recent years. The absence of naming does not imply an absence of the phenomenon or experience.

The absence or incommensurability of terms to experience is important to examine because it tells us about the gaps in our social contexts that are not often acknowledged. Dominant languages often do not take into account the experiences of the marginalised. Terms such as *sharam*, *haya* and *apmaan* in our South Asian context are applicable to only those bodies which are inherently associated with or expected to maintain a certain respectability or honour that they must not transgress. Upper-caste women are told to have *laaj sharam* to maintain their chastity and the family's honour. Upper-caste women are told to have *laaj sharam* to maintain their chastity and the family's honour. On the other hand, Dalit and trans bodies struggle to survive and find themselves acceptable. The gaps in language to denote the interiorities of shame in discriminated bodies tell us that these are experiences that have never been considered worthy of examining. The gaps in language to denote the interiorities of shame in discriminated bodies tell us that these are experiences that have never been considered worthy of examining. This shame remains hidden not only from language but often from the ones feeling it too.

This is not to argue that the failure of language to illuminate experiences means that there can be no way to articulate and listen to them; rather, what is necessary is embodied listening. At this moment, I am reminded of an article in the *Indian Express* (Sarangan 2020),[10] which pointed to the difficulty of diagnosis and appropriate treatment when words describing mental health are rare or missing in regional languages. The article began with the author's memory from school days,

9 'Lynching is alien to Bharat' RSS Chief Mohan Bhagwat (*The Print* uncut, available at https://www.youtube.com/watch?v=4itygYWl1gg, accessed on 8 October 2019).

10 Ram Sarangan, 'Finding a Language to Talk about Mental Health', *Indian Express*, 22 February 2020.

> ... it feels like your heart is about to explode when your name is called in the classroom. Or, perhaps, right before a school play, you find yourself buckling down, gasping for air. A thousand ants form a straight line and march around furiously in your stomach a day before an important exam.

A therapist treating in English offers translates and provides words such as anxiety, depression, shame and so on to name mental states; but it isn't solely naming the experiences, but making meaning of the breathless embodied states that allows the listener to grasp with experience. This requires immense self-reflexivity on the part of the listener and the capacity to communicate without the necessity of precision that words produce. An embodied state of listening may even allow us to notice shame in places in the sites we do not as listeners expect it to appear. Eli Clare, an American writer, writes about shame in the context of their disability and transness:

> I want to strike at the center, to talk directly about the raw, overwhelming mess that is shame. How it wakes us up in the morning and puts us to bed at night, whispering to us as we have sex, tracking our every move as we dress to go out, lying to us as we sit in job interviews. Shame visits us in the bedroom and at the beach, in the medical exam room and at the therapist's office. Shame lives in the mirror and the camera, and its impact is huge, ranging from low self-esteem to addiction, from infrequent healthcare to suicide. This afternoon I want to talk about the ways in which shame inhabits our bodies and how we can resist that habitation. (Clare 2010: 456)

Even though they use the term shame with precision, it is shame's affective location in everyday life that lends to its potency. We only realise this when we listen closely, taking account of the often invisible, yet manifold circulations of shame. While language may help gesture towards an experience, experience also has the capacity to articulate itself in its own right. As we bring this essay to a close, we are left with the incompleteness of words in different contexts; a process marked by the fact that language and experience simply cannot keep pace with each other. Add to this the fact that language is also a political ploy; a malleable clay in the hands of the powerful and evinces the interest of those who set both social and linguistic terms. If such is the case within a given language or between language and the inner world, it is not surprising that translation between languages is forever in a state of transition. The ineffability and illegibility of shame this essay has gestured towards is an important lesson to remember, especially for some of us upper castes. It reminds us that there is much that remains hidden from us for we do not seek to know. We may think we don't know for there is no name for it; but really speaking, our wilful ignorance produces the absence of words. Shame is not legible to us for we have protected ourselves from its knowledge. The more legible stories of humiliation have drawn our attention. They are uplifting for us upper castes too for they satiate our need to see radicalism that does not involve us. Shame's is a quieter and more disturbing story for us. We may want to notice it, understand it. We could begin with language.

6

Saying It, Not Saying It: The 'Hindi' Film Song

> Love and the lyrical impulse of its narration are indeed universal, one of the few constants left in a world that makes a fetish of cultural relativism. Erotic passion, with love's tender discoveries, sudden torments and consuming desires, is one of the last bastions of our common humanity. However, if we subscribe to the premise that modes of experiencing and expressing emotions are constructed in specific and cultural ways; it is possible to see that 'heart' and 'dil' may have only a linguistic commensurability.
>
> —Kakar (2009: 62)

> Translation is capturing the feeling that words evoke—that's more important to me than the meaning of the words.
>
> —Gulzar (2018: 9)

Pushpa comes to my house every day at 9 a.m. She does the dusting, sweeping and mopping. Once done, she and I have tea together and listen to a song. I asked her, '*Pushpa, kya sunogi?*' She asked me to play any Rajesh Khanna song. Pleased by the prospect of listening to Kishore Kumar, I played on my phone, '*Kuchh to log kahenge, logon ka kaam hai kehna*' from the film *Amar Prem* (1972). The song translates as 'People will say something, it is their job to say things'. Pushpa has been having a hard time ignoring comments about her heartlessness. She has finally sent off her brother-in-law to a mental health institution. While he lived with her, she had fed him, nursed him, but he had begun to assault her in recent times. Pushpa has felt judged but seldom mentions it. The 'log' (people) who criticise her have no idea what she had been going through. The song proceeds to say, '*Kuchh reet jagat ki aisi hai, har ek subah kee shaam huyi/ tu kaun hai, tera naam hai kya, Sita bhi yahaan badnaam huyi*' (That's how the world works, for every morning there follows an evening, who are you to complain, when Sita was not spared either). Women have been told this story often; they are not unique in what they go through; others have preceded them. This dubious consolation may not work for modern and privileged women; for it is easy to see how much normalisation takes place here, especially through mythology. Listening to this song must have helped Pushpa, who, before leaving said, '*Kitna achha gaana hai*.' The solace songs provide makes their subjects realise that they are not alone in their predicaments, making the songs sometimes unacknowledged sources of self-help. The reassurance may or perhaps works better for what has been Hindi cinema's historical constituency—the labouring groups. They turn to it as one would to living forms of mythology. The subjectivity, not allowed the leisure or space through humdrum chores, finds at least a song. This is particularly true of people finding themselves caught in difficult predicaments that elude individual agency and decision. There are two things happening in songs of the kind I illustrated. First, the lack of agency is subsumed into the common sense of simply being human and social. Secondly, and particularly for the listener, the song itself becomes an entry into a proxy world of actors and characters who have also not had the agency. The experience of being in the social, of having one's desires thwarted is the theme of the many so-called 'sad' songs sung by singers of yesteryear.

As such many of us owe our sanity to the insane numbers of films we watch and songs we hear. Surely the images, names, sentiments, emotions, stories, words—whether in 'dialogues' (such an Indianism!) or songs settle somewhere, in non-immediate ways, forming a lexicon of seeing and feeling. Hindi film songs accompany our life; defining it, naming it, inspiring us to live amidst sorrows and reminding us that no one in this world is spared from their share; bringing joy to hearts when filled with despair and in short adding a texture to the experience of life. Innumerable YouTube comments below sad and melancholic songs show the admission of drawing such consoling philosophies from film songs. To this end, film songs justify the ways of god to men, without taking a resort to a religious or even spiritual explanation.

This mode of being in the world, in the social, of living through obligations and duties comes across in many songs about *zindagi*, *duniya* or *waqt*. Songs on life, the world and the times we live in often employ an accompanying vocabulary of a puzzle, coincidence or the powerlessness of human will against insurmountable circumstances (for instance, *paheli*, *ittifaq* or invocations to the caprices of *waqt* or time we discuss later). In the process, they engender an acceptance of the bewilderment that characterises life—the vicissitudes that elude understanding. However platitudinous they may sound to the readers of this book, they play an important role in situating the limits and expanse of being in life, of being in the social. The individual is reminded of how her position is not a singular one. This sliding into the collective reduces the loneliness of being singled out and in that sense, this phenomenon echoes the flight from particularism to universalisms discussed in the first chapter of this book. At the same time, desires are felt in the individual body, and they also need validation. How is that singularity to be reconciled with the collective experience of being in the social that songs engender? I believe it is in the terrain of romance and desire that the language of songs becomes more complicated. If the 'sad' songs provide solidarity with the collective, romantic ones hide from the collective by deploying surrogate words and metaphors. In doing the work of being-with-all and hidden-from-all, songs create their own language and internal codes which would make little sense as forms of linguistic translation. In that sense, songs create their own linguistic universe. To the listeners who seek consolation, songs provide solidarity of experience. To the ones seeking an expression of romance, the songs provide surrogate metaphors which are also a form of solidarity. Both desire and melancholy find a place in the repertoire of songs and this effect is achieved by specific uses of language. It may be interesting for us to deepen our understanding of this linguistic universe by asking how is it constituted and seeing how the audiences are socialised into non-commensurability of meanings. In simpler words, this essay hopes to show through a dialectic of self and subjectivity, songs and experience that the language of Hindi film songs demands an act of faith and tests of translation that is unique to that universe. It is only by staying with the semantic and semiotic world of the songs that we might be able to understand a universe that is at once coded and fluid in its movements. The two strands—how the experience of songs shapes our responses and the constitutive nature of the language of songs—intertwine in this essay. *The question of language is not separate from one of translation, which in this case, is not of equivalent meanings but social and emotive meanings that form a community of listeners and help situate both human predicament and desire.* The stock images and words in the song reappear and make metonymic references to all that it is not possible to say—living through the experience of both desire and regulation and having to take resort to proxy and surrogate language. In some sense, songs are the elsewhere of desire but operate in the social. Through the demonstration of certain ubiquitous words from Hindi film songs, I show in this essay, the process of walking the tightrope of romance; building memory upon memory; merging life's stories with that of songs and vice versa. In short, I show that the experience of being with the songs also shapes the experience of being in the body and the world at the large. This complexity and profundity surrounding the popular subject are difficult to see and understand; but it is precisely this grasping and gasping nature of language that I wish to struggle with, without the anxiety of building its resolution. So really speaking, the movement from the body to words and back; the employment of symbols to say the 'real' thing; the creation of surrogate words in lieu of direct sensuality—all these are questions of commensurability, equivalence and hence translation.

Hu Gaano to Yaad Ache ...

The 'experience' of films shaped my reality. I saw bereaved husbands seeking refuge in grief-filled songs; I heard creditors using 'dialogues' to extract money out of borrowers; I witnessed women in the house guarding their dimples to look like Sharmila Tagore, and I overheard my mother quoting Meena Kumari from a film when she wanted to say she'd had enough. The fashioning of life out of lives watched, heard and consumed through films made my 'reality' and made me grow up without thinking of films as an object of a gaze; but thinking of the 'self' as an object of cinema—shaping, morphing, re-forming under its alluring influence.

Here's an entry from my journal to convey that the world of songs is not an object of study (alone); rather it is mediated by most non-linguistic and non-cognitive sources of meaning:

> *A yellow tape recorder. Its yellowness poked the eyes. It would play all day in the kitchen when my mother listened to entire stories of Trishul and Shakti while she cooked. In films where Amitabh died, moistness filled my mother's eyes creating a thin film between her and the onions she assiduously* bhuno-*ed. I still don't have an English word for* bhunna, *that act of sheer commitment when you sauté onions to the extent that they were brown and oily and the tomato gravy had hidden them so well as to not know where they disappeared after going from purple to brown to invisible. Amitabh was in our kitchen every day. And when he met with an accident during the shooting of the film Coolie, a pall of gloom lay over the kitchen. The yellow tape recorder witnessed these deep relations between my mother and Amitabh Bachchan. It was like a puppet from folk stories, it just knew a lot. Then, during the day, sometimes it would move to my brother's room where it would be perched on top of a cupboard. The songs played louder; men could do these things. They were not these good-for-nothing women who listened to stories. At night, the yellow tape recorder was next to my father. It played Ceylon news, smack in the middle of the night. One day, a list of songs landed in our house. Songs from the 40s and 50s, written in Hindi, and along with that came a magical discovery that the yellow tape recorder was also a recorder, not just a player. My father made me and my sisters sing songs from the list, and he recorded our voices. Such was his optimism that each one acquired a label of Lata Mangeshkar, Asha Bhosale and Usha Mangeshkar. Those eight years in the* tekre vaaro ghar, *the house on a mound, the yellow tape recorder also lived with us. It brought a new purpose to my father's dull, hiding-from-the-world, life.*
>
> *The little girl comes to haunt me sometimes. Sometimes, I see her lying in bed with her sisters and they listen to Chhaya Geet. Chhaya Geet. Kanta Gupta* ka namaskar. *Mala is a perfect impersonator. Mala is her sister, named after Mala Sinha. She just knows from the opening bar what song is being played. The little girl smiles at this game.... For the moment, I am glad the songs existed, the radio existed. Her sister Sangita has drawn*

the exact design of Rekha's kurta in the film Khubsurat. She is confident that the tailor would be able to stitch one for her exactly like this. She wants to look like Rekha. She is Rekha of Khubsurat, *chatty, spirited, sharp-featured. But she also became Rekha of another film, cotton saree, single woman, earning for the rest of the family. The little girl had grown by this time. The adult little girl had left the little one behind. She didn't want to meet her or think about her. She only wanted to make sure all the children in the family, including her own, didn't stand with their backs to her. The only time the little girl and her old self meet is when a song reminds them to.*

In the home where I grew up, film songs played not just in the background and in the head but formed a substratum of life. The voices of Shamshad Begum and Talat Mehmood were the voices of childhood; the ones of Kishore Kumar and Lata Mangeshkar belonged to my adolescence. Lines from songs were quoted in the midst of intensely serious conversation, only to lend more seriousness and credibility. The presence of songs made everything seem like spoken in mid-conversation with lines, *hu gaano to yaad ache* ... or I am reminded of that song. The film was *pikchar*, the song was *gaano*. The former lived, the latter outlasted. Desires for objects and touch; places and people were couched in songs which were mobilised to make the 'self' a look-alike of someone else; an image, a word, a song hovering always on the horizon making humdrum life a little more liveable. In this process of being an approximation, nobody asked questions about the original or the authentic. In fact, authenticity lay in not being entirely like the original but in the intensity of that commitment. I must have learnt one of my first lessons of translation here; which is we don't just love to translate, we translate to love (Young 2006: 19).

Travel and Migration of the Song

It may be worth asking how 'Hindi' are Hindi songs? Whether it is the Marathi *bhaavgeet* or Rabindra Sangeet, the 'Hindi' song has oftentimes had other linguistic traditions, making its 'Hindi' a placeholder. There are umpteen occasions when cinema adapts itself to a linguistic register needed for the moment. It may also of course, and it does rather, caricature. Consider, for instance, one of the first 'mixed' songs, '*Kis liye kal ki baat*' from the film *Aadmi* (1939) directed by V. Shantaram. It is sung by and picturised upon Shanta Hublikar, a sex professional, who is being asked by her male clients to sing a song. The group of men that make a demand are from different regions, made evident in the semiotics of the film by the turbans they wear. The song that begins with Hindi/Urdu begins to take on words from Punjabi, Marathi, Gujarati, Tamil with the *pugree* or turban she borrows from each of them. This symbolic life of a song that puts on a new hat on demand for desire recognising no linguistic boundary is a significant one. This may not happen all the time; however, it would be safe to say that, unlike Hindi poetry, for instance, an artefact called 'Hindi' film song manages to break a considerable number of barriers. As such, the familiarity with the written word poses its own set of challenges in a way that orality does not. It also cannot be gainsaid that the hegemony of Hindi and the circulation of the Bollywood industry may be responsible for the dissemination. That being said, the Hindi song's commitment to its 'Hindi' is also quite flexible. The songs wear language lightly, enabling far more inclusion than other artefacts of the Hindi language such as the oral and written announcements, speeches and forms of writing on government platforms. Songs are heard and hummed, and they travel the most through circulations and repetitions. The 'Hindi' of a song is capacious (albeit more so in the North Indian context) enough to make room for languages it needs—from Awadhi and Braj to Punjabi and English, and in the last two decades Hinglish. It may be worthwhile to consider if cinema has manyness even if it appears to be spoken of in one language.

The point I want to emphasise is that the affective life of a song and its non-reliance on script or campaign for dissemination enables the migration and travel of the song, and so does its half-serious relationship with its supposed 'Hindi'. It is not uncommon to hear in parts of India and far-flung places that people relate to the emotions of the songs and do not feel inhibited by a lack of comprehension. From Russia to Jerusalem to Switzerland to Africa, the reach of the Hindi film song is phenomenal, without its being processed as 'Hindi' but rather a sensory treat with an emotional charge to it. In the southern and northeastern states of India, this phenomenon has much less purchase. At the same time, it may have a little more currency than other forms of communication associated with 'Hindi' and mainland India.

The Symbolic Language of Songs

Hindi film songs abound with stock words. And these get parodied, used, abused and embraced in everyday life. Their earnestness and repetition make them both serious and non-serious. However, we might want to stop and examine some in particular, not the least because they are ubiquitous and seem to occur every second song. The excess of their appearance hides in plain sight the reasons why they are needed so often. To say that there is a lack of innovation and repertoire of vocabulary, and ditties are churned out mindlessly may not be far from the truth. It is equally true, as Gulzar points out, that people relate first to a hummable tune and an interest in words comes later (2018: 24). However, both observations do not reveal to us the full truth that even some of the most accomplished lyricists of yesteryears use certain words again and again. It may also be interesting to see why certain words that one would have thought would be needed more often simply seem obsolete. Did they represent meanings that we don't need anymore? For instance, the word *waqt* appeared powerfully in the decades of the 1950s and 1960s with a range of meanings—destiny; time; occasion; opportunity; circumstance; fate; accident. *Waqt* then is not only time; in fact, it may intervene in time, and create a simultaneous moment of triumph and tragedy. In the song '*Waqt ne kiya kya haseen sitam* ...', written by Kaifi Azmi, the irony of a beautiful tragedy wrought by time was as much about the film *Kaagaz ke Phool* (1959) as the Partition of India. In the years when Sahir Ludhianvi was writing '*Tu Hindu banega na Mussulaman banega*' (film *Dhool ka Phool*, 1959) or '*Yeh kis ka lahu hai kaun mara*' (film *Dharmaputra*, 1961) was also the period when he wrote the elegy of parting that was grieving over the loss of selves. Partition also changed the 'me' and 'you' making each unrecognisable, setting people on journeys whose destinations remained unknown ... *jayenge kahaan sujhta naheen, chal pade magar rasta naheen....* The debris of human achievement in the song '*Waqt ke din kin aur raat*' gestured in the film *Waqt* (1965) towards the earthquake but may well have been the debris of dreams during Independence. This one example, among many, has been used to illustrate how the obliqueness is now a refuge; now a form of translating the unspoken into the spoken or the other way round. In his study on Partition cinema, Bhaskar Sarkar argues persuasively how working with the trauma of Partition in films 'requires thinking through the unthinkable; speaking about the unspeakable: it is a task that is neither routine nor transparent but which places unusual demands on our cognitive and psychic resources' (Sarkar 2010: 31). In a well-known song sung by Mukesh, '*Waqt karta jo wafa to aap hamare hote, ham bhi auron ki tarah aap ko pyaare hote*' (had time stayed constant, you would have been mine; I would have remained dear to you like the rest), the responsibility of the individual is shifted to time. The idea that individuals do not act only out of their agency but are determined by time provided an explanation of life and not just a set of actions. Meanwhile, the word *waqt* has now all but disappeared. Have we ceased to need the all-consuming, all-powerful notion of time, the one that subjects states and people to its own whim and fancy? It's possible that the ascendancy of the individual will to change a life and set its terms may have placed the metaphysics of *waqt* on the backburner and appeared to emerging generations a fatalistic idea or a relic of another India. And on a rare occasion that it does appear, it needed an English subtitle that supplemented its meaning thus—*Waqt: Race against Time* (2005). Is *waqt* not time alone? The point is it is not. As Sudhir Kakar points out of 'dil' and 'heart,' waqt and time also have only a 'linguistic commensurability'.

While the linguistic universe of film songs shows a complex understanding of responsibility and will in the social world, it evokes a gamut of gestures and signs in its romantic arena. Really speaking, there is a displacement of symbols in both instances: in one, it is a moving away from the person to fate; in another, it is communication through allusions and half-said confessions. As a telling example of the gestural love, a song penned by S.H. Bihari comes to mind. Bihari's lyrics in the song, '*Ishaaron Ishaaron mein dil lene wale, bata yeh hunar tune seekha kahaan se*' offers a peek into the world-making repertoire of gestures and non-linguistic cues. The song begins by asking a rhetorical question in Asha Bhosale's voice, 'Where did you learn to take the heart away like this, through eyes/gestures?' The word 'gestures' has a burden of physicality, although not entirely. So that serves our purpose better than indications, which also serves as an approximation to the Urdu word *ishaara*, which includes not only signs made through the eyes but also other gestures. The response in Mohammed Rafi's voice, '*Nigaahon nigaahon mein jaadu chalana meri jaan seekha hai tumne jahaan se*' (Same place where you learnt to cast a spell with your glances). This back and forth between gestures and eyes are followed by words that still do not use the first person to profess love or allure but become an archive of the non-linguistic and non-verbal nature of love. They happen to be voiced; but we hear them as hints, rather than as fully semantic entities. Notice the continuation of displacement from the self; an avoidance of the first person—*Mere dil ko tum bha gaye, meri kya thee iss mein khata*—My heart took to you; what fault that is of mine. The separation of the 'I' from the *dil* (a discussion we come to in greater detail later) reinforces the non-volitional nature of love, and that may well be inherent in the English expression—to fall in love. However, it is interesting to note the word fault, for why would that be necessary? At the risk of digression, it must be noted how songs use a gamut of words around guilt—*khata*, *gunah*, *paap*. At times, these are merely literary or rhetorical devices; however, they frame the disjunct between actions and comfort about the actions taken. It is in the zone of non-action, of much achieved merely through eyes that film songs show greater confidence. We will turn to the eyes again, meanwhile, a crucial aspect of this worlding is that love may be intense; its challenges are hard; life may have miseries, but we've been there before. There are others who have been. The song provides a fitting insight into the continuity of affect—*Yeh Ranjha ki baatein, yeh majnu ke qisse, alag to naheen hain meri dastan se*; these legends of Ranjha or the accounts of Majnu are no different from my own story. It is to be noted that these are in a male voice, perhaps we need to see whether female subjectivity is allowed such flamboyance or is that true only of the suffering. Meanwhile, the words straining to mimic silence are once again evident in *Mohabbat jo karte hain wo mohabbat jatate naheen*—those who love, do not profess, nor do they let others hear the heartbeat. The song proceeds to say what is left of enjoyment when one expresses love with one's own tongue. The word *zubaan* is both tongue and language. What happens to the elusive idea of love when spelt out, and how avoidable it is to spell it out yourself? Doesn't its affect, sanctity diminish in its expression? This emphasis on not saying it but saying it all the time, makes songs rely on an extended and expansive understanding of language.

The Protean Heart and Synecdochic Eyes

If saying it is either not possible nor desirable, how is desire to be conveyed, how are interests to be received and covenants to be formed? Songs employ, among many other words, two words—*dil* (heart) and *aankhen* (eyes)—the most to do this work. The word *dil* is particularly instructive in this regard. I have argued elsewhere that it lies between two seemingly contradictory positions of seething desire and heavy regulation (Kothari and Shah 2017). The distance between what one wishes to do and what one is allowed to do produces *dil*—an overfamiliar trope and a highly polysemantic word. The *dil* is also sometimes set in opposition to regulating entities such as *duniya* (world) or *log* (community). The semantic and semiotic field of *dil* in Hindi film songs forms part of what Rachel Dwyer (2006) calls 'discourses of the intimate', in which a range of cues from visual to non-visual aid the expression of romance. Also, *dil* draws from poetic traditions and metaphors of Persian and Urdu, frequently overlain by other conventions and idioms of love in South Asia. In fact, a gamut of traditions that distance desire from the 'I' and project it onto seasons, eyes, heart and so on are part of the Indic poetic conventions also (Orsini 2006). The conditions under which the unspoken is spoken through the *dil* is a legacy of society and poetic conventions with specific psychoanalytic meanings of 'self'. *Dil* is a site of desire and is simultaneously intimate and external, that is, extimate. Through a combination of linguistic, cultural and psychological perspectives, *dil* becomes a site of negotiation, an alternative possibility of expression, a transferred epithet that serves situations where desires lack legitimacy.

The terrain of *dil* in Hindi film songs is a slippery one. Notwithstanding that it itself is contained within the body of the subject and/or the beloved, *dil* eludes summarisation by being too many things at the same time. It is a container of love and desire, of the beloved or god and crucially, is also the seat of secrets. It is something tangible, measurable, locatable and all-too-fragile—it is frequently broken, even fragmented. Yet, it is an abstract entity that is exchanged freely between lovers. It is bi-gendered—linguistically masculine; it often takes on distinctly feminine characteristics. The *dil* is restless, infantile, even insane, clearly outside the control of the subject. The figure of speech called transferred epithet taught to English school students how a property associated with the self is transferred to another object for poetic effect. *Dil* is a recurring epithet upon which both the desires and responsibilities of the self are transferred. Take this song, for instance:

> *Yeh dil na hota bechara* (This heart would not have been desolate),
> *Kadam na hote aawara* (These steps would not have been wayward),
> *Jo khubsurat koi apna humsafar hota* (Had there been a beautiful companion).

The speaker chooses to refer to the desolate heart as if it were another person and steps (again, without a subject position) that are wayward. Such conditions of both loneliness and promiscuity (implied in the *aawara/kadam* or wayward steps) could have been avoided had there been a beautiful companion. It would seem that the consequence of the absence of a beloved absolves the heart and steps. Meanwhile, the 'I' that could have taken the responsibility is absent. The subject position remains diffused over body parts that take on a life of their own; leaving the individual both helpless and absolved.

Meanwhile, *dil* is also the seat of secrecy; it whispers its secrets to the speaker who talks about *dil* as if it were another person altogether. The speaker 'shares' the secret with his beloved as an (other) person's truth. *Mere dil mein aaj kya hai; tu kahe to main bata dun* comes to mind as one of the best-known songs from the 1970s: 'I could, if you wish, tell you what is on my heart today'. In the triad of the speaking self, body and heart, who is ultimately the one feeling and the one expressing it? The song elaborates on the wishes of the heart: '*Teri zulf phir sanwaroon teri maang phir saja doon*.'

The words 'to caress your hair again, to adorn your hair with vermillion again' are both sexual and euphemistic, referring to consummation and remarriage that the speaker wishes with the widowed beloved. But who is the one wanting to caress the hair? Is this reported speech with an elliptical subject so that *zulf phir sawanroon* (to caress your hair) is the heart's desire but merely reported by the speaker? Or has the heart emboldened the speaker to say this on its behalf? The structure of self split across the speaking 'I' and the desiring subject as represented by the secretive *dil* is not unique to this song. A similar split across the self/body and *dil* is evident in '*Yeh dil tum bin kahin lagta nahin,/hum kya karein*'—It is difficult for this heart to attach to anything since you are not around. This song from the 1970s is a popular duet and provides a good example of the multiple significations of *dil*. The female voice expressing love and separation is followed by a male voice: '*Lute dil mein diya jalta nahin hum kya karein*.' The male voice expresses the inability of a desolate house-like heart to light another flame, or to put it literally, to find love again. The recurring refrain *hum kya karein* (what can I/we do?) absolves both the desire and responsibility from the individual self which now rest squarely upon the *dil*. But if *dil* is outside of the self, where exactly is this desire located? Who is the one feeling the desire?

A series of verbs suggestive of arousal, pining, longing, feeling restive or lonely attach themselves to *dil*, and it is possible to see some of the roots going back to Urdu poetry.

See the following lines by Jaleel Manikpuri:

> *Aap pehlu mein baithein to sambhaal kar baithein* (When you sit next to me, do be careful),
> *Dil-e-betaab ko aadat hai machal jaane ki* (The restless heart has a tendency to fidget).

Once again, language allows for a missing subject so that the speaker can distance himself from the action ascribed to *dil*. Does *dil* here act as a substitute for an unconscious phallic–aggressive desire? It does make a certain temerity of expression possible for both men and women. For instance, this song from 1973:

> *Betaab dil ki tamanna yahi hai* (The restless heart wishes this alone),
> *Tumhein chahenge tumhein pujenge* (To love you, to worship you),
> *Tumhein apna khuda banayenge* (To make you my God).

It would be tempting to read a gendered meaning into what appears in the above as testimony to ultimate submission and self-effacement rather than a full-throated sexual desire. However, the blurring of the devotional and romantic is integral to expressions of love in South Asia and a part of its symbolic language. One of the multiple strands stemming out of the discussion on *dil* is a perception that *dil* is constant and authentic in a world of temptation and transience. Having to contend (as the Indian subcontinent did) with flows of different cultures, the body is left with the mark of such colonial encounters; *dil*, on the other hand, is uncontaminated. The famous song below, used quite often by cinema studies scholars as an example of national–cosmopolitan imagination, supports this argument:

> *Mera joota hai Japani,*
> *Yeh patloon Inglistani* (My shoes, they are Japanese, and my trousers English),
> *Sar pe laal topi Roosi*
> *Phir bhi dil hai Hindustani* (The cap I wear is Russian, but the heart is Indian).

If the *dil* is authentic and steadfast, a view invoked even in diasporic films that advocate an incorruptible inner core, it is also fragile, brittle and wavering. By itself, heartbreak is a common and clichéd metaphor for betrayal in love. In Hindi songs, it is often set up in opposition to a more powerful adversary, such as social class: '*Chaandi ki deewar na todi, pyar bhara dil tod diya*' (You could not break the walls). A broken heart or '*tuta huya dil*' is the death-knell, making life pointless, as in '*jab dil hee tut gaya, hum jeeke kya karenge*' (When the heart is broken, why should I live?).

Hence, the lover warns his beloved, '*chudi nahin yeh mera dil hai, dekho dekho tute na*' (This is not a bangle, but my heart, make sure it doesn't break). The fragility of the heart and the danger of its breaking at the hands of a merciless beloved is a recurring theme in Persianate style poetry in South Asia. See Daag Dehlvi's couplet below:

> *Tumhara dil mere dil ke barabar ho nahin sakta* (Your heart cannot be like mine),
> *Woh sheesha ho nahin sakta yeh pathar ho nahin sakta* (Yours cannot become glass, nor can mine turn into stone).

The finality of presumable essences of the male and female heart sometimes makes an oblique appearance, unlike the couplet above. There are several instances of gendered *dil*/s in Hindi film songs. For instance, *dil* as an object that can be given away, stolen, sold, bartered, etc., may appear far more as a theme in female songs. An entreaty such as the one below is but one example: '*Chura liya hai tumne jo dil ko, nazar nahin chura na sanam*' (Now that you have stolen my heart, don't steal the glance away). Or an offer such as the following:

> *Dil cheez kya hai aap meri jaan lijiye* (What price the heart, take my life away if you will)
>
> Or a more blatant invitation:
>
> *Yun to premi pachattar humare* (As such numerous lovers seek me),
> *Leja tukar satattar ishaare* (You can be the next one to make gestures),
> *Dil mera … muft ka* (Go on then, my heart sells for free).

The self-effacing *dil* peeping through female songs notwithstanding, we should be cautious by not overemphasising this for *dil* is polysemic and protean. It assumes many forms, shapes and meanings, depending upon the circumstances. It can be a receptacle for divine grace (*dil ek mandir hai*—The heart is a temple) or an alcove (*dil ke jharokhe mein tuj ko bitha kar*) and so on. It can be stolen from both men and women, and, like a naughty child, it can hide itself unbeknownst to the owner/parent. For instance, in this well-known song from 1990:

> *Koi aaye zara dhoondh ke laaye* (Someone please go and fetch),
> *Na jaane kahaan dil kho gaya* (I don't know where I have lost my heart).

In its restlessness, the heart is beyond control, as the popular expression in much Hindi film dialogue goes: '*Dil par kissi ka zor nahin*' (No one has power over the heart). One of the most common elements for making a compound word with *dil* is *bekaraar* (without rest). Songs such as '*Bekaraar dil tu gaaye jaa*' (Pining heart, keep on singing), '*Afsana likh rahin hun dil-e bekraar ki*' (I am writing the story of the pining heart) or those that suggest insanity of the *dil* in '*Dil deewana bin sajnake*' (The heart is crazy without my lover) and '*Dil to pagal hai*' (The heart is foolish) are much too numerous to cite here, but all these instances add up to make the heart unreliable, infant-like, passionate and recalcitrant. Once again, the separation of the heart from the head/body/self may be platitudinous, but it being a child and the locus for desire begs for attention. Is *dil* then an erogenous zone or a conscious and transgressive social agency that serves as a counterpoint to a regulating society? Is *dil* a symbolic and rhetorical device for hiding love or a convenient proxy for expressing one? It is this indeterminacy that makes *dil* a poor equivalent of heart, an impossibility of translation.

Aankhon Mein Kya Jee?

What do the eyes have? Do they hold secrets that the world doesn't know about? If *dil* is the testimony of desire transferred elsewhere, do eyes inhere the consensus over desire? Are they the sites of mutuality? I am reminded of my teenage years when I witnessed a friend exchanging glances with her boyfriend every day. In a neighbourhood where I used to live, a young girl named Meena would daily, unfailingly, go to the terrace of her house. Her eyes were glued to the main road that she could see from the terrace. And at a fixed time, Harish (a young boy from my neighbourhood) would pass by on his two-wheeler on that road. The two of them exchanged glances every single day. The family was none the wiser. As a friend and confidant, I had been allowed to 'witness' and my eyes had the permission to see this intimacy that spoke volumes without words. Meena and Harish's eyes managed to convey so much for that is all they had—an exchange of glance. And that moment of being visible to each other was accompanied by the fear of being visible to other unwanted eyes. In this circuitous visuality, there was simultaneous hiding and revealing. *Aankhon hi aankhon mein ishara ho gaya*. Commitments of a lifetime were made through the eyes. They didn't need to speak.

The stock word *aankhen* has a distinct significance in the semantic world of film songs. If *dil* is a protean abstraction which is spoken for or sought refuge in, the eyes are unmistakably present in the seeing they do and their own visibility to the other. They form the first sensuous connection by being locked in another pair of eyes and many film songs pay a tribute to this moment. They become a springboard upon which other sensations are built; and in fact, it is not unusual to go from the eyes to the heart. For instance, a song says, '*Aankho se dil me utar ke too mere dhadkan me hai*'—it is through the eyes that love was felt and eventually descended upon the heart, making it a heartbeat. This strange anatomical journey would make no sense outside the universe of the song. However, we must imagine it through affect and social experience than pre-conceived linguistic meanings. The first experience of frisson is through the eyes for if touching is 'watched' even at a more evolved stage of a romantic relationship, it has no place in the initial one. It is the intensity of the gaze that many songs rely upon for conveying nascent feelings of love. The spoken word is as difficult as the touch; it identifies, pins down and marks out the speakers. But eyes both convey and elude, say it and don't say it. The gradual process of embodiment in the films songs, especially in a period from the early to the late 1970s or so, was non-linguistic. In fact, even a late 1990s song from the film *Ghulam* (1998) has a similar grammar but with a greater sense of play—*Aankhon se tune yeh kya keh diya, dil yeh diwana dhadhakne laga*, which translates as 'What is it that you said with your eyes that my crazy heart began to beat'. Eyes are arguably the foreplay, the first invitation, a part of the body that has in it the corporeal concentration of the entire sexual act, impossible to enact. The expression of this seething desire relies then upon the *dil*, though not always. Relatedly, songs about sleep going away from the eyes and being replaced by the image of the lover abound, for instance, *Meri aankhonki neend lagaya balam daga dega ya.* The ease and comfort with which a covenant has been formed without using language speak volumes of how a unique language of desire is carved.[1]

Eyes convey much more when there persists the fear of other eyes that see us. The surveilling Indian family has its gaze upon romantic love, and it is in those shadows that romantic love invents its language and cues. The eyes are in the body; but they also enable us to see, they create a spectacle, a *nazara*. And in the absence of touching, they touch. The liquid pools of silence create their own words. Film songs show a yearning to understand, interpret and decode this language. '*Sharbati teri aankhon ki jheel see gahrain mein main doob jaata hun*'—I drown in the juicy and ocean-like depths of your intoxicating eyes. Are eyes being used to refer to body parts that cannot be named, a euphemism for a phallocentric fantasy? It's difficult to say if the listeners knew these dual meanings or if the lyricists intended them. But a covenant of meanings that needed no articulation stood between the songs and their listeners; one in which eyes are not only about eyes. They are much much more for they hold secrets and also dreams. The song '*Aapki aankhon mein kuchh mehke huye se raaz hain*' suggests an oceanic depth, almost like the unconscious, where secrets lurk. What comes over strongly is how language-as-we-know does not serve the purpose. Its ambit expands and sometimes language bypasses the conventional meanings.

To translate a song is therefore to translate this embeddedness of the social and corporeal experience and therefore time and again, the eyes that say and tongue that cannot say stand in contrast to each other. For instance, the words '*Kaho na kaho, yeh aankhen bolti hain*' suggest to the beloved that regardless of her admission or lack of it; the eyes have done the saying. This difference between unsaying of language

1 In an insightful paper, Taylor (2002) draws attention to *nazar* or 'gaze' as a mode of expressing desire that draws simultaneously from devotional and romantic contexts of eyes-meeting-eyes. Like *dil*, the word *nazar* also comes to us as a stock metaphor via Indo-Persian poetry.

and the speaking of the eyes may seem true in many situations, not unique to romantic songs in films. However, if love fears being found out and comes with a baggage of illegitimacy, eyes are the only means of dialogue—*aankhon aankhon mein baat hone do* (Let the conversation happen through eyes). Is the conversation tactile or verbal; perhaps the burden of both rests upon the eyes that see and eyes that look back, the seer and the visible, as it were. Perhaps it is the eyes, more than the *dil* that make the binary of the body-world more nuanced for they diffuse the distance but also remind us of the impossibility of tactile pleasure. This reversibility of the visible and the seeing eyes creates a complex loop of meaning in film songs.[2]

For instance, a song from the film *Dharmaputra* manages to pay a tribute by the male lover to his beloved by talking about her eyes. The eyes remain even when other details are unknown to the speaker. The opening line begins by saying how could anyone forget these lovely eyes (*Bhool sakta hai bhala kaun, pyaari aankhen*). The hero is taciturn and has not laid eyes on women, engrossed as he has been in a fairly puritanical regime of becoming a Hindu nationalist. However, it is the eyes that profess romance and it is to the eyes that he can manage to say what he has to. The lines of the song appear in the male lover's poem and reciting his poem is one pre-text; the eyes become another pre-text, rather a synecdochic reference for the person. The second line builds on how the eyes are sleep-filled—deep pools of allure. The male voice avoids the first-person reference and appears to emphasise the larger impossibility of ignoring such 'lovely eyes'. The second-person reference is also missing so that 'one' may substitute for *bhala kaun* and the eyes appear detached from a body. Gradually, the speaker musters the courage to say the eyes have been part of every breath he takes, every thought he possesses (*meri har saans, har soch ne chaha tujhko, jabse dekha* ...). The 'seeing' eyes see the eyes of the beloved, creating one loop of visibility. While he does that, there are also eyes of the rest of the family upon the couple, as they watch the couple indulgently. This circuit of

2 For an excellent discussion, from a phenomenological point of view of inside/outside and how sight is on the threshold of the two (if they are two indeed), see Sundar Sarukkai (2002).

visibility is also about being invisible; for really nothing has been said that can lead to shame and embarrassment. Language has been bypassed, manipulated and made disingenuous through transferring epithets from the body to the eyes. Some songs also refer to the desire to possess the beloved's eyes. For instance, the song '*Yeh aankhen dekh kar ham saari duniya bhool jaate hain*' (when I/we see these eyes, I forget the existence of the world) goes on to say in the next line, '*inhe paane ki dhun mein har tamanna bhool jaate hain*' (in order to possess these, I forget every other longing). What is to want to possess someone's eyes? Why would eyes be the object of desire? How can eyes suffice for a body; a life; a self? One could argue that eyes are not overtly erogenous or a sexual part of the body; and hence it involves no effrontery to seek them, talk about them. On the other hand, they inhere possibilities of the sexual but again safely circumventing reference to rest of the body, appearing innocuous but also suggestive. Elsewhere, a song begins, '*Teri aankhon ki chahat mein main yeh sab kuchh luta doonga*'. The eyes compress as the self and body to be desired; and they also become the language, in fact rendering verbal language redundant. Note the next few lines:

Bahut kuchh tumse kehne ki
Tamanna dil mein rakhte hain
Magar jab saamne aate hain
Kehna bhool jaate hain
Mohabbat mein zubaan chup ho to
Aankhein baat karti hain
Woh keh deti hain sab baatein
Jo kehna bhool jaate hain

Female voice:
I carry the wish in my heart
To say so much to you
But when we appear before each other
I forget what I wanted to say

Male voice:
When lovers' are tongue-tied
Eyes speak, they say
All that the lovers forget to say

Given the gendered dialogue in the example above; we may think that the eyes become particularly significant for an assigned female body. But this is not a consistent pattern, even if it appears common. The point I want to make is that eyes are the tongue of the body; they are its language.[3] But eyes are also the erotic object, evoking desire by conveying desire. They speak so that they are not heard by the rest; and they touch and caress, making language incidental. Like *dil*, eyes contain; but unlike *dil*, they also spill over in more physical terms, so that love can become a tear that is shed—'*Aansoon samaj ke yunh mujhe aankh se tumne gira diya*'. They may also spill over with happiness—'*Mujhe khushi mili itni, ke man mein samaya palak band kar lun, kaheen chhalak hee jaye*'. Eyelids safeguard the fantasy, that's broken by opening them. '*Palak band kar lun*'. But eyes also let his happiness spill over in the form of tears. They are like overfilled chalices. They are the bearers of affect.

Closing Thoughts

The two examples of words creating proxy possibilities for expressing desire are part of a large repertoire of verbal, non-verbal and visual cues that Hindi film songs use to express emotions. The social obligations to keep love hidden and understated produces a gamut of supplementing material to draw from. As audiences and listeners, we understand the constraints as well as the desire to transgress boundaries and in this consensual understanding songs become as much 'theirs' as 'ours'. Language or its bypassing possibilities allow for it to be a quiet collective, making the experience both individual and common, laying

3 See this song from the film *Haasil*
Aankhen bhi hoti hai dil ki zubaan - 2
Bin bole kar deti hai haalat yeh pal mein bayaan
Aankhen bhi hoti hai dil ki zubaan
Bin bole kar deti hai haalat yeh pal mein bayaan
Aankhen bhi hoti hai dil ki zubaan
Khaamoshi bhi to pyaar mein
Rakhti bahut hi asar hai
Kab ishq ho jaaye yahan
Dil ko kahan yeh khabar hai

out as it were the pedagogy of being desirous in an inoffensive manner. Experience of the body and being in a social world intertwine to do both—suggest a mutual conflict but also provisional ways out of this conflict. The affective matrix of film songs also demonstrates the limits of language and puts pressure on the idea of verbalising, articulating and making its actors and listeners join a community that understands that all need not be said. In simpler words, we could hear Gulzar hinting at the ineffability of language. In an interview with Nasreen Munni Kabir, this snippet may be helpful to us:

> NMK: If I understand correctly, many of your songs talk of the 'experience of feeling,' rather than being a description of events.
> Gulzar: [pauses] Absolutely right.
>
> I am not trying to give a simile or paint an image—I want to create an experience of feeling. And what is that feeling? I might be fumbling to catch an image—that fumbling itself becomes the expression. (Gulzar 2018: 61)

Hindi film songs are evidence of both fumbling and circumvention of language. Or should one perhaps say that they create their own language; in as much as a linguistic universe whose codes are shared amongst a community may be considered adequate for the formation of a language. Finally, we may ask if the language of songs is so gestural and symbolic, what does that say about translation? Does it enhance the impossibility of translation? I believe that the language of songs demonstrates to us most accurately that the biggest challenge to translation is language itself; its ability to carry emotion. Film songs also demonstrate the central role of translation which is one of standing in; stepping in for the thing itself, for being a surrogate presence when the 'original' is elusive (as it always is). This proxy brings it closest to translation; in that sense, our inquiry about the language of film songs may be rephrased to say all expressions of affect in songs are an ongoing event of translation. As we bring this discussion on the eyes to a close, it is perhaps a song that expresses the inarticulateness of language that may help us here. Interestingly, the song does another displacement—it makes eyes exude fragrance. More importantly, the song provides an insight into all that we have been trying to say; it says it better. It reminds us that Hindi film songs have a theory of language: meaning is achieved through deflection and displacement, and surrogate words are also accompanied by surrogate experiences. Its impossibility of translation lies in the fact that language itself is a highly suspect phenomenon. As scholars, we may also remember with some humility, that this theory is best understood not only through songs but in a song such as the one below.

Humne dekhi hain un aankho ki mahakti khushbu
Hath se chhuke ise rishto ka ilzaam na do
Sirf ehsaas hain ye ruh se mahsus karo
Pyar ko pyar hi rahne do koyi naam na do

Pyaar koi bol nahi, pyar aawaz nahi
Ek khamoshi hain sunti hain kaha karti hain....

I/we have seen the fragrance of these eyes
Don't touch it with your hands and give it the name of a relationship
This is mere feeling; felt through the soul
Leave love alone; do not give it another name

Love is neither a word, nor sound
It is silence, that listens and speaks

7

Uneasy Translations

Translations too, being poems, are 'never finished, only abandoned'.
—Ramanujan (1985: Introduction)[1]

> Nothing is exactly the same in one language as in another, so the failure of translation is always necessary and absolute. Apart from its neglect of the fact that some pretty good equivalencies are available, this proposition rests on a mystification, on a dream of perfection we cannot even want, let alone have. If there were a perfect equivalence from language to language, the result would not be translation; it would be a replica. And if such replicas were possible on a regular basis, there would not be any languages, just one vast, blurred international jargon, a sort of late cancellation of the story of Babel. (Apter 2014: Preface, Chapter xiv)

Although we are nearing the completion of the book, this essay is about incompleteness, the incompleteness in the business of translation. Or I could say the 'unfinished' business but the associations with that word are overburdened by cataclysmic historical contexts. The examples in this essay cannot claim such arrogance of significance. However, they (also) remind us of slapdash borders made around translation projects, ones that remind us of the 'task' that had to be done; whilst especially avoiding the question of why it had to be done; or what makes it appear so easy but remains uneasy in memory. There is no pattern to the examples of texts discussed in this essay. There is a recurring theme—forms of othering in the Indian subcontinent—especially caste and religion. Very often these are inseparable. By reading them through translation, I hope to show the challenge of this language that resists translation. This involves re-visiting and re-reading some works that I had 'concluded,' and in one case, not even started. However, they

1 Ramanujan (1985: xv).

refused to leave me alone. This divergent and collage-based archive under discussion avoids a pattern but merely helps me document the uneasy and incomplete translations as an exercise that helps us reflect. In other words, this essay documents the lingering and haunting meanings that persist and irritate us into thinking of how translation remains inconclusive. One could even rephrase that and say what remains uneasy, unsmooth, forever reminding us of an interminable series of approximations is, in fact, translation. Philosophically, we may want to avoid saying and thinking that a translation is complete, over and done with, concluded. For, it is forever beckoning us to notice what we might have missed, even if we 'translated' accurately. When I look back upon the self-conscious journey of translation, one particular example sticks out the most. The example is one of failure; hence it is not effervescent but has stayed tugging at the horizons of the mind, asking what exactly happened. Now it's interesting that I should use those words, 'What exactly happened' when the poem is itself about not happening. Herein lies the main question: My English has been asking accountability of what the Gujarati language and the ghazal form did not want to be too definite about.

Na Thaya: The Language of Non-action

Failures bring rich lessons. Particularly if they leave us guessing for the rest of our lives the reasons why they happened. As such, every act of translation fails to meet its idealised self. Some particularly don't. Their incompleteness has persisted in my mind and finds its place in this essay that asks what exactly happened. However, sometimes nothing happens, like my mother's non-writing. I am reminded of one of the early ghazals, the only one, I translated (in collaboration). The title of the ghazal is '*Na Thaya*', which in Hindi would mean '*Naheen Huya*' or even '*Naheen Bana*'. In English, we needed a subject positioning word. The pronoun we used was 'it' and called it, 'It Did Not Happen', although even 'that' did not happen was also a possibility. The English grammar did not allow us the uncertain or missing subject. Therein lies the story of this failure or incompleteness. The indicative pronoun stubbornly defined what did not happen; a responsibility an Indian language was not willing to take, or rather a naming an Indian language did not want to do. Really speaking, translation is the realisation of small things. It is not the irreconcilability of grand cultural gestures, which of course, do not have an equivalence. However, we surely don't go through life thinking that everything has an equivalent for that would be an ultimate act of arrogance, almost hubris. But how was one to know that the 'it' will haunt like this? A subject position repressed in Gujarati has returned like a spectre to demand at least an explication of the phenomenon of translation. The ghazal in Gujarati goes like this:

આમ અછતા ન થયા આમ ઉઘાડા ન થયા,
હાથ ફૂલોમાં ઝબોળ્યા ને સુંવાળા ન થયા.

સ્વપ્ન તો આંખમાં આવીને રહે કે ન રહે,
ઘેર આવેલ પ્રસંગો ય અમારા ન થયા.

તાગવા જાવ તો – ખોદાઇ ગયા છે દરિયા,
અર્થ શોધો તો – અમસ્થા ય ઉઝરડા ન થયા.

એક વરસાદનું ટીપું અમે છબીમાં મઢ્યું,
ત્યારથી ભેજભર્યા ઓરડા કોરા ન થયા.

સમુદ્ર લોહીમાં ખીલ્યો, ખીલ્યો, ઝૂલ્યો ને ખર્યો,
બળી 'ગ્યો છોડ લીલોછમ ને ધુમાડા ન થયા.

આજ ખાબોચિયાનાં થાય છે શુકન રણમાં,
તો ય ભાંગી પડેલ જીવને ટેકા ન થયા.

આજ વરસાદ નથી એમ ના કહેવાય, રમેશ,
એમ કહીએ કે હશે, આપણે ભીના ન થયા.

- રમેશ પારેખ

(Parekh 1988: 373)

Aam achhta na thaya, aam ughaada na thay,
Haath phulo maan jabolya ne sunvaala na thaya

Swapn to aankh maan aavi ne reh ke na reh,
Gher aavel prasongo-e amara na thaya

Ek varsaad nu teepu ame chhabi maan madyu,
tyaar thee bhej bharya orda kora na thaya.

Samudra lohi maan khilyo, khilyo, jhulyo ne kharyo,
Bali gayo chhod leelo chham ne dhumada na thaya.

Aaj varsaad nathi em na kehvaaye, Ramesh,
Em kahiye ke hashe, aapne bheena na thaya

English Translation:

Things were neither hidden, nor were they revealed
flower-drenched hands somehow didn't smell sweet.

Dreams lingered or didn't perhaps in our eyes
but ceremonies at home were somehow not ours.

Taking measure, we found ourselves digging the sea
seeking meaning we found merely shavings and scraps.

A raindrop caught and framed was hung on the wall
dampness in our rooms since then has not dried.

Red sea-flowers bloomed, swayed and were shed
green twigs burning but no smoke in the air.

The portent today was water in sand
but pieces of a life still broken lie around.

Don't say, Ramesh, it didn't rain today
Say: perhaps it did, but we didn't feel the rain.

(Ramanathan and Kothari 1998: 52)

The first couplet does not have a self-reflexive pronoun. It refers to (a/the) palms that were dipped in fragrance but did not become fragrant. *Na thaya* or did not happen in the second line refers to the not happening of fragrance. The second stanza qualifies how even dreams may not stay for long in (one's) eyes, implying that they do not belong to the eyes and hence they merely visit. The second line of the second stanza continues with this thought by adding the conjunction 'but' and says that even festivities at home did not become ours. The Gujarati language often refers to festivities as *prasang* and uses the verb 'to come', to accompany it. This is to say festivities that came. In this case, they came home, for that's where they belonged, occasions of joy in the family. However, they were ours but did not become ours. *Na thaya* is now an act of becoming as well as belonging. Both did not happen. The second stanza uses the self-reflexive pronoun *amara* (ours). The singular and specific person is missing. 'Ours' could be any or all of us—the indeterminate body to which things happen, the *veetak*. The third stanza refers to rooms that did not become dry for one drop of rain remained captured in an image; while the fourth refers to verdant shrubs that were set on fire but produced no smoke. What did not happen in these cases? What are the shadows of past life that hang and keep the memories damp, or what are these infertile plants that singe and burn without producing even smoke? This existential futility or bewildering unfulfilment characterises the rest of the stanzas. However, the last stanza is an important one to dwell upon:

> Don't say, Ramesh, it didn't rain today
> Say: perhaps it did, but we didn't feel the rain.

If fulfilment remained tantalisingly close, and yet elusive, who is to be blamed? Let us not blame the rain, for it may have rained or it probably did, but we find ourselves dry. Did we choose not to get drenched or did the raindrops touch us in vain? Who's to know? The poem does not wish to pin the blame on anyone. The missing subject and passive construction of the poem posits a predicament in which a web of contexts may underlie a lack. It is not interested in identifying a source or reason for this lack; in fact, it reminds us to make sure that we do not use the active voice nor blame any one factor in particular. The failure may well have been ours, or fault lay in our stars. The English act of this poem demanded accountability and reacted to the passive construction. The Gujarati *aapne* in the last one for 'we' is an inclusive 'we' but also non-specific to who's included and who's not. The uncertain subject is commensurate with the uncertain circumstances that produce situations of promise but ironically also a gap between owning and belonging, having and possessing, touching and remaining untouched. The agency-driven English found this excessive and strained to put subject positions. The poem did not work, *na thaya*. Universes in literature are formed not only by beautiful words but also by positions of the subject and object in the syntax of life. The passive construction in Indian languages is a metaphysical condition which produces two results—at a philosophical level, it disallows the individual hubris as being the author of all actions; at the level of the social, it suggests a lack of autonomy in the order of things. At a political level, it absolves the individual from taking any responsibility, but that is a phenomenon I will come to shortly. Meanwhile, I am reminded of a talk on 'failure' by Pratap Bhanu Mehta, and some insights might help us to deepen this discussion on the social life of language that an incomplete translation has revealed for us. Mehta asks what might be the conceptual conditions under which a historical category like 'failure' becomes available to us? Let me hasten to clarify that Mehta's invocation of 'failure' has less to do with the incompleteness in my translation effort, but one that might be useful to put in conversation with failure or unfulfilment *within* the poem. Mehta argues that the conceptual category of 'failure' has much to do with seeing agential presence; the individual as the cause of consequences rather than an effect. To put this in simpler words, I am the person and I have potential, and I made the effort but I still failed. In this conception, the 'I' (note how it's missing in the poem) is the originary source from which all action is perceived to emanate. This, according to Mehta, is a culturally contingent phenomenon. Philosophical traditions from Augustinian Christianity to Buddhism do not account for the individual as the originary source; in fact, they remain 'deeply suspicious of this idea'. The preoccupation with failure or rather the ubiquitous language of success, according to Mehta, is a product of neoliberal anxiety.

With this in mind, if we were to move back to the poem, how does the English language force us to ascribe an originary source when none exists? And if it does, does the translation into English intervene in its philosophy by intervening in its grammar? This also helps us think about what might be the role of language; not in its special designation as a repository of cultural references, but in its structural arrangement that also contains the architecture of world views and social outlook? Really speaking, we could be merely demonstrating here the Sapir-Whorf theory of language constituting worlds than merely reflecting them. However, breaking down incompleteness to small things of translation unfolds its elusive possibilities and reminds us that the unfinished business of translation may be allowed to linger to mine rich possibilities. It is no mere coincidence, or perhaps it is, that the last word of Paul Ricoeur's major work, 'Memory, History, Forgetting' is 'incompletion' (inachèvement), as pointed out by Richard Kearney (2006). This incompleteness was to remain, to survive, as history does, packed compactly between memory and forgetting, between translatability and untranslatability, regardless of Ricoeur's naming it. However, naming this incompletion as it is matters, 'for it acknowledges that translation, understood as an endlessly unfinished business, is a signal not of failure but of hope' (ibid.). The impossibility of Derridean terms also is both a hope and failure.[2] It is in sitting with translation that the incompleteness survives both the translator and the translation, the doer and the doing, like a spectre of small things, like shadows of memory—now revealing and now hiding.

Meanwhile, I mentioned earlier that the passive construction combined with an uncertain subject also has a political dimension to it. It is time to turn to that, especially with regard to Gujarati. The Spanish Jesuit priest Father Carlos Vallés spent over four decades in Gujarat. In keeping with the tradition of Jesuit commitment to learning the language of the provinces, he also learnt the Gujarati language. However, he went beyond learning and emerged to be one of its most reputed and read prose writers. On the thread of the missing subject, Fr. Vallés' observations are worth attending to; for he responds to Gujarati both as an insider and outsider. His observations appear quirky but draw from a range of sources in both textual and everyday life. Upon encountering

2 'In a sense, nothing is untranslatable; but *in another sense*, everything is untranslatable; translation is another name for the impossible' (Derrida 2001: 56–57).

the missing subject in expressions like *bolai gayu* (words came out) or *kehavai gayu* (words happened to be said), Fr. Vallés comments:

> As a foreigner I have had some advantage in the course of learning Gujarati. What has appeared normal and ordinary to a native speaker has stuck for me, and I notice new things. For instance, 'bolai gayun.' An ugly and unnecessary utterance. Not that I spoke. But without my volition, thought, planning, words escaped me, 'kehvaayi gayu.' Words mine, but not my matter. Voice mine, but not my thought. Words have been used, but not by the speaker . . . words are unanchored, in the air, orphan, and if I had no agency, I am a mere ghost, a remain, a maya then. How can I be held responsible? (Valles 2015: 50)

The refusal to lend a singular person to an utterance, according to Fr. Vallés, makes the Gujarati speaker hide in safety. This is especially true in unpleasant situations where the upper-class and upper-caste Gujarati relies upon the uncertain pronoun *apana* or ours (or *aapne*, us people) instead of *maara* or mine. Commenting on the difference between *maari* and *aapni* in Gujarati, Fr. Vallés instantiates how the *aapne* hijacks responsibility in Gujarati. Instead of saying 'I speak like this', I could have said, 'We speak like this'. The plural—*bahuvachan*—expressed by words like *aapne badha* (all of us) or *aapne* (us) makes the individual hide in the collective; and disallows not only taking responsibility for oneself but also expressing one's dissent with the rest. It is quite common to find references to caste and inter-religious violence referred to by the genteel class in Gujarat as '*aapne tyaan tofano thaye, pan aapne nathi karta*'. Literally translated, 'there are 'troubles' at ours, but we people are not the ones initiating it'. Language colludes to engender a universe in which the hubris of action is allayed, but also one in which ethical questions of responsibility are hijacked and hidden behind the collective pronouns.

To sum up, this paradoxical effect of language bears itself out the most in translational readings of Gujarati and reminds us that the so-called challenges of translation are not ones of finding equivalent words, but of unravelling a world/word in its own context. The 'loss' is effected by the gain of a definitive pronoun in English. On the other hand, the subject position in English lends itself to a more responsible and accountable position in charged political contexts. It would be simplistic on our part to see this interaction between Gujarati and English in terms of absences and presences, and we may therefore go back to the question of the 'missing' subject—missing from whose point of view and from which point of view? The incompleteness has allowed the possibility of rich questions regarding self, language and experience that would not be possible had the poem felt 'complete'. We would do well to think of this incompleteness as an invitation to continue thinking, revising, translating and collaborating on uncovering the laws governing the linguistic organisation of world-views. To reconcile with a settled (and hackneyed) view about how all translation is an approximation is to let go of the fecund possibilities that underlie the ongoing nature of translation. As Judith Butler remarks, 'the reciprocal and ongoing way that a translation acts upon both languages suggests that the translation does not simply arrive on the date of publication: that arrival is ongoing, uneven and incomplete' (Butler 2016: Introduction).

Angaliyat: Wisdom and Assertion

We come to translation and at times, translations come to us. The grandiose claims we translators make of making the best works available to the world and so on, are partly true, but often specious. Texts haunt us into forming a deeper and longer relationship with them. For instance, I first heard of *Angaliyat* at St. Xavier's College in Ahmedabad where I taught; there were a large number of Christian employees from the region of Anand and Petlad. This is where early conversions to Christianity had been made. Some of them had found jobs in various institutions run by the Society of Jesus. Peterbhai Macwan was amongst them. He provided tea to us during breaks and did odd jobs. He saw me reading in Gujarati often. 'Read about my community,' he said. He mentioned *Angaliyat*. I didn't catch the name. I heard *angadia* as in a courier. He reminded me again the next day and the day after. 'Alright, bring it,' I said. This early framing of the novel as a story about the weaver community and one that the educated Vankars (weavers) took great pride in was intriguing. The Gujarati copy of *Angaliyat* has a little boy on its cover, holding the finger of his mother. His face looks distraught, angry, unhappy. I saw the title and the photo and didn't understand any connection as if something was lost in communication. This reminds me of Vivek Shanbhag's *Ghachar Ghochar*, a novel in Kannada and carrying the same title in every single language it has gone into. The words *ghachar ghochar* do not mean anything outside the context of the novel. As such even within the novel and its title, they are a set of nonsense words. They first occur when Anita, the narrator's wife, is not able to untie the knots of her petticoat. The entangled web is what she refers to as *ghachar ghochar*, a family code for situations and objects that eluded a clean understanding or solution. This private sphere of language extends just enough to allow the entry of the fifth person beyond the family—the narrator himself. The privilege of knowing the nonsense words of a family is an extension of intimacy, and the narrator knows somewhere he has been both burdened and privileged. Language as such is neither public nor private. Gradually, we readers also know that life is *ghachar ghochar* on most days. The word *angaliyat*, on the other hand, is not a nonsense word that a bunch of siblings made up. However, it is inseparable from the novel; it sits not only on the title page but is the framing device of the story. It is a word the Vankars of Gujarat use for a child who accompanies the mother and comes to their stepfather's house. Presumably, the mother has remarried, a practice frowned upon by the upper castes and common among the Dalits. If the word *angaliyat* reminds the child of their lack of entitlement, the remarrying act reinforces the perception of impurity. In traditional Gujarat, the Dalits are referred to by the upper castes as *natariya naat*—the caste that remarries and hence remains impure, or rather, from the upper castes' point of view, becomes even more impure. The perceived impurity of the caste finds its locus in the woman who remarries, but it is also the Dalit women that are often molested by the Patidars and Darbars in the region. Meanwhile, I 'translate-d' *Angaliyat*. The past tense attending to the word 'translate' appears forced in the light of the interminable afterlife of the book. And a massive dose of affect has characterised my relation with it all along, refusing to be sealed away as 'translated' and over and done with. 'We are accustomed to reading translations as products, as finished texts, inscriptions, and not as congealed moments of a process,' remarks Joshua Price (2021: 14). The entire ecology of the *angaliyat* stands next to a colon with the English word 'stepchild' on the book cover of the English translation. The supplementing meanings rely on the readers' motivation to not just read the novel but read it carefully enough to know this, ensuring that nothing is lost in communication. The colon is a reminder of both the possibility and impossibility of this important word; nay, a pejorative word that Macwan both resents and builds upon. The utterance of the word *angaliyat* by the upper caste towards the Dalits and by the Dalits towards each other creates in the novel situations of sapping confidence, of sucking out legitimacy. And people give what they receive. So much happens because the word is uttered; and yet not for the fact of its utterance, of it being said. Ortega y Gasset says, 'The effectiveness of speech does not simply lie in speaking, in making statements, but, at the same time and of necessity, in a relinquishing of speech, a keeping quiet, a being silent'! (2000: 57). Through such social and epistemological landscapes, *Angaliyat* became an entry point to understanding caste hierarchies in Gujarat, and I was enriched intellectually and emotionally by this new relationship with translation.

Angaliyat is arguably India's first Dalit novel, and it set the benchmark for Dalit literature in Gujarat. Like all symbolic beginnings, it has its flaws. However, it is an intense novel, written with the pace and plot arrangement of a bestseller. Now, that is indeed a strange thing to say for a novel that also documents the struggles of the community of Vankars (weavers). I say this because Joseph Macwan was a flamboyant person and a master storyteller. He had a sense of drama and theatre. He brought to life the quotidian and the heroic and peopled the landscape of Gujarati literature with characters it had not encountered; language it had not heard, and pathos and tears it had not experienced. This profound relation with his environment and centrality of experience lent to *Angaliyat* an immediacy and power that is difficult to describe in words. He also wanted the community to see its own heroism, to not internalise the slurs of 'low-caste' directed at it, and provide (without spelling it out thus) almost a Kshatriya-like tale of valour. That being said, Macwan would contest that such heroism and larger-than-life people existed only in his fiction; his portraits in *Vyatha na Veetak* (a collection of character sketches) testify to the living characters that find their way into *Angaliyat*. The characters in *Angaliyat* are people Macwan lived with and observed when he was a little boy and they were adults. Through such portraits, the novel gives its people a memory to be proud of, an object to return to and a sense of the past, perhaps. It must be for this reason that I was recommended this novel by Peterbhai. When does life become a story, a memoir and acquire a literary form? Rather, is it still the form of life, but to its readers, it appears like a story? *Angaliyat* belongs to the world of the formidable and receding tradition of orality, incidentally produced as written literature. An embodiment of this tradition, one character that stayed with both Macwan and me was Bhavaanbhagat:

> Bhavaankaka had inherited from his forefathers a natural intuitiveness and foresight. People looked up to him for his knowledge, wisdom, and presence of mind that he brought to bear upon intricate problems. . . . That's why it was said even among the upper castes that 'there was none like Bhavaankaka within a hundred miles', and it was only through a quirk of fate that a person like Bhavaankaka was born in an inferior caste like the Vankars! (Macwan 2012: 52)

At the start of the novel, Teeha wakes up and strains to hear Bhavaankaka's sarangi, but the roosters' calls fall on his ears and he sights the deevo in Savli's house dimming. The 'time' for the novel comes through from the senses, especially seeing and listening and touching—creating, as Guru and Sarukkai note, the everyday social. The regularity of rituals that marks the beginning of *samskara* appears here as well but involves instead the networks of labour and singing and being one among others. In tandem with the rhythmic '*khat* ... *khat* ... *khat*' of Teeha's loom, Bhavaankaka eventually begins to sing:

> Look, there sits the swan on the edge of the brimming lake,
> Over him stretches the pearl-filled sky,
> Where should he peck, he knows not Ram
> Where should he peck, he knows not Ram
> What can I know of its fate, O Ram!
> (ibid.: 2)

Does the swan have so much plenitude or is neither place—the sky and the lake—available to him? Or does his being on the edge—almost there yet neither within nor without—indicate a sense of not belonging to either world? 'What can I know of its fate,' confesses Bhavaankaka, as if speaking about himself. Dwelling on the edge between the two worlds like the swan, he was both dependable and unreliable. It is to him that Teeha, Valji and others turned when in times of dilemma or crisis. Valji, keen on getting Teeha married, once declared him totally unreliable: 'But you couldn't rely on Bhavaakaka. He was entirely capable of rubbing holy ash instead of the peethi' (3). How does Bhavaankaka come to become the voice and conscience of the community, its archive and also its exception? How does he remain a soothing and provocative old man, singing with simplicity but also dwelling upon abstractions, drawing from experiences of what others call *anubhav vaani* but remaining sceptical of the social world in general? An old man, who sings philosophical songs at the sarangi and sometimes goes away for long periods, walking to places of pilgrimage. His is the voice of the morning, for his notes on the sarangi merge with the sounds of his immediate world when Teeha begins his day and sits down at the loom to weave. The sounds of weaving and the notes on sarangi keep pace with each other, giving us a sense of the rhythm of both the now and the forever—the world and its labour and the longing for the other world, respectively.

The two characters also represent for me the different modes of experience. If Teeha stands up to the upper castes in the novel and becomes the carrier and initiator of Dalit assertion, Bhavaanbhagat beckons us to think of the spiritual in the political. He lends to the Dalit struggle against the upper castes an understanding that is not specific only to this time but rather an insight into how the *ujaliyat* (fairer-skinned people) hide their faults and project them onto the Dalits. In this service, he draws from mythology, common sense, songs and stories that are like pearls animating his very own sky. His anecdotes appear from deeply paradoxical experiences of life in which both the worldly and the other-worldly coalesce and compete. He believes the world to be illusory, a maya, and would like to devote time to *paramarth*, a pursuit of spiritual meaning. But is that spirituality available to a Dalit life that needs to protect its life and dignity on an everyday basis? It must be noted that Bhavaanbhagat is not a designated Praneshacharya, although he may have understood more through life. There is little on the surface that could make me compare Praneshacharya with Bhavaanbhagat. The former is the crest jewel of the Vedas, the Agrahara's most virtuous expression who is made to carry the burden of its sin by remaining pure himself. The latter is a member of the Dalit community of Vankars. He has seen how the Dalits announce their embarrassments from rooftops, while the upper castes hide them, perpetuating a myth of their purity. He has seen how women during widowhood long to have company and asserts that the stigma of remarriage is the upper castes' hypocritical judgment for we don't know what happens behind their closed doors. When Bhavaankaka advises Teeha to get Kanku remarried, a startled Teeho asks:

> In that case how do widows in these high castes spend their lives? What happens in the nooks and corners of their houses does not travel through their walls Teeha! Our caste is a foolish one and so announces these things from the rooftops. I can tell you, I have not seen fair crows even in Kashi! (Macwan 2012: 116)

The dignity, wisdom and courage of Bhavaanbhagat are created in this novel through the trust that people invest in him. This is visibly different from the trust Praneshacharya enjoys—a phenomenon that rests upon knowledge, an intimacy with the scriptures, a knowledge of distinguishing the right from the wrong as dictated by the sacred books. Bhavaanbhagat's notions of *maya* and *paramarth*, on the other hand, are not the spatially demarcated worlds of the Agrahara; they are the inventiveness of an old man who, through wisdom, decides upon the spiritual and the political. At one point, responding to the innocence/ignorance of his caste, he laments:

> In which moment did you create us, my Lord
> O Potter, on which wheel did you cast the pots? (ibid.)

The narrator suggests that Kaka often sang this song and explained to his listeners that he is asking the maker, 'What kind of time it was when he made us; why doesn't our single effort find fulfilment?' (ibid.: 56). The novel time and again makes references to *na-gani jaat*—

an inconsequential and useless caste—that Teeha and Bhavaanbhagat themselves use. What kind of pots are these, o potter, Bhavaanbhagat asks when he sings. His listeners think those are references to someone else and miss the tears in Bhavaanbhagat's eyes. The lack of anger and indignation that Bhavaanbhagat finds missing in his community provides us with a deeper understanding of the Dalit assertion—manifest here not in anger but pain and disappointment. Bhavaankaka's frustration with the shackles of his caste identity is made clear here. The couplet also reveals Bhavaankaka's spirituality and his bond with a god or a *paramatma*, the supreme soul, whom he invokes in various instances.

Bhavaanbhagat knows that the stories of mythology inspire confidence and valour and teach the philosophy of life, but also that sometimes solidarity and collective fight and the project of being-in-this-world must supersede the transcendental. This is illustrated effectively when Valji's death, almost like Rohith Vemula's in our time, becomes a pivot around which the community is politicised. Bhavaankaka, who lived the life of an ascetic, soon mobilises people into collective action. Known for consoling people on such occasions with the tale of the transience of the body and the immanent journey of the soul to heaven, Bhavaankaka, however, refuses to use the story to console this time. Not only the denizens of the Vankar vas but also those from the Harijan and Rohit vas populated Valji's verandah and the neighbourhood square. Amongst them, Raidas the cobbler and Kasno the sweeper sat next to Bhavaankaka, longing to hear the story of Ahilochan and Abhimanyu. The hovering soul of Ahilochan had resided in Abhimanyu to find a release in a death done through treachery. The death itself was an answer to an earlier act of treachery in which Krishna had killed Ahilochan through treachery. This story of karma, of fate, and pre-ordained and well-served actions and consequences made no sense to Bhavaankaka today. When asked to heal and provide the story to understand the loss of Valji (also killed through treachery), Bhavaankaka says:

> Now just forget about Ahilochan and Abhimanyu or Arjun and the Lord Krishna. Enough of all other-worldly and spiritual matters. What's the point of it all? . . . We live here in this world, this is what should concern

> us now. If we need to improve anything, it should be this world.... What does our caste know of detachment and renunciation? . . . You people may think that he [Valji] died in pursuit of worldly matters. In my opinion, he died in pursuit of a higher truth, of true Paramarth. He did not privilege his life over his friend Teeha. (Macwan 2012: 97)

Bhavaanbhagat has given up on worldly *maya* but the atrocities wreaked upon the Vankars of Ratnapaar make him participate again in *vyavhar*, the bonds of sociality and this-worldliness. For someone who has seen dharma through detachment, he realises that situations of contingency demand of us dharma of an exceptional kind as well. At first sight, it seems as though Bhavaankaka is eschewing a spiritual discourse altogether and replacing it with a political one. He firmly locates his discourse in 'this world' and even invokes a larger identity of caste. It could be argued that this is not the language of spirituality at all. However, it can also be read as a response to the kind of apolitical spirituality that often gets appropriated into the upper-caste Hindu fold, losing all of its political potential. In that regard, Bhavaanbhagat's spirituality aptly responds to the question that Hawley asks.[3] Honestly, he is but a reluctant representative of the community, a waning light and an old man who for most times be rather left alone. The economy of his vocabulary that incorporates the *paramatma* and *paramarth* in the *vyavhar* of the everyday creates a unique and elastic epistemology via which he navigates the world. Quietly, when the time comes, he bids farewell to the village: 'the nail did not have either the sarangi or the bow hanging on it' (ibid.: 229).

More haunting than this visual picture of loss is the ungraspability of Bhavaanbhagat in language. Macwan confessed: 'I could not fathom him [Bhavaanbhagat] fully; how could I then translate him into words? I wrote him as I saw him.' For me, too, Bhavaanbhagat's wisdom, his experience, remained one of the major ungraspable—and,

3 The question that lingers here is whether the message of bhakti is a message of social protest. Is the equality it celebrates fundamentally a social reality—and therefore something revolutionary in its Indian context—or is it only spiritual, in which case it can coexist with Brahminical hinduism even if it does not endorse it? (Hawley and Juergensmeyer 2008: 16).

consequently, untranslatable—aspects of the novel. It is neither merely a literal or linguistic residue nor a cultural one that resists being carried over into a new register. It is not even a heterogeneity of sorts that could be assigned to and identified from 'the half-silent connotations . . . which drift, as it were, between the signs, the sentences, the sequences' (2006: 6) that Ricoeur mentions. Elsewhere, he remarks that '[e]very language's struggle with the secret, the hidden, the mystery, the inexpressible is above all else the most entrenched incommunicable, initial untranslatable' (ibid.: 33). Meanwhile, much like Bhavaanbhagat's journey, the translation was over, but not quite; its retrieval from particularities of caste, region and temporality made it an unfinished business. Bhavaanbhagat had gone away from the text, leaving behind the community that mourned for him. He had also slipped away from me because I had not provided him with the ecology which made room for his situated spirituality and politics.

At some level, translating Bhavaanbhagat's *svabhav* is not so much a secret or mystery of language; rather it is the incompleteness of reading, and, therefore, rendering. It is an example of Derridean aporia that makes the translation untranslatable (1998: 66). Bhavaanbhagat operates through a bewildering mix of things that we think are oppositional, and his decisions do not allow us to slate him, especially from the point of view of modernity. This aporia—not on his part, but on ours—causes aphasia in us as readers, thereby pushing for the need for a new language of understanding experience and a new framework for translating such a *vyavharic* epistemology. *Vyavhar* or social transaction is not reducible to transactionality. It is a negotiation with the social, political and economic and involves weighing the primacy of one or the other as the situation demands. If the judgment is so dynamic, how is one to define it comprehensively? One fathoms it but not quite. Neither the word *Angaliyat* nor its unsatisfactory equivalent *The Stepchild* stayed with me. It was the colon between them that reminded me of how this leftover was not about comparable illegitimacies. It was about the person called Bhavaanbhagat whose wisdom, knowledge, this-worldliness and otherworldliness, *vyavhar* and *parmarth*, attention and absentmindedness, caste assertion and transcendental abstractions that were slipping away constantly. Joseph

Macwan's translation both captured and demonstrated the maya-like elusiveness of Bhavaanbhagat. The modernity of my language defined him perhaps, shrank him, made him legible. I mourn this loss, effected by modernity. This uneasy translation lies beneath language.

Owning and Belonging: The Possessive Pronoun

Once upon a time, a man named Jokhu and his wife Gangi lived in a nameless village. We don't know which caste they belonged to, but we do know that they were very poor and must have belonged to a 'lower caste'. They were not allowed to draw water from the well that only belonged to the Thakur (Rajput by caste) or the Sahuji (Bania by caste). We also know that they were dominated by all three upper castes—the Brahmins, the Kshatriyas, and the Vaishyas. Jokhu does not have clean water to drink, and as a man convulsed by cough and fever, he is also feeling worse from drinking unclean water. Gangi goes to 'steal' water from the Thakur's well but fails to bring any. Just when she manages to fill up the pitcher with clean water from the well, the Thakur emerges, bellowing, from his home. In a flurry of fear, Gangi drops the pitcher and rushes home to save her life. She finds the sick Jokhu drinking stench-filled water from a lota.

This brief story provides a peep into the subhuman existence of Dalits in a caste-ridden village. The story, *Thakur ka Kuan*, or Thakur's well, is written by Munshi Premchand—a fact that many readers of this essay may have known. Characteristic of Premchand's oeuvre of rural and subaltern lives, the story is dark and relentless in its critique of the upper castes and its 'sympathy' for the poor Dalits. Critiques about Premchand's representation of the poor Dalit are well documented, and there is much to be said about the limits of ideology as well as experiential location.[4] However, I want to discuss neither the Hindi original story nor its English translation, but a retelling and translation of the story by another author in another mode first. In other words, it is Omprakash Valmiki's Hindi poem,

4 See for instance, Laura Brueck, *Writing Resistance: The Rhetorical Imagination of Hindi Dalit Literature*, Columbia University Press, 2014.

a retelling and response to Premchand's story, that forms the crux of the discussion below, as another example of an act of translation that unseals concluded meanings and reminds us of the inseparability of the syntactical and political role of language. My concern today is also based upon the shaping power of language and the politics of caste and acts of translation that set up divergent world views between a well-meaning upper-caste writer and a Dalit writer.

चूल्हा ठाकुर का
मिटटी तालाब की
तालाब ठाकुर का

भूख रोटी की
रोटी बाजरे की
बाजरा खेत का
खेत ठाकुर का

बैल ठाकुर का
हल ठाकुर का
हल की मूठ पर हथेली अपनी
फसल ठाकुर की

कुआँ ठाकुर का
पानी ठाकुर का
खेत-खलिहान ठाकुर के
गली मोहल्ले ठाकुर के
फिर अपना क्या ?
गाँव?
शहर ?
देश?

Chulha Thakur ka
Mitti Taalab ki
Taalab Thakur ka

Bhookh roti ki
Roti bajre ki
Bajra khet ka
Khet Thakur ka

Baiyl Thakur ka
Hal Thakur ka
Hal ki mutth par hatheli apni
fasal Thakur ki

Kuan Thakur ka
Paani Thakur ka
Khet-khalihaan Thakur ke
Galli mohalle Thakur ke
Phir apna kya?

Gaun?
Shahar?
Desh?

Characters like Jokhu and Gangi live a precarious existence with a fear of assault upon their lives and bodies, and even basic resources are denied to them. The upper castes, on the other hand, are complicit in hoarding resources, manipulating power and essentially, they take it all, always. As an affective memory of Premchand's stories, readers went away with the visuals and heartrending details of the poor and their suffering. However, seldom did questions of systemic and structural exploitation arise or persist in the reading of Premchand's oeuvre. In contrast, after a distance of almost half a century, Omprakash Valmiki's 'version' of this account, in an intra-lingual translation of the form from a story to a poem, raises the question of resources and their ownership. Valmiki troubles the category of ownership/belonging/constitution all at once through the simple, unseen, insignificant-looking, possessive word *ki/ka* (former feminine, latter masculine) in Hindi. The English language needs explicating and different words each time, diffusing and dispersing the politics of language from its ubiquity and innocuous-looking role by making it seem enumerative. My point may be made clearer by dwelling closely upon the poem:

The first stanza (*Chulha Thakur ka / mitti taalab ki / taalab Thakur ka*) sets up a hierarchy of resources from their very material foundation of food. The cooking stove belongs to the Thakur. The possessive suffix *ka* denotes both belonging and ownership. The earth that has gone into the making of the stove belongs to the pond. The *ki* here also denotes a constituent element, which is to say that the earth used to make the stove is 'from' the pond. The pond, in turn, belongs to/is owned by the Thakur. The second stanza (*Bhookh roti ki / roti bajre ki / bajra khet ka / khet Thakur ka*) deepens the meanings around owning and belonging and also lends further a semantic and pragmatic complexity by using *ki* and *ka* as prepositions and genitive. For instance, the hunger is 'for' the roti; the roti is made 'of' bajra; the bajra is 'from' the field, and the field is owned by/belongs to the Thakur. The missing subject in the opening line of the second stanza is significant. Who is hungry, whose hunger is to be satiated by the roti that is made of bajra, which grows on the Thakur's field and thereby makes the satiation of hunger depend upon the Thakur? The chain of command as well as of supply is established from the upper caste's resources to a Dalit body that does not have a self-reflexive pronoun to refer to the self. The third stanza inserts a context of labour in this chain of supply, thereby showing how the production of resources is made possible through Dalit labour without establishing a Dalit's right to it. The oxen that plough on the Thakur's field (*Baiyl Thakur ka*) belong to him and the plough is also his (*Hal Thakur ka*), but the fist upon the shaft of the plough are 'ours/mine' (*Hal ki mutth par hatheli apni*) whereas the harvest produced through this labour belongs to the Thakur (*Fasal Thakur ki*). The well that appears in Premchand's story as the chief locus of injustice is not an object by itself. It is a sign in a larger system of signification. The next stanza brings us to this truth.

Kuan Thakur ka
Pani Thakur ka
Khet-khalihan Thakur ke
Gali mohalle Thakur ke

The well belongs to the Thakur
The water belongs to the Thakur
The farms and fields belong to the Thakur
The lanes and mohallas belong to the Thakur

The possessive verb *ki/ka* has shed its constituent roles, suggesting elements forming other elements; it has rather stayed purely with the idea of possession. The Thakur of Premchand's story did not own the well in a vacuum; he did that by owning the field and the water and all the neighbourhood around it. The well is symptomatic of an unbroken and impermeable web of power around it, criminalising Gangi's act of taking water into an act of stealing. If Premchand's story touches upon the sympathetic chord of an upper-caste reader by showing how Gangi was denied water, the progressively used possessive verb in Valmiki's poem builds momentum to show that an upper-caste reader can only read isolated signs without the system accompanying and sustaining them. From this point on, the dispossession of the Dalit is easy to see. For what belongs to one, the poem asks at the end, village, city, country? The caste network of the village is but a microcosm of a larger republic of caste, and the unsuspecting role of this climax or anti-climax has been performed by the smallest word in the poem (*ki/ka*).

Valmiki's telling, we must note, is both 'responsive' and 'reflexive' to Premchand's in that, based on Ramanujan's definitions (2012: 189), it responds to Premchand's in ways that define both these tellings, and it reflects on Premchand's by relating itself to it directly or inversely. It thus becomes both a 'co-text' and a 'counter-text' to it, making use of the possibilities that lie in the space and time between the two, possibilities carved on the map of experience. If we were to distinguish Valmiki's retelling from Premchand's and assess that by the much-discussed parameters of accuracy and difference, we may miss how grammar and experience combine to see the world the way Valmiki sees it. The significance of this example also lies in the fact that it rescues from a possible fallacy of thinking that incomplete forms of translations are only products of linguistic difference. As such, the movement from Hindi to Hindi allays the overdetermined emphasis on the impossibility between two distinct and different languages. It is by shifting the terms of grammar within the 'same' language that Valmiki reminds us of how possessive pronouns are not merely elements of grammar but of material conditions of possession. It is also in the small elements of language that questions of owning one's story lie, like *hinnan jee ain muhinji atamkatha*.

The Blindness of Translation

During the first phase of lockdown in India from March 2020, the Partition archive of India invited me and Furrukh Khan (a scholar based in Pakistan) to have a conversation about teaching Partition to our respective students. Those were early days before the webinar fatigue had set in, and the imagination of bringing two scholars together despite the boundaries and lockdowns to a well-attended audience excited all of us. At one point in the discussion, Khan mentioned that the Muslim generation that left India mourns over many things, but also says that the Hindus put Muslims in the caste system. The comment appeared and disappeared; nobody noticed, and it was not picked up in the discussion. Questions of why Partition happened, who is to be blamed, and how is that past to be erased but also made peace with continued as usual. Like the audiences who heard Furrukh Khan, I also unheard of caste in my focus upon translating the 'Partition' stories (Ghulam 2019). The anthology *Unbordered Memories* brought together stories from both sides of the border, which I translated from Sindhi. Resistant to the notion of performing 'nations' through translation, I focused on the hollowing out of Sindhi Hindus from the lives of Sindhi Muslims in Pakistan and upon memories of Sindh among Sindhi Hindus. Partition framed the choice of the stories as did my understanding of them, and it is to this incomplete task that I turn in this essay.

Gordhan Bharti, a well-known Sindhi writer who moved to Ulhasnagar camp near Mumbai during Partition, is a fine storyteller. One of his stories is called 'Boycott'. Based in the small village of Aarazi in Sindh, the story focuses on a character named Jaman. Jaman is a Koli, an untouchable caste in both India and Pakistan today, although, in India, many variations bring Kolis into 'tribes' and 'Rajputs' as well. Meanwhile, Pakistan has been formed and a large number of Hindus have left the new state of Pakistan to go to India. The early wave of the exodus had been from urban Sindh; hence the village where Jaman lived still had some 20 odd Hindu trader families that had continued to live in Pakistan. Before we move further, it is important to remember that the upper-caste and well-to-do Sindhi Hindus were referred to as *vaanyas* (bania). Sindh had a negligible number of Brahmins, and as such, they held no special position or privilege in the highly trade-based network. The sacerdotal functions of the Brahmins had also been adjusted need-wise as and when the bania saw them fit. So, in Jaman's story, the Hindu traders were middle-caste, rather than upper-caste, but economically the most powerful group. The Muslims, on the other hand, had two main blocks of the cultivating and labouring castes (Dalits) and the landowning Wadheros (feudal lords). Sindh's political muscle was formed from the Wadhero class, who ruled over the poor and maintained a mixture of cordial and hostile relations with the Banias. When we begin the story, Jaman receives the summons from the Wadhero to see him: '*"... sainjin has asked you to come to the otak this evening," Khamiso snapped*' (Bharti 2009: 28).

An *otak* is a meeting place attached to every rich person's home in Sindh—somewhat away and outside from the women's quarters of the home. For a poor Dalit Koli to be summoned to the Wadhero's *otak* was frightening business. Jaman presented himself before the Wadhero the next day. The writer provides us with an insight into new configurations of power in Pakistan—so that along with the Wadhero is Abdulatak Salero, who had done recruiting for the National Muslim Guard, and also a bunch of young unemployed men who had taken to reading the Quran. Abdulatak was clad in a sherwani, churidar and Jinnah cap. Jaman had also been a part of the National Muslim Guard for a brief period and had followed the routine of stomping about the village, joining in shouting slogans against the infidel *vaanyas*. By doing this, you could get four annas a day. Jaman was now recruited to help stop the business of the *vaanyas* so that the remaining ones would also leave. He is told, 'We will boycott these vaanyas. Do you follow me? Boycott means *bahishkar*, which means we will not buy anything from them. Right?' Abdulatak explains to Jaman. What ensues from this point is Jaman's exploitation to this end which involved making him start a sweet shop by using his own money and selling Islamic *pakodas* and mithai. The entire endeavour leaves Jaman in a worse state of penury than he was, and he finds no compensation for his labour or money in this driving-away-the-Hindus enterprise. When Jaman opens his mouth to say how it was the rich that benefited from Pakistan, while he remained even poorer, he is thrown away like a dog.

> 'I will not hold my tongue. Pakistan has been formed for heavy-turbaned people like you, not for us poor.'
>
> 'How dare you? Arre Khamisa, kick this son of a Koli and throw him out.'
>
> Jaman wanted to say more, but before he could do that Khamisa picked him up and threw him out of the *otak*.
>
> 'Son of a pig, how dare you violate sainjin's dignity?'
>
> Jaman fell to the floor, and kicks rained down on him. He felt dizzy, a cascade of abuses continued to flow from the *otak*. 'Son of a Koli, I have driven you out of the *otak*, next time you say something, I will have you thrown out of the village. Bloody cur ...'
>
> A stumbling and staggering Jaman made an effort to rise from the ground and dust his clothes. He realized that long before the vaanyas, it was he who had been boycotted. (Bharti 2009: 31)

Jaman did not need the translation of the English word; he had its meaning through experience. The story throws up an insight into the project of Pakistan that rested upon old forms of feudalism and caste. Dalits are instrumentalised in hate campaigns against the other, and the profits accrued in the process remain with those who wield power, regardless of religion. The mirroring of a similar phenomenon is present in a recent autobiography by Bhanwar Meghwanshi in India. Translated from Hindi by Nivedita Menon, this memoir tells the story of a Dalit who joins the Rashtriya Swayamsevak Sangh (RSS), only to realise that he was merely an instrument of Hindutva. His Dalitness would not make him a fully legitimate member of the RSS. Access to the Hindu fold was for him like Jaman Koli's to the Muslim fold. Religion and nation policed their borders to keep the Dalits out in both cases. The narrator, Meghwanshi, is warned of this by his father:

> My father was a hard-core Congress supporter, and would often stop me as I set out in my khakhi shorts and black cap, saying, 'This party of Banias and Brahmins will never be with us farmers and lower castes,

> they just use us to start fights with our miyan brothers, the Muslims. They themselves can never fight, the cowards. They use us'. (2020: 77)

However, it is also interesting how the Hindu shopkeepers are absolved by being absent from both the story 'Boycott' and Pakistan. The writer, Gordhan Bharti, a post-Partition Sindhi Hindu, externalises the treatment of the Dalit onto the Muslim body, which is the chief perpetrator. This externalising gaze is a form of blindness, common to all caste Hindus, including me. At the time of translating this story, it had seemed to be a critique of the idea of Pakistan and its fragile foundations that rested upon the poor. Not only did I not see the mirroring that is cited above but what might be the relation between a Jaman Koli and Hindu merchants remained invisible to me. What is, then, to miss a crucial link in understanding and translating? Is that a form of action carried out in blindness? The blindness of insight, as Dilip Menon puts it, or blindness of translation? In an important essay titled, 'The Blindness of Insight: Why Communalism in India is about Caste', Dilip Menon draws attention to a not-so-accidental schism between 'communal' (2010) and 'caste' studies in the social sciences. While the former subject forms one of the more urgent issues, the latter remains less discussed, relegated in terms of experience to Dalits and, therefore, externalised. Methodologically, caste 'news' remains confined to journalistic reportage, and it seldom speaks to the studies on communalism and by extension, matters of religion and secularism. Menon describes the separation of spheres as a historical process, situated in the colonial logic of the 'public' and the 'private'. For a moment, I want to dwell on the term 'blindness' as both a lack of and refusal to visual access to a field of meanings. Menon uses blindness to qualify it at the level of insight—modes of perception by which caste (through its relegation to a pre-modern sphere) escaped the notice of social scientists who engaged with what appeared to them as questions of religion. The blindness is generated by a false logic and false conception, which in itself is a product of an upper-caste neurosis about modernity. One of the consequences of this 'blindness' is the secular biography of the nation-state. Meanwhile, I use the word 'blindness' to evoke many things. In his well-known play, *Andha Yug*, the writer Dharamvir Bharati lays bare the debris of the Kurukshetra war. The war is both a result and testimony to many forms of blindness.

> Following the great war
> descended this blind age
> in which all affairs, attitudes, and spirits are perverse.
> . . .
> [Except Krishna] all the others are blind
> misguided, self-lost, and depressed
> dwelling in the dark caverns within themselves. (Bharati 1954: 2)
> (translated by Sanchit Toor)

The chief locus of blindness is Dhritrashtra whose blind love for his son and physiological blindness characterise what remains invisible to the human eye through inability, denial and lack of imagination. He says, '[Since] I was born blind, how could I have comprehended the external reality or recognised its social codes?' (ibid.: 9). Bharati uses only one verb *grahan*—meaning: to assume, accept, comprehend or simply experience—a single word that allows Dhritrashtra to place himself on the other side of reality and absolve himself of all the blame. He has divided the world and, consequently, himself and his (in)experience from the world, courtesy of his blindnesses. As a justification, this may leave much to be desired. However, it serves as a useful allegory for us to understand how texts continue to unravel meanings past the moment of translation. The narratives are also teased out for the meanings they open up, revealing and hiding caste, central but implied, instrumental but displaced from language. The afterlife of the text is rendered not so much by the translation that *happened* but by the one that happens in the course of re-reading and re-thinking.

To sum up, translations are like intimate relationships—built upon selective truths. We ignore, sometimes without realising, things so that an intimacy is formalised. In a novel called *Intimacies* (2021) by Katie Kitamura, the protagonist-interpreter finds herself complicit in the fate of a despot. She has heard him intimately, recreated his side of the story with accuracy but failed on another ethical ground. Doing right by every translation is perhaps not a possibility, we can only commit to being a part of its wanderings. After all, for Rilke and Benjamin, too, translators are but wanderers—wanderers who become wonderers on the path of exile, migration, restlessness, and longing—as Robert Young cautions us: 'Translation perpetuates the translated into eternity, an eternity of proliferating reproduction of uncertain memories from which the translator can never return, the afterlife of a text that turns the translator into a wanderer over the face of the earth, and exile across its seas' (Young 2006: 7). Really speaking, this wandering is, in fact, translation. Sometimes, like Bhavaankaka, the wanderer leaves unannounced, abandoning the un/finished matters of the word/world, indeed destined to never return. At other times, like Praneshacharya, he falls into the accidental company of a co-wanderer like Putta, only to return home, to return to the translated, feeling restless to re-read it and re-touch it and, through the process, re-become, before deciding to abandon it once again. To that extent, this exercise is true to the translation, which is not a deed concluded, but a verb and work in progress, travelling with us as it were.

Afterword

Experiencing Language

After reading this book, *after* immersing in its words, sounds, images, concepts, ideas and poetry, what remains? What comes after, afterwards—more experiences, understanding, knowledge? What is the space of the 'after'? Is it even a space or is it only a temporal extension? A period of time following an experience?

Normally, 'after' is a period following the experience and before language intrudes to describe that experience. It is neither experience nor language but is the gap that connects the two. Experience has an afterlife before it is gathered into language. So many of our difficulties in understanding language and its relation to experience are embodied in this gap. Poetry exists in this gap, exists as an experience that constantly resists being reduced to language. Rita Kothari's book is an attempt to embody this gap, to illuminate it for our consideration. It cannot be done by mere analysis and description; it has to be affective, incomplete, and with pockets of silence. For that is the nature of the after and any attempt to understand it involves asking these difficult questions that this book consistently keeps asking: What is the experience of language? What (languages?) do you need to articulate this experience?

There is a difference between the use of something called language and the experience of being-in-language. Language in the former sense is a given, an 'object', an entity that is present already before us that we can use to communicate, express and use. But there is another type of engagement with language which is not about language as a given entity but as a kind of experience in itself. I will use the word 'languaging' to suggest this experiential aspect of language. I want to use 'languaging' as the experience of language just as seeing is an experience of an object of sight that we see.

Objects of experience should not be confused with the experience catalysed by and associated with, the object. Objects may catalyse experience but are distinct from it. After all, the same object can cause different experiences in different people and different contexts. The simple fact that experience is the state that is an inseparable mix of the object and the experiencing subject means that experience can never be reduced to objects of experience.

With language as an object of experience, there are new complications. Most importantly, language is not just any object as far as experience is concerned; it is, somehow, essentially connected with the experience itself. Language captures the urgency by which experience wants to be heard, to express itself, make itself visible and escape the first-person ontology into which it is always bound. Not all experience can be uttered and this point is often put under the category of ineffability. But the interesting question is the site of ineffability—is it merely a limitation of language that is not able to express the experience? But there is an experience of experience that is ineffable—that is, our own experiences are not transparent to us, there is always leakage of that experience and parts of our experience are always occluded to ourselves. It is not the problem of language alone that is the problem of ineffability but also the very nature of experience itself. This observation is most true when we consider the experience of language. In this case, the experience is always effable (in that the experience is already linguistic) but the experience of language seems to be ineffable. The 'after' of this experience can be expressed as follows: Language is not the immediate after of the 'experience of language'.

We speak, read and write a language so effortlessly that we forget to experience it. The closest experience we have of language is through music or just listening to the unending sounds around us in our daily lives. The truest experience of sound comes when it is not contaminated with meaning or intentional attempts to discover meaning, structure, information and knowledge. It is truly in the nature of being-with and not knowing-that. This is a dichotomy that Guru and I invoke to understand the nature of the social in a text that arises as an after text through Kothari's references to it. To extend this dichotomy to language is to recognise that language is social, not in the usual way we understand the social nature of language but more as an experiential social. It is this aspect of language as an experiential social that Kothari keeps pointing us to. It is also to recognise that we do not colonise and occupy language (however proficient one might be in it) but that we are in a human relationship to it. We have to be in a silent companionship with language just like we may sit silently with somebody we want to be with.

I like this image of being-with language in silence: it is an image that Kothari's text is trying hard to articulate. That is why she keeps coming back to the experience of language. In so doing, she has to engage with ineffability and silence, of course, but also with multiple words in multitudinous languages. Sounds flow effortlessly from English to Hindi to Gujarati to Sindhi. In order to be-with words that I don't understand in Sindhi or Gujarati, I remain in silence. It is in that silence of being-with that I can begin to get a sense of the experience of language as such and not through the specific words that are used in a text.

Learning to experience language is important; following Kothari's deeply reflective and evocative remarks, I must perhaps say that it is necessary. Meaning in poetry is not found in the words of the poem, not even in the interstices of the reader's imagination. It is found in the sense of being-with that characterises a poet's creation of the poem. Reading is to experience—not the story, the images, the words in the poem—but the experience of the poetic moment present in the 'after'—after experience and before language intrudes.

To experience language is to observe it as well as participate in it at the same time. I am thinking of anthropology here, and reading this book reminds me of anthropology, except that here it is an 'anthropology of language'. It makes me wonder about the anthropological imagination in literature, particularly when we read about the many intersectionalities of caste, gender, class and religion that Kothari writes about. What is the possibility of an 'anthropology of language'? Drawing from a well-known anthropological 'method', we could view an anthropology of language as involving participant-observation of a language or languages. To be a participant-observer, the anthropologist lives the life of the subjects, learns their language, customs, etc. In a deep sense, it is more of being-with, which sometimes, unfortunately, gets converted to only knowing-that. While there is a problem in reducing participant-observation only to knowing-that (knowing about the people we are with), the primary strength of this approach lies in the possibility (and sometimes the impossibility) of being-with without wanting to impose oneself on the other. Being-with language is also like this: finding a way to inhabit the language, its sounds, its words, sentences, idioms, phrases, incompleteness, sense of lack and many other such qualities that characterise a language. Being-with is the way towards languaging, an experience of language as language and not as a set of words that mean something, that talk about some subject matter and so on.

Language and experience are not like other dyads. Every experience has an after, an after that is sought to be filled with language—these become the language of that experience. However, this filling the after is not possible since language itself can be an experience that cannot be followed by more language. The ambiguities of poetry—the expressions that are always referring to what is not said—are only signs of the inherent difficulty in experiencing language, given the troubled relationship between experience and language.

Kothari has already written the afterword even as she wrote her text. This book is filled with the experiences and the language of after. So many terms arise in the aftermath of what she wants to say. It is not merely about the relation between experience and language. It is also a striving to find a language for language, to describe the nature of languages and the experience of language. What could be the language of the experience of a language? When I eat a fruit and I experience a sweet taste, I can use English to say: 'This fruit is sweet.' Maybe in saying this, I am satisfied that language has 'captured' my experience and bound it within some sounds. But when I experience English—when I experience the sentence 'This fruit is sweet'—in what language is this experience expressible? Do we even need language to express this experience? How should this experience be expressed? It cannot be in English for that does not obey the fundamental distinction between experience and language since English (or a sentence in English) is the object of experience. There is a fundamental ontological distinction between experience and language, but what happens to this distinction in the case of the experience of language?

I experience English—how then do I speak about that experience? If I express it in English again, then I am still in the domain of the language-experience and have not stepped out of that domain. I experience sweetness, I use language to express it. In so doing, I am using something other than experience in order to describe it. One might say that I have translated the experience into a language. Yes, this is how translation begins, not as some matching game as if it is a game of tennis between two languages, where words in different languages are lobbed across the net. Rather, translation first arises in the moment of finding a language for the experience of language. It arises in knowing that the experience of language has to encounter another language. Translation signifies the difficulty in *experiencing language*. We move to translation because we do not know how to speak about the experience of a language. Or equivalently: *After* the experience of language, then what? When I experience English as a language (and not about what the words mean), then I am at a loss for 'words' to express this experience.

To translate a text into a given language, it is necessary to experience the language of the text first. It is not enough to 'know' the meaning of the words in the text and to know the structure of the text. Unless one experiences the language (in every sense of the word experience), translation in its true sense is not possible. We can understand this claim as follows: *Translation is the language that tries to express the experience of the language of the text.* Translation itself is a language and is not just another language into which a text is translated.

Traditionally, translation is misunderstood as the after of language, something which comes after language has been given. But that is not true. Translation is the space of the after of the experience of language. Kothari cannot let go of the after in her text. A text that is filled not just with words but also with afterwords, afterthoughts, afterimages—not only through the recurring idea of translation in the book but also repeatedly through various other concepts in each chapter. When she speaks about theory, it is about theory after experience. Placing the relation between theory and experience in this context is to ask for the dynamics of the space of the after that captures the difference between theory and experience. Is it that theory is aptly an afterword to experience, words written after the text of experience has had its say?

I cannot help seeing the space of the after when she discusses the role of I and the We, leading us to the image of the I as the afterword of the We and vice versa. Modernity might insist that the experience of the We comes after, and from, the experience of I but, as Guru and I argue in our book, it may well be the case that the sense of I comes after a sense of the social, a sense of the We. In another chapter on the mother tongue, I stumble upon the possibility that the daughter is the afterword to the mother and in asymmetrically gendered stories, the image of women arising as an afterword to men. In the chapter on the incompleteness of language and translation, I read the incompleteness of translations as an experience felt by the reader. Translation is the act that reminds us that we consciously keep spaces of silence and hide what we want to say. Every language is then unique not because of its words and meaning but in what it does not want to reveal. The uniqueness of language is its resistance to being used to reveal all the time, to be a handmaiden to experience. Poetry arises in this space of resistance. Translation has become too much of a positive activity—positively showing what is already present in the original text. But languages are unique because of what and how they hide. Translation, as the experience of language, has to discover these absences in a language and a text. When translators think that their task is to make the new tongue reveal what it does not want to, they are not experiencing language but only reducing it to its functionalities.

Sundar Sarukkai

Bibliography

Abdi, M.A. 2015. 'Performing Blackness: Disrupting "Race" in the Classroom'. *Educational and Child Psychology*, 32 (2), ISSN 0267.

Adalaja, Varsha. 2011 (2009). 'Nayana Rasik Mehta'. In *Shataroopa*, edited by Sharifa Vijliwala. Ahmedabad: Gurjar Grantha Ratna Karyalaya, pp. 200–206.

———. 2022. 'Nayana Rasik Mehta'. In *The Greatest Gujarati Stories Ever Told*, edited and translated by Rita Kothari. New Delhi: Aleph Publishers.

Agamben, Giorgio. 1998. *Remnants of Auschwitz: The Witness and the Archive*, translated by Daniel Heller-Roazen. New York: Zone Books.

Ahmed, Sara. 2017. *Living a Feminist Life*. Durham: Duke University Press.

Akhtar, Salman. 2015. *Shame: Developmental, Cultural, and Clinical Realms*. Routledge. London.

Ambedkar, Babasaheb. 'Untouchables or The Children of India's Ghetto'. In *Dr. Babasaheb Ambedkar: Writings and Speeches*, Vol. 5. Compiled by Vasant Moon. Mumbai: Education Department, Government of Maharashtra. Rpt. 2014.

Appiah, Anthony Kwame. 2000. 'Thick Translation'. In *The Translation Studies Reader*, edited by Lawrence Venuti. London: Routledge, pp. 417–429.

Apter, Emily. 2014. 'Preface'. In *Dictionary of Untranslatables: A Philosophical Lexicon*, edited by Barbara Cassin, translated by Steven Rendall et al., translation edited by Emily Apter, Jacques Lezra and Michael Wood. Princeton: Princeton University Press.

Ananthamurthy, U.R. 2012. *Samskara: A Rite for a Dead Man*, Oxford India Perennials Series, 2nd ed. New Delhi: Oxford University Press.

Bagul, Baburao. 2018. *When I Hid My Caste*, translated by Jerry Pinto. New Delhi: Speaking Tiger.

———. 2000. *Jevha Me Jaat Chorli Hoti*. Mumbai: Akshar Prakashan, pp. 78–89.

Baldwin, James. 2017. *Notes of a Native Son*. Penguin Modern Classics. London, England: Penguin Books.

Bama. 2000. *Karukku*, translated by Lakshmi Holmstrom. Oxford University Press: New Delhi.

Basile, Elena. 2012. 'Scars of Language in Translation: The Itchy Poetics of Jam Ismail'. In *Literature for Our Times*. Brill Publishers.

Bhatt, S. n.d. *Search for My Tongue*. Available at: https://genius.com/Sujata-bhatt-search-for-my-tongue-annotated (accessed on 5 June 2021).

Bharati, Dharamvir. 1954. *Andha Yug*. Allahabad and Delhi: Kitaab Mahal.

Bharti, Gordhan. 2009. 'Boycott'. In *Unbordered Memories: Sindhi Stories of Partition*, edited and translated by Rita Kothari. New Delhi: Penguin India.

Biddle, Jennifer. 1997. 'Shame'. *Australian Feminist Studies*, 12 (26): 227–239.

Behar, R. 2003. *Translated Woman: Crossing the Border with Esperanza's Story*. Boston: Beacon Press.

Benjamin, W. 1999. *Illuminations: Essays and Reflections*, translated by Harry John. New York: Schocken Books.

Butler, Judith. 1997. *Excitable Speech: A Politics of the Performative*. New York and London: Routledge.

———. 2016. 'Introduction' of *Grammatology* by Jacques Derrida. Trans. Gayatri Chakraborty Spivak. Maryland: John Hopkins Press.

Chamberlain, Lori. 2000 (1988). 'Gender and the Metaphorics of Translation'. In *The Translation Studies Reader*, edited by Lawrence Venuti. London and New York: Routledge.

Chandra, Shefali. 2012. *The Sexual Life of English: Languages of Caste and Desire in Colonial India*, 1st ed. New Delhi: Zubaan Books.

Chatterjee, Partha. 1993. *The Nation and Its Fragments: Colonial and Postcolonial Histories*. Princeton, New Jersey: Princeton University Press.

Clare, Eli. 2010. 'Resisting Shame: Making Our Bodies Home'. *Seattle Journal for Social Justice*, 8 (Spring/Summer).

Collins, Patricia Hill. 1989. 'The Social Construction of Black Feminist Thought'. *Signs*, 14 (4): 745–773.

Das, Veena. 2018. 'The Life of Concepts and How They Speak to Experience'. In *The Composition of Anthropology: How Anthropological Texts Are Written*, edited by Morten Nielson and Nigel Rapport. Oxford and New York: Routledge.

Derrida, Jacques. 2001. 'What is "Relevant" Translation?'. *Critical Inquiry*, 27 (2), Winter: 174–220.

———. ed. 2016. *Of Grammatology*, translated by Gayatri Chakravorty Spivak. Baltimore: John Hopkins University Press.

Detha, V. 2009. 'Jhupdi ro Gyan'. In *Baatan ri Fulwari*, Vol. 5. Jodhpur: Rajasthani Granthagar.

Detha, V. and V. Kothari. 2020. 'The Learning of Toil'. In *Timeless Tales from Marwar*. New Delhi: Penguin Random House, pp. 44–52.

Devy, G.N. 2017. *The Crisis Within: On Knowledge and Education in India*. New Delhi: Aleph Spotlight.

Devika, J. 2008. 'Being "in Translation" in a Post-colony'. *Translation Studies*, 1 (2): 182–196.

Du Bois, W.E.B. 2018 (1903). *The Souls of Black Folk*. New Delhi: Gyan Publishing House.

Dutt, Yashica. 2019. *Coming Out as Dalit*. New Delhi: Aleph Book Company.

Dwyer, Rachel. 2006. 'Kiss or Tell? Declaring Love in Hindi Films'. In *Love in South Asia: A Cultural History*, edited by Francesca Orsini. Cambridge: Cambridge University Press, pp. 289–302.

Eliot, T.S. 1970. 'The Metaphysical Poets'. In *English Critical Texts*, edited by D.J. Enright and Ernst de Chickera. Oxford University Press.

Erikson, Erik. 1956. 'The Problem of Ego Identity'. *Journal of the American Psychoanalytical Association*, 4 (56): 56–120.

English, Fatima. 1975. 'Shame and Social Control'. *Transactional Analysis Bulletin*, 5 (1), January: 24–28.

Fanon, Frantz. 2008 (1952). *Black Skin, White Masks*, translated by Richard Philcox. UK: Penguin Books.

Flotow, Luise von. 1991. 'Feminist Translation: Contexts, Practices and Theories'. *TTR: Traduction, Terminologie*, Rédaction, 4 (2): 69–84.

Gandhi, M.K. 2018. *Satya Na Prayogo or An Autobiography or The Story of My Experiments with Truth*, translated from Gujarati Mahadev Desai. A Critical Edition introduced with notes by Tridip Suhrud. New Delhi: Penguin, India, p. 106.

Ganeri, Jonardan. 2011. *Artha: Meaning*. New Delhi: Oxford India Paperbacks.

Geetha, V. 2009. 'Bereft of Being: The Humiliations of Untouchability'. In *Guru*, 95–107.

Ginzburg, C. 1992 (1980). *The Cheese and the Worms: The Cosmos of a Sixteenth-Century Miller*, translated by John Tedeschi and Anne C. Tedeschi. Baltimore: Johns Hopkins University Press. Revised edition.

Godard, Barbara. 1984. 'Translating and Sexual Difference'. *Resources for Feminist Research*, 13 (3): 13–16.

Gulzar. 2018. *Jiya Jale: The Stories of Songs* (in conversation with Nasreen Munni Kabir). New Delhi: Speaking Tiger.

Guru, Gopal. 2012. 'Experience, Space, and Justice'. In *The Cracked Mirror*, pp. 71–106.

———. 2012. 'Egalitarianism and the Social Sciences in India'. In *The Cracked Mirror*, pp. 9–28.

———. ed. 2009. *Humiliation: Claims and Context*. New Delhi: Oxford University Press.

Guru, Gopal and Sundar Sarukkai. 2012. *The Cracked Mirror: An Indian Debate on Experience and Theory*. New Delhi: Oxford University Press.

———. 2019. *Experience, Caste, and the Everyday Social*. New Delhi: Oxford University Press.

Hallisey, Charles, trans. 2015. *Therigatha: Poems of the First Buddhist Women*. Cambridge, Masachusetts: Murty Classical Library of India.

Hawley, John Stratton and Mark Juergensmeyer. 2008 (1998). *Songs of the Saints of India*. New Delhi: Oxford University Press.

Heidegger, Martin. 1971. 'A Dialogue on Language between a Japanese and an Inquirer'. In *On the Way to Language*, translated by Peter D. Hertz. New York: Harper and Row, pp. 1–54.

Hess, Linda and Shukdev Singh. 2002 (1983). *The Bījak of Kabir*, translated by Linda Hess and Shukdev Singh, essays and notes by Linda Hess. New York: Oxford University Press.

Hess, Linda. 2018. 'When a Text Is a Song'. In *A Multilingual Nation: Translation and Language Dynamic in India*, edited by Rita Kothari. New Delhi: Oxford University Press.

Hussain, Ghulam. 2019. 'Appropriation of Caste Spaces in Pakistan: The Theo-Politics of Short Stories in Sindhi Progressive Literature'. *Religions*, 10 (11): 627. Available at: https://doi.org/10.3390/rel10110627 (accessed on 5 June 2021).

Ilaiah, Kancha. 2009 (1996). *Why I am not a Hindu?* Calcutta: Samya.

Ingalls, Daniel H.H., et al. trans. 1990. *The Dhvanyaloka of Anandvardhana with the Locana of Abhinavagupta*. Harvard Oriental Series. Harvard: Harvard University Press.

Jaaware, Aniket. 1994. 'The Silence of the Subaltern Student'. *Subject to Change: Teaching Literature in the Nineties*, edited by Susie Tharu. New Delhi: Orient Longman, pp. 107–124.

———. 2012. *Destitute Literature*. Mumbai: Mahatma Jyotirao Phule and Babasaheb Ambedkar Chair, University of Mumbai, pp. 5–43.

———. 2018. *Practicing Caste: On Touching and Not Touching*. New York: Fordham University Press.

Jaffrelot, C. 2015. *The Pakistan Paradox*. UK: C. Hurst & Co Publishers Ltd.

Jani, Manishi. 2012. *Koni Koni Chhe Gujarati?* (To Whom Does Gujarati Belong?) Ahmedabad: Gujarati Lekhak Mandal.

Joshi, Svati. 1991. *Rethinking English: Essays in Literature, Language, History*. New Delhi: Trianka.

Joshi, Umashankar. 2011 (1941). *Akho: Ek Adhyayan*. Ahmedabad: Gujarat Vidya Sabha.

Johnson, Mark. 2014. 'Experiencing Language: What's Missing in Linguistic Pragmatism'. *European Journal of Pragmatism and American Philosophy*, 6 (2): 14–27.

Jyoti, Dhrubo. 2018. 'A Letter to My Lover(s)'. In *Eleven Ways to Love: Essays*, edited by Shreshtha. New Delhi: Penguin India.

Kakar, Sudhir. 2009. *Mad and Divine: Spirit and Psyche in the Modern World*. Chicago: University of Chicago Press.

Kamala, N. ed. 2009. *Translating Women: Indian Interventions*. New Delhi: Zubaan Books.

Kawade, Ankit. 2019. 'The Impossibility of "Dalit Studies"'. *Economic and Political Weekly*, 54 (6): 20–23.

Kearney, Richard. 2006. 'Introduction: Ricoeur's Philosophy of Translation'. In *On Translation*, by Paul Ricoeur, translated by Eileen Brennan. New York: Routledge, pp. vii–xx.

Kitamura, Katie. 2021. *Intimacies*. Penguin, UK: Riverhead Books.

Kothari, Rita. 2009. *The Burden of Refuge: Partition, Sindh, Gujarat*. New Delhi: Orient Blackswan.

———. 2011. 'The Paradox of a Linguistic Minority'. In *Interrogating Reorganisation of States: Culture, Identity and Politics in India*, edited by Asha Sarangi and Sudha Pai. New Delhi: Routledge, pp. 129–143.

———. 2013. 'Caste in a Casteless Language'. *Economic and Political Weekly*, xlvi, II (39), September: 60–68.

———. 2017. *A Multilingual Nation: Translation and Language Dynamic in India*. New Delhi: Oxford University Press.

———. 2019. 'Farewell, Neeravbhai'. *Economic and Political Weekly*, 54 (22), June.

———. guest ed. 2021. 'Dil Ki Zubaan: A Symposium on the Language of Songs'. *Seminar*, May.

———. 2022. *The Greatest Gujarati Stories Ever Told*. New Delhi: Aleph Book Company.

Kothari, Rita and Abhijit Kothari. 2021. 'Past Continuous: K.M. Munshi, Gujarat and the Patan Trilogy'. *Economic and Political Weekly*, LVI (18), May: 36–42.

Kothari Rita and Apurva Shah. 2017. 'Dil Se: Love, Fantasy and Negotiation in Hindi Film Songs'. *Interventions*, 19 (4): 1–19.

Kumar, Udaya. 2013. 'Consciousness, Agency and Humiliation: Reflections on Dalit Life-Writing and Subalternity'. In *The Political Philosophies of Antonio Gramsci and B. R. Ambedkar*, edited by Cosino Zene. Routledge, pp. 158–170.

———. 2016. *Writing the First Person: Literature, History and Autobiography in Modern Kerala*. Ranikhet: Permanent Black.

Levinas, Emmanuel. 2003. *On Escape*, translated by Bettina Bergo. Stanford: Stanford University Press.

Macwan, Joseph. 2012 (2003). *Angaliyat: The Stepchild*, translated by Rita Kothari. New Delhi: Oxford India Paperbacks.

———. 2018 (1986). 'Maari Dharti nee Mehak'. In *Angaliyat*. Ahmedabad: Divine Publications.

———. 2018 (1985). *Vyatha na Veetak: A Collection of Pen Portraits*. Ahmedabad: Divine Publications.

Maitreya, Yogesh. 2019. 'Three Poems'. Sunflowercollective. Blogpost, 6 August. Available at: https://sunflowercollective.blogspot.com/search?q=yogesh+ (accessed on 18 May 2022).

Mani, Lata. 2013. *The Integral Nature of Things: Critical Reflections on the Present*. New Delhi: Routledge.

Matilal, B. 2001. *The Word and the WORLD: India's Contribution to the Study of Language*. New Delhi: Oxford University Press.

Malouf, D. 1999. *An Imaginary Life*. London: Vintage Books.

Mehta, Ila Arab. 2011. *Vad*. Ahmedabad: Gurjar Granth Ratna Karyalaya.

———. 2015. *Fence*, translated by Rita Kothari. Delhi: Zubaan Books.

Menon, Dilip. 2010. 'The Blindness of Insight', in *Indian Political Thought: A Reader*, edited by Aakash Singh and Silika Mohapatra. London and New York: Routledge.

Mewaram, Parmanand. 2002 (1933). *A New English-Sindhi Dictionary*. New Delhi: Sahitya Akademi.

Miller, William Ian. 1993. *Humiliation: And Other Essays on Honor, Social Discomfort and Violence*. Ithaca and London: Cornell University Press.

Morrison, T. n.d. *Toni Morrison Nobel Lecture*. NobelPrize.Org. Available at: https://www.nobelprize.org/prizes/literature/1993/morrison/lecture/ (accessed on 6 June 2021).

Mutfi, Aamir. 2016. *Forget English!: Orientalisms and World Literature*. Cambridge, Massachusetts: Harvard University Press.

Meghwanshi, Bhanwar. 2020. *I Could Not be Hindu: The Story of a Dalit in RSS*, translated by Nivedita Menon. New Delhi: Navayana.

Mehta, Pratap Bhanu. 2021. 'Failure, Self-Worth and Agency in Modern Liberalism'. Symposium on Failure hosted by Ashoka University, February 2020. Available at: https://www.newwriting.net/2020/07/ (accessed on 2 March 2021).

Nagaraj, D.R. 2010. *The Flaming Feet and Other Essays: The Dalit Movement in India*, edited by Prithvi Datta, Chandra Sobhi and Ashis Nandy. Ranikhet: Permanent Black.

Nandy, Ashis. 2001. 'A Report on the Present State of Health of the Gods and Goddesses in South Asia'. *Postcolonial Studies*, 4 (2): 125–141.

———. 2007. *An Ambiguous Journey to the City: The Village and Other Odd Ruins of the Self in the Indian Imagination*. New Delhi: Oxford University Press. New edition.

———. 2009. 'Humiliation Politics and the Cultural Psychology of the Limits of Human Degradation'. In *Humiliation: Claims and Context*, edited by Guru Gopal. New Delhi: Oxford University Press, pp. 41–57.

Naik, Purnachandra. 2016. 'Baluta and Joothan amid Humiliation'. *Economic and Political Weekly*, LI (26–27), June: 19–21.

Nussbaum, Martha C. 2010. *Not for Profit: Why Democracy Needs the Humanities*. The Public Square Book Series. Princeton: Princeton University Press.

Orsini, Francesca. 2006. 'Introduction'. In *Love in South Asia: A Cultural History*, edited by Francesca Orsini. Cambridge: Cambridge University Press, pp. 1–39.

———. 2022. '*Aukaat*'. In *Changing Theory: Concepts from the Global South*, edited by Dilip Menon. New Delhi: Routledge India.

Ortega y Gasset, José. 2000. 'The Misery and the Splendor of Translation', translated by Elizabeth Gamble Miller. In *The Translation Studies Reader*, edited by Lawrence Venuti. London: Routledge, pp. 49–63.

Parekh, Ramesh. 1988. *'Na thaya' in Ekant Nee Sabha*, edited by Jagdish Joshi. Ahmedabad: Vora Publishers.

———. 1998. 'It Did Not Happen'. In *Modern Gujarati Poetry: A Selection*, edited by S. Ramanathan and R. Kothari. New Delhi: Sahitya Akademi, p. 52.

Parekh, Bhikhu. 2009. 'Logic of Humiliation'. In *Humiliation: Claims and Context*, edited by Guru Gopal. New Delhi: Oxford University Press, pp. 23–40.

Palshikar, Sanjay. 2009. 'Understanding Humiliation'. In *Humiliation: Claims and Context*, edited by Gopal Guru. New York: Oxford University Press.

Patel, Neerav. 2010. 'Creamy Layer'. In *Nisbat*, edited by Mohan Parmar and Yashvant Vaghela. Ahmedabad: Gujarati Dalit Sahitya Pratishthan.

———. 2022. 'Creamy Layer'. In *The Greatest Gujarati Stories Ever Told*, edited and translated by Rita Kothari. New Delhi: Aleph Publishing.

Pawar, Daya. 1978. *Baluta*. Mumbai: Granthali Prakashan.

———. 2015. *Baluta*, translated by Jerry Pinto. New Delhi: Speaking Tiger.

Premchand, Munshi. 2017. 'Thakur's Well'. In *The Complete Short Stories*, Volume 4, edited by M. Asaduddin. New Delhi: Penguin.

———. 2020. '*Thakur ka Kuan*'. In *Premchand Pratinidhi Kahaniyaan*, edited by Bhisham Sahni. New Delhi: Rajkamal Prakashan.

Pawde, Kumud. 1994. 'The Story of My Sanskrit', translated by Priya Adarkar. In *Corpse in the Well: Translations from Modern Marathi Dalit Literature*, edited by A. Dangle. Orient Longman, pp. 110–124.

Phillips, Adam. 2000. 'On Translating a Person'. In *Promises, Promises: Essays on Psychoanalysis and Literature*. London: Faber and Faber, pp. 125–147.

———. 2015. *Unforbidden Pleasures*. New York: Farrar, Straus and Giroux.

Phipps, A. 2011. 'Travelling Languages? Land, Languaging and Translation'. *Language and Intercultural Communication*, 11 (4): 364–376.

Price, Joshua. 2021. 'Translation as Epistemicide: Conceptual Limits and Possibilities'. *Palimpsestes: Revue de Traduction*, 35.

Rajan, Sunder Rajeshwari. 1992. *The Lie of the Land: English Literary Studies in India*. New Delhi: Oxford University Press.

Ramanathan, S. and R. Kothari. 1998. 'It Did Not Happen'. In *Modern Gujarati Poetry: A Selection*, edited by New Delhi: Sahitya Akademi, p. 52.

Ramanujan, A.K., ed. and trans. 1985. *Poems of Love and War: From the Eight Anthologies and the Ten Long Poems of Classical Tamil.* New York: Columbia University Press.

———. 1989. 'Where Mirrors Are Windows: Toward an Anthology of Reflections'. *History of Religions*, 28 (3): 187–216.

———. 1997. *The Collected Poems of A. K. Ramanujan*. New Delhi: Oxford India Paperbacks.

Ricoeur, Paul. 2006. *On Translation*, translated by Eileen Brennan. New York: Routledge.

Rushdie, Salman. 1983. *Shame*. London: Jonathan Cape.

Sadana, Rashmi. 2012. *English Heart, Hindi Heartland: The Political Life of Literature in India*. Ranikhet: Permanent Black.

Sarangan, Ram. 2020. 'Finding a Language to Talk about Mental Health.' Available at: https://indianexpress.com/article/express-sunday-eye/all-the-light-we-cannot-see-6279757/ (accessed on 30 May 2022).

Sarangi, Asha. 2009. 'Languages as Women: The Feminisation of Linguistic Discourses in Colonial North India'. *Gender and History*, 21 (2): 287–304.

Sarkar, Bhaskar. 2010. *Mourning the Nation: Indian Cinema in the Wake of Partition*. New Delhi: Orient Blackswan.

Sarkar, Tanika. 2013. *Words to Win: The Making of Amar Jiban*. New Delhi: Zubaan Classics.

Sarukkai, Sundar. 2002. 'Inside/Outside: Merleau-Ponty/Yoga'. *Philosophy East and West*, 52 (4), October: 459–478.

———. 2012. 'Understanding Experience'. In *The Cracked Mirror: An Indian Debate on Experience and Theory*. New Delhi: Oxford University Press, pp. 46–70.

Saarth, Jodnikosh. ed. 2012 (1929). *M.K. Gandhi*. Ahmedabad: Gujarati Vidyapith. Ninth edition.

Mohanty, Chandra Talpade, Foreword. Sangtin Writers. 2006. *Playing with Fire: Feminist Thought and Activism through Seven Lives in India*. Minnesota: University of Minesota Press.

Shepherd, K.I. 2019. *Why I Am Not a Hindu: A Sudra Critique of Hindutva Philosophy, Culture and Political Economy* . New Delhi: Sage Publications Pvt. Ltd., 1st edition.

Shivaprakash, H.S. trans. 2010. *I Keep Vigil of Rudra: The Vachanas*. New Delhi: Penguin Books, p. 92.

Scheff, Thomas J. 2003. 'Shame in Self and Society'. *Symbolic Interaction*, 26 (2): 239–262.

Shanbhag, Vivek. 2015. *Ghachar Ghochar*, translated by Srinath Perur. Harper Perennial.

Sila-Khan, Dominique. 1997. *Conversion and Shifting Identities: Ramdev Pir and the Ismailis in Rajasthan*. Delhi: Manohar Publishers.

Tagore, Rabindranath. 1954 (1924). *Gora*. London: Macmillan and Company Limited, 1st edition.

Tharu, Susie. ed. 1994. *Subject to Change: Teaching Literature in the Nineties*. New Delhi: Orient Longman.

Tolani, Dharmendra. 2020. 'The More I Seek the More I Find'. In *Sindhi Tapestry: Reflections on the Sindhi Identity*, edited by Saaz Aggarwal. Pune: Black and White Fountain Publishers, pp. 11–20.

Taylor, Woodman. 2002. 'Penetrating Gazes: The Poetics of Sight and Visual Display in Popular Indian Cinemas'. *Contributions to Indian Sociology*, 36 (1 and 2): 297–322.

Vaidik, Aparna. 2020. *My Son's Inheritance*. New Delhi: Aleph Publishing.

Valmiki, Omprakash. 2020. 'Bhaya'. In *Salaam*. New Delhi: Radhakrishan Prakashan, pp. 39–47.

———. 1981. '*Thakur ka Kuan*'. Available at: https://dalitawaaz.com/dalit-literature-poems/omprakash-valmiki-poetry-on-dalits-hindi-dalit-literature/6570 (accessed on 16 July 2021).

Valles, Father. 2015. *Vanee Tevun Vartan: Reflections on Language*. Ahmedabad: Gurjar Granthratna Karyalaya.

Williams, R. 1985. *Keywords: A Vocabulary of Culture and Society*. New York: Oxford University Press.

Yengde, Suraj. 2019. *Caste Matters*. New Delhi: Viking, India.

Yildiz, Yasmin. 2011. *Beyond the Mother Tongue: The Postmonolingual Condition*. New York: Fordham University Press.

Young, Robert J.C. 2006. 'Writing Back, in Translation'. In *Writing Back in/and Translation*, edited by Raoul J.Grandqvist. Frankfurt am Main: Peter Lang, pp. 19–37.

Index

About the Author

Rita Kothari is Professor of English at Ashoka University where she also runs the centre for translation. A distinguished translator, Kothari is also a leading theoretician of translation studies; she is internationally known for *Translating India: The Cultural Politics of English, A Multilingual Nation* and her co-edited books, *Chutnefying English* and *Decentring Translation Studies.* Her translations of note include *Angaliyat: The Stepchild* from Gujarati, *Unbordered Memories* from Sindhi and the *Patan Trilogy* by K.M. Munshi from Gujarati (a translation in collaboration). Her work on Partition and borders brings forth the unusual Sindhi experience in books such as *The Burden of Refuge* and the study of the Indo-Pak border region in *Memories and Movements.* Kothari is a multilingual scholar, and her translation interest is manifest in the way she moves between various languages through research and pedagogy. She also writes extensively on language politics, Partition, the literary and social traditions of Gujarat and Sindh and Hindi cinema. Her most recent publication is *The Greatest Gujarati Stories Ever Told* (2022).